DESCARTES AND THE

Descartes is often accused of having fragmented the human being into two independent substances, mind and body, with no clear strategy for explaining the apparent unity of human experience. Deborah Brown argues that, contrary to this view, Descartes did in fact have a conception of a single, integrated human being, and that in his view this conception is crucial to the success of human beings as rational and moral agents and as practitioners of science. The passions are pivotal in this, and in a rich and wide-ranging discussion she examines Descartes' place in the tradition of thought about the passions, the metaphysics of actions and passions and sensory representation, and Descartes' account of self-mastery and virtue. Her study is an important and original reading not only of Descartes' account of mind–body unity but also of his theory of mind.

DEBORAH J. BROWN is Senior Lecturer in Philosophy at the School of History, Philosophy, Religion and Classics, The University of Queensland.

DESCARTES AND THE PASSIONATE MIND

DEBORAH J. BROWN

CAMBRIDGE
UNIVERSITY PRESS

CAMBRIDGE UNIVERSITY PRESS
Cambridge, New York, Melbourne, Madrid, Cape Town, Singapore, São Paulo, Delhi

Cambridge University Press
The Edinburgh Building, Cambridge CB2 8RU, UK

Published in the United States of America by Cambridge University Press, New York

www.cambridge.org
Information on this title: www.cambridge.org/9780521857284

© Deborah J. Brown 2006

First published 2006
This digitally printed version 2008

A catalogue record for this publication is available from the British Library

ISBN 978-0-521-85728-4 hardback
ISBN 978-0-521-08809-1 paperback

This book is dedicated to my parents,
Margaret and George, and
to my sister, Catherine,
for their love, laughter and generosity.

Contents

Acknowledgements

The surprisingly lush vegetation around where I live grows out of the notorious 'Brisbane shale', a flaky mixture of mud, silt and brittle sedimentary rock. Clinging precariously to a cliff of this rubbish is a loquat tree, whose roots are few and frantically gripping whatever stable soil it can find, and whose trunk is spindly and clawed by possums, but whose fruit, for those willing to work around the many obnoxious stones, is delicious. Descartes locates his account of the passions among the fruits of his 'tree of knowledge', but most, finding the roots insecure and the trunk inevitably thin, do not venture that they will find anything at the end of the branches. Sometimes though you just have to follow the possums.

My own possums are Lilli Alanen and Calvin Normore. Lilli provided the initial impetus to write on the passions for a conference in Helsinki in 1996, and has kept the pressure steadily up since then. She has been an inspiration, a mentor and a friend, and I am so very grateful to her for her comments on earlier drafts and discussing these topics with me over the intervening years.

There are many obnoxious stones in Descartes' philosophy, and he would have seemed much less interesting to me had it not been for Calvin Normore, who directed me towards the metaphysical fun stuff in Descartes' philosophy of mind: the union of mind and body, action and passion, sensory representation, the will and virtue – and towards the medieval traditions against which Descartes must(!) be understood. I thank him for his encouragement and attention (without devotion), his sound advice on matters of text, translation and argument, and for the two suns of our cosmos.

Many thanks also to friends of the inter-Nordic community of scholars who graciously accepted a Queenslander as an honorary Viking. Thanks especially to Mikko Yrjönsuuri and Henrik Lagerlund, and to the regulars of the inter-Nordic mind fests: Christopher Martin (for advice on floating men), Peter King (for a good time, always), Simo Knuuttila, Sten Ebbesen,

Eyolfur Emilsson, Fred Stoutland, Dennis Des Chene, Rega Wood, Jon Miller, Pauliina Remes, Sara Heinämaa, Martina Reuter, Lorenzo Casini, Thomas Ekenborg and Minna Koivuniemi.

For interesting conversations in other contexts, I would like to thank Michaela Boenka, Peter Harrison, Jeremy Hyman, Jack MacIntosh, Amy Schmitter, Lisa Shapiro, John Sutton, Martin Tweedale and Catherine Wilson. I am especially grateful to Stephen Gaukroger for his superb advice about texts and ideas, and for his general encouragement. Ronald de Sousa and Mohan Matthen inspired a number of lines of thought in chapter 3. A version of chapter 3 was presented at RSSS at the Australian National University and at the Centre for Cognitive Science at Rutgers University, which gave me the opportunity to rethink its content in useful ways. Many thanks especially to Jerry Fodor, Ernie Lepore and Philip Petit for stimulating discussions.

This book was written and taught in two cities: Brisbane and Los Angeles. At the University of Queensland, I would like to thank my colleagues for their support and helpful conversations, in particular, Aurelia Armstrong, Michelle Boulous Walker, Mark Colyvan, Dominic Hyde and Roger Lamb, and my students, Maria Caltabiano, Paul Murray and Peter Van Geuns. For being there in more ways than I can count, I thank especially my colleague, Julian Lamont.

The UCLA philosophy department provided a particularly hospitable environment in which to write this book and present the material contained within it. I extend a special thanks to John Carriero for sharing his depth of knowledge about the *Meditations* and conversations about the passions. Joseph Almog, Tyler Burge, Brian Copenhaver, Gavin Laurence and Terry Parsons asked the right questions at the right times. I am grateful also to Ahmed al-Wisha for our discussions about Avicenna.

The referees for Cambridge University Press provided exceptionally generous and astute comments, which helped me avoid a number of gaps and gaffs. The remaining ones are all mine. I am very, very grateful to them and to Cambridge University Press's editor, Hilary Gaskin, as well as JackienWarren and Gillian Dadd, for bringing this project to fruition. I thank also the copy editor, Audrey Cotterell, for her excellent advice on editorial matters. Institutional support has come from three Australian Research Council Grants, an Early Career Research Grant and generous leave from the University of Queensland. Various travel expenses between 1999 and 2004 were covered by the Nordic Research Council in the Humanities (NOS-H) project. Research for chapter 2 was conducted at the Bodleian, Taylorian and Christchurch libraries at Oxford. I am grateful to these institutions for their support during the research for and preparation of this book.

For maintaining a good *complexio* of humours (and spirits) at various times during the writing of this book, I would like to thank Susan Croteau, Christi Favor, Darryl Heiner (and the boys, Scott and Dominic), Annette Johnson, Joanne Johnston (beach retreats and a fine friendship), the Lavery-McColls, Damien Ledwich (more beaches), Mark Lovewell, Victoria McGeer, Peta Orbach, Katya Rice, Joseph Vaughan and Marina Vitkin. Damien Ledwich offered good-humoured technical support (and technical good humour), and designed the magnificent cover. For keeping my son, George, distracted and happy, I thank the Cooney–Carillo family, the staff of the Cornerstone Preschool of Santa Monica and its wonderful director, the late Nancy Brooks. I am also grateful for the happy and independent disposition of the George in question, and for that of his little brother, Joseph, who joined us for the final revisions of this book, and to his Paty (Patricia Palomino), who loved her new 'boyfriend' for a few hours each day while I scribbled.

Note on references

I have utilised the standard edition of the works of Descartes by Charles Adam and Paul Tannery, *Oeuvres de Descartes*, 12 volumes (1897–1913), hereafter cited as AT. References to *Les Passions de l'âme* from the AT edition are hereafter cited as PS. Unless otherwise indicated, all translations are my own. I have benefitted from consulting the following English translations: John Cottingham, Robert Stoothoff, Dugald Murdoch and Anthony Kenny, *The Philosophical Writings of Descartes*, vols. I–III, (Cambridge: Cambridge University Press, 1985–91); John J. Blom's translation of the Elisabeth corespondence, *Descartes: His Moral Philosophy and Psychology* (New York: New York University Press, 1978) and *René Descartes: The Passions of the Soul*, trans. Stephen Voss (Indianapolis, IN: Hackett, 1989). Quotations from Descartes' correspondence with Princess Elisabeth, other than those with an AT citation, are taken from the 'Past Masters' CDRom: *Oeuvres Complètes de René Descartes*, ed. André Gombay, Connaught Descartes Project; all translations are my own.

Introduction

As Descartes saw it, the real *you* is not your material body, but rather a nonspatial thinking substance, an individual unit of mind-stuff quite distinct from your material body.

(Churchland, 1984: 8)

What Dualist philosophers have grasped in a confused way is that our direct acquaintance with the mind, which occurs in introspective awareness, is an acquaintance with something that we are aware of only as something that is causally linked, directly or indirectly, with behaviour.

(Armstrong, 1980: 25)

Descartes is often accused of having invented the modern mind by having invented the modern notion of consciousness, the unmediated awareness that the mind has of itself and of its thought contents.[1] Although not denied an important part in the constitution of the human being, the human body and its worldly acts appear to have no obviously indispensable role in the functioning of the Cartesian mind, and it is this very autonomy of the mental that many find so unpalatable. This senti-ment hasn't prevented us from continuing to feed Descartes to our children. The *Meditations* is still core reading for every philosophy major, but the pedagogy behind this is often like that of the conscientious parent whose idea of moral instruction is a family outing at a public flogging. We can't accept the Cartesian mind but we can't seem to avert our gaze either, and we despair of finding a better way of introducing the mind–body problem to our kids.

---

[1] Richard Rorty (1979: ch. 1), for example, accuses Descartes of begging the question against materialism by assuming that diverse mental phenomena can all be classified as thoughts of a single entity, the mind, considered in isolation from the body, and then as inconsistently arguing that some of those thoughts depend on the functions of the body. John Carriero (1990: 230–1) argues that Rorty underestimates Descartes' non-sceptical arguments for the autonomy of pure understanding from sense and imagination.

There have been various attempts to diagnose why we remain in the grip of the Cartesian mind-set. With the ascension of physicalism as the one true theory of everything, few are inclined to subscribe to the dogma of 'the ghost in the machine', as Gilbert Ryle famously put it (Ryle, 1949: 15–16), or to the 'forlorn' and deeply *unscientific* view that the immaterial and material can interact [Dennett, 1991: 33], but we have retained a 'Cartesian' orientation in the study of the mind. The term 'mind', as it has come down to us from Descartes, seems to describe a self-contained entity, completely transparent to itself and only accidentally connected to things outside it. It has spawned an entire industry of thought directed at undoing the scepticism that led Descartes to it, and another aimed at reconciling what follows from it – the primacy and irreducibility of subjectivity – with the objective perspectives of the natural sciences. Daniel Dennett diagnoses the problem as a tendency to view the mind as a theatre, a place where intellectual thoughts and sensations, the ghosts of neural activity, dance before the spectral observer we call the conscious mind.[2] The theatre metaphor is supposedly the root of all Descartes' epistemological woes. Because the Cartesian mind has immediate access only to its ideas, it is thus Descartes himself who made possible the very sceptical worries he had to overcome, as well as the various forms of idealism and phenomenalism that threaten our direct cognitive access to the world.[3]

Despite the awful consequences of the Cartesian mind, we retain the insidious identification of the self with the Cartesian ego, the 'I' that Hume and Kant failed in their different ways to stumble across on their introspective forays. What is left of our essence – the thinking thing – is something that we can neither understand nor yet conceive differently. Thomas Nagel laments this horrible predicament – 'the view from nowhere' – to which Cartesian thinking has led us thus:

The apparent impossibility of identifying or essentially connecting the self with anything comes from the Cartesian conviction that its nature is fully revealed to

---

[2] Dennett argues that the anti-scientific attitude rests on the false 'Cartesian' intuition that consciousness has some kind of unity, some point at which information comes together and awareness happens, the physical substrata of which is the pineal gland. It leads theorists to postulate an obscure 'centre' of the mind/brain, a Cartesian Theatre, where 'it all comes together' and consciousness happens. This idea does not accord with the hierarchical structure of the brain (Dennett, 1991: 39).

[3] Miles Burnyeat has argued that Descartes' sceptical arguments represent the first moment in the history of philosophy where knowledge of the subjective realm was thought to be immune from doubt (Burnyeat, 1982). Fine [2000] and Groarke [1984] reject the idea of a great distance between Cartesian and earlier forms of scepticism.

introspection, and that our immediate subjective conception of the thing in our own case contains everything essential to it, if only we could extract it. But it turns out we can extract nothing, not even a Cartesian soul . . . Identification of myself with an objectively persisting thing of whatever kind seems to be excluded in advance. (Nagel, 1986: 34–5)[4]

Justifiably lamentable to be sure, but attempts to ground the mind or self in the objective, publicly observable properties of the body or behaviour have not proved terribly successful either. The very perspectival quality of conscious experience seems hard to ignore, as Nagel himself has noticed, and makes it difficult to see how the mind could be defined from the third-person perspectives belonging to the natural sciences. We may not like the Cartesian concept of mind, but we seem to be stuck with it.[5]

I want in this book to establish some distance from these 'Cartesian' conceptions of mind and self. I do not intend to offer a panegyric to substance dualism, or to rewrite Descartes as some kind of closet materialist. There is no getting around the dualism, or the autonomy he perceives the mind as having. But it is our failure to set the Cartesian mind in the wider context of Descartes' thought that exacerbates the problems associated with this notion. What it is like to be a Cartesian mind is not the same as what it is like to be a spectator watching a private performance, someone who is left wondering about what is going on outside the theatre or backstage. When we look at those texts in which the union of mind and body is under discussion, what we find is not an inward-looking mind reflecting its metaphysical distinction from the body, but a kind of phenomenological monism – an experience of being one unified and embodied substance.[6] This book is an attempt to explore why it is important to Descartes that our experience is like this.

It is generally assumed, for example, that if there were a genuinely Cartesian science of the mind, it would have to resemble nineteenth-century introspectionism, a study of the conscious mind based on direct inner awareness, and a dismal prospect to many if ever there was one.[7]

---

[4] See also John McDowell's rejection of the identification between self-consciousness and the Cartesian ego (McDowell, 1994: 99–104).

[5] Nagel (1974) is arguably Cartesian on the irreducibility of the first-person perspective.

[6] For recent discussions emphasising mind–body unity rather than distinction, see Alanen (2003), Almog (2002), Baker and Morris (1996), Broughton and Mattern (1978), Cottingham (1998), Gaukroger (1995) and (2002), Hatfield (2003), Radner (1971) and Rorty (1986a).

[7] Introspectionism in psychology is generally associated with the German psychologist, Wilhelm Wundt (1862) and his student, E.B. Titchener (1898). Introspectionists catalogued mental events, particularly sensory experiences, from the point of view of the conscious subject. Their techniques were more scientifically respectable than is usually supposed, involving, for example, objectively

The reasoning behind this is as follows. The real distinction of mind and body entails a disintegration of the human being into two completely separate realms of activity, mental and bodily, the functions of which are specifiable independently of each other. Since nothing is defined by anything outside itself, the mind cannot be defined in relation to the body, and so cannot be known in relation to the body. This reasoning seems to leave only the mind's awareness of itself as a possible point of entry to the study of the mind. But although it is true that the Cartesian mind is not defined by its relation to matter, it is created conjoined to matter with which it forms a system of coordinated functions, and with which it causally interacts. Many of the functions of the mind concern its relationship to the body and the world it inhabits, and when Descartes turns to the study of these, he turns not inward to his own consciousness but to the natural science of his day, mechanics, and to his own practical experience. It is highly doubtful, therefore, that Descartes would ever have favoured the introspectionist psychologies that have taken his name over the neuropsychological perspectives that purport nowadays to be reactions against all things Cartesian.

Descartes' account of the embodied mind is present in the *Sixth Meditation,* but its presence tends to be eclipsed by the emaciated notion of the mind that dominates the early parts of the *Meditations.* By the end of the *Second Meditation,* Descartes takes himself to have established that he cannot know with certainty whether anything other than his mind exists, that his mind is essentially thinking, and that body in general, including his own human body, should it exist, is essentially extended, non-thinking stuff. It seems natural to assume that at this point he has committed himself to the conclusion that *self* and *mind* are the same thing and metaphysically independent of his or any other body. But this, as Hobbes pointed out, would be too quick. It is fallacious to move from 'I know *only that p*' (where p in this case is the proposition: *I am a thinking thing*) to 'I know that *only p*.'[8] By the end of the *Second Meditation,* Descartes cannot claim to have established anything about the relation-ship between mind and body. But, as he replies to Hobbes, the proof comes not there but in the *Sixth Meditation,* where the veracity of clear

---

measurable and repeatable response time and attention tests, and tests designed to measure a subject's sensitivity to changes in sensory stimuli. It was not so much the methodology as the assumption that conscious experience can be analysed into primitive 'elements' that accounted for its demise. Descartes' enumeration of the passions bears some similarity to this analytic project.

[8] See Brown and de Sousa (2003).

and distinct ideas and the separability of that which can be clearly and distinctly conceived apart can (he thinks) be assumed. Whether his reply to Hobbes suffices or not is irrelevant to our concerns here. The point is that the placement of the real distinction argument is significant because the conception of the mind we are left with at the end of the *Second Meditation* is not the conception of mind developed in the *Sixth Meditation,* where *both* the mind's real distinction from and substantial unity with the body are argued for in the same train of thought. Having been reduced in the *Second Meditation* to a thinking thing who knows only that it thinks and exists, the mind in the *Sixth Meditation* is reunited through sensation with its body and redeposited in a world teeming with more bodies than it began with (or one big continuous one, depending on your view). The mind of the *Sixth Meditation* may still be incorporeal, but its experiences of itself are not the out-of-body ones of a spectral observer. Fail to understand Descartes' conception of the human being, the mind *in corpore* rather than incorporeal, and one fails to understand Descartes' mind.

Why have we tended to miss or de-emphasise the discussion of the union in the *Sixth Meditation?* Part of the answer to this question, Descartes tells us, is that we cannot easily digest at the same time both the argument for the real distinction of mind and body and the conception of their union (AT III, 693). Yet, it is instructive to reflect on why it is Descartes, and not the countless other dualists in the history of philosophy, whom we regard as having severed the connection between the self or person and the whole human being. Among Descartes' chief opponents, the 'Scholastics' (by and large, commentators on Aristotle), the immateriality and immortality of the soul were largely uncontested doctrines. Descartes' way of arriving at the conclusion of the soul's immateriality – through the application of hyperbolic doubt – certainly differed from preceding approaches, but the conclusion was much the same. Yet no one would have accused an Aristotelian, for example, Aquinas, of identifying the self with the immaterial and intellectual part of the soul, or with anything less than the whole human being. And the reason why no one would level such an accusation is that, on the standard Aristotelian view, the soul's relationship to the body was conceived of not as that of one substance united with another substance, but as a form inhering in matter, and form and matter are not distinct substances, capable of existing completely apart from one another, but principles of one and the same unified nature. The notion of form explains why a material object is the kind of thing (*quid*) it is and why, consequently, it behaves as it does.

The separability of the human intellectual soul from matter was not, for the Scholastics, in conflict with the idea of their union, for regardless of the intellect's separability, the doctrine of the soul as informing matter, and on those accounts faithful to Aristotle's *De anima*, as relying on matter (particularly, the matter of the sense organs) for its proper functioning, entailed that the mind *could not be conceived of in any intelligible way apart from matter.*[9] It was this dependence of the rational soul on the body for its proper functioning that made Scholastic forms of dualism more palatable than Descartes', though not in the end more coherent.

What is particularly hard to grasp about Descartes' dualism is how, therefore, in the face of the metaphysical independence of mind and body, it is possible to conceive of them as constituting a system of integrated functions. To conflate the 'I' of the *Sixth Meditation* and the whole human being seems disingenuous. Descartes' assertion to Regius that the soul is the 'true substantial form of a human being', and indeed the only substantial form (separable from matter), did little to ease his contemporaries' suspicion that having separated mind and body so successfully, he would be hard-pressed to get them back together again (AT III, 505). But his preparedness to use the terminology of substantial forms in this one special context is illuminating. The sense in which the mind 'in-forms' the body is the sense in which, at any given time, a parcel of matter through its relation to a mind becomes a human body, matter being otherwise undifferentiated (AT IV, 166–7). The Cartesian mind does not in-form the body in the way the soul does on Scholastic accounts, that is, in the sense of determining all the functions of the body. But by its relationship to a mind, matter is promoted to a special status and subject to new modes of explanation. Human beings stand in need of teleological explanations, which make reference to the integrated functions of their components, and to the 'artistry' of God who creates them, in much the same way that clocks are understood as integrated systems, the parts of which function in accordance with the specifications of their designers. The human body cannot properly be understood apart from the mind to which it stands in a non-accidental relationship and with which it comprises a functional unity.

[9] The separated soul proved especially difficult for Christian thinkers committed to Aristotle's account of understanding as relying on sensory images. According to Aquinas, the separated soul has a less perfect knowledge of its proper objects, the natures of material things, although it can know things which are directly intelligible through divine illumination. *Summa Theologiae*, I, q.89.

The study of the integrated functions of mind and body is centred, for Descartes, around the study of passions. The passions are the lynchpins of mind–body unity, and to play this role passions must have a dual status, consisting in bodily processes and thoughts. That passions have this integrating function is reflected in the definition offered at article 27 of the *Passions*. The term 'passion' refers in the broadest sense to anything that happens in the soul independently of the will (PS, arts. 17–19), but passions in the strict sense are modes of the soul that are 'absolutely dependent' upon certain motions in the body (PS, arts. 27, 41). The definition of the passions states that they are 'perceptions, sensations or emotions of the soul, which we refer particularly to it, and which are caused, maintained and strengthened by some movement of the spirits' (AT XI, 349). The primary function of the passions is to protect the union of mind and body, specifically, 'to incite and dispose their soul to want the things for which they prepare their body' (AT XI, 359; see also PS, art. 52). How the passions achieve their biological ends is by a vigorous presentation to the will of objects for its consent and action upon. Biological success depends on being able to make quick evaluations of and responses to situations, a job for which the passions are particularly apt. Because the passions depend upon the body, the will, however, has only indirect control over the passions (PS, art. 45).

With this brief sketch of what a passion is and how it functions, the following eight chapters explore some of the more prominent themes of Descartes' account of the passions. The aim is to show that it is the passions more than any other modes of mind that are fundamental to our experience of unity, and to show why that experience is necessary in both our practical and theoretical enterprises, insofar as these depend on the co-operation of the body.[10]

In the following chapter, I examine the philosophical background to the passions, as presented in the exchange between Descartes and Princess Elisabeth. The problem of reconciling dualism with the experience of embodiment is the problem occupying Princess Elisabeth at the start of her correspondence with Descartes in 1643, and this and many other problems she raises set the agenda for his subsequent account. The fruit

---

[10] The *Passions of the Soul* is the culmination of work on sensation that begins with several earlier treatises (published and unpublished) concerned in part or whole with the functions of the human body – *La Dioptrique*, *Le Monde* and *Traité de l'homme*, all written between 1629 and 1633, and parts of the *Principia Philosophiae*, written between 1640 and 1642 – and represents Descartes' most mature formulation of the integration of rational and sensitive functions of the human being.

of their exchange is a treatise which complements and extends the project of the *Meditations* into the practical domain, and over which the *Meditations* also had a demonstrable influence. A comparison of the two texts is undertaken in the final section of this first chapter

Despite his claims to the contrary, Descartes' reflections on the passions do not emerge *ex nihilo* from the well-springs of his understanding, but are grounded in a number of traditions influential in debates about the passions during the Renaissance. Chapter 2 explores Descartes' place in these traditions, and argues that despite the continuity with a past he disparages, his treatise on the passions is revolutionary in the particular scientific perspective it adopts and in its treatment of passions as ideas of a unified soul.

Chapter 3 addresses the question why phenomenological monism is important to Descartes. I argue that passions and sensations are necessary for embodied rationality. Rational decision-making and action requires that one experience oneself as if one were a single embodied substance. We are not to our bodies as pilots are to their ships, and importantly, *we could not be*. Our navigating the world depends on our direct awareness of our bodies and the spatial orientation with respect to other objects that that provides. The passion of wonder plays a central role in explaining our spatial awareness and abilities. In his broader theory of the integrated functions of sensation and emotion, Descartes thus demonstrates a sensitivity to some strikingly modern problems in philosophy and the cognitive sciences, in particular, the relationship between attention and sensation, and the question of the indispensability of phenomenal content.

Passions inform our moral judgements and rational decision-making by virtue of their representational properties. Chapter 4 examines the intentionality of Cartesian passions, in terms of how they are referred to the soul. Descartes' treatment of how sensations and passions represent is puzzling and constrained, on the one hand, by his official account of representation, understood in terms of the objective reality of ideas, and, on the other, by his need to allow that sensations and passions often contribute to false judgements. A study of the referring function is useful for understanding Descartes' account of sensory representation generally, but also helps to solve certain perennial problems in Cartesian scholarship concerning the notion of material falsity. A study of these issues provides evidence that Descartes' realism is direct not representationalist.

In chapter 5, I return to the metaphysical issues surrounding the union of mind and body, and, specifically, to the relationship between passions in the soul and actions in the body. The union is more than an accidental conglomerate of substances but less than a single substance itself, although some have argued that if we understand 'substance' broadly enough, we can count the union as a substance.[11] In the *Passions*, at least, Descartes is seeking a conception of mind–body unity or oneness compatible with his dualism. Although he does not postulate any kind of metaphysical identity between the substances of mind and body to account for this unity, there are passages that suggest a metaphysical oneness of modes across the two substances. Descartes expresses this view by referring to actions in the body and passions in the soul as being *une mesme chose*. Understanding what this means for Descartes brings us closer to understanding what the union entails for him and helps to resolve the question of Descartes' alleged occasionalism.

It is hoped that the present study will foster new ways of looking at the *Meditations* and many of its core ideas. Chapter 6 revisits the passion of wonder and argues that far from presenting the disembodied knower as an ideal, the *Meditations* should be read as providing certain principles by means of which the embodied knower may investigate natural phenomena. Knowledge of the natural world presupposes some affective engagement with it, an engagement that can be only imperfectly mimicked by a pure act of will. The passions of wonder and love are crucial to the practice of science and to our self-understanding, as particular individuals and as human beings. The 'self' that emerges from this study is both embodied and socially embedded. The social aspect of the self entails that its boundaries are to some extent flexible. We are capable of extending our selves to incorporate other persons, at least as parts of our moral if not metaphysical selves.

The last two chapters concern the *Ethica Cartesiana*, as Descartes' skeleton of a moral theory was oddly portrayed in some quarters during the seventeenth century. Moral advancement depends upon mastering and utilising passions. The final presentation to the will before action is the work of desire and controlling desire, as we shall see in chapter 7, is no trivial matter. We cannot avoid having some 'vain' desires, desires for things that do not come to pass, but a novelty of Descartes' account of desire is the introduction of something akin to the regret strategies of modern decision-theories, strategies for acting under conditions of total ignorance so as to minimise and, with practice, eliminate regrets.

---

[11] See Hoffman (1986) and Cottingham (1985).

Unlike the Stoics and Kant, Descartes does not believe that the path to virtue lies in extirpating one's passions. At the very end of the *Passions* we learn that all the good and pleasure of this life depend upon the passions (PS, art. 212). Whatever knowledge we attain of the good and evil for us in this life depends on our affective engagement with the social and natural world. Ethics is not an a priori study, but one that depends upon experience and acceptance of the providential order. This is a fitting end to a treatise that argues that happiness can only be achieved by recruiting a 'master' passion, *générosité*, to serve one's moral self-development. As will be argued in the last chapter, the treatise provides an elegant and simple solution to one central problem of ethical motivation: how can we be rationally motivated to act when action depends on desire and desires are not themselves the product of rational processes? Descartes' solution utilises the forces of reason and the body: to control what you desire and how you act, control what you esteem. It also marks Descartes' ethics as a virtue ethics grounded in the essential goodness of the free will, an ethics with some sinister precursors. The generally underplayed connection between Descartes and Machiavelli, and the problems with elevating the will above knowledge of the good, are explored in this final chapter.

The recommendation of this book is that Descartes' concept of mind, and the attendant concept of self, should be reconceived in light of those texts in which his attention is turned towards our experience of ourselves as whole human beings. If this picture is correct, the *Passions* should be as much core reading for our students as the *Meditations* is, for as Genevieve Rodis-Lewis eloquently describes it, the value of the 'little treatise' extends beyond the narrow topic of the passions and bears upon a proper understanding of Descartes' whole thought.

'From metaphysical roots, through physiology and its action in union with the soul, and through the soul's reaction to it, the treatise offers the most complete branch of the Cartesian philosophy and its ripest fruit' (Voss, 1989: xxv).

This ripened concept of mind, understood in terms of its complex relations to the body, the world, and others, this is Descartes' passionate mind.

CHAPTER I

Volo ergo sum: *the unity and significance of* Les Passions de l'âme

Until fairly recently, *Les Passions de l'âme* was a work relatively ignored in Cartesian scholarship. This may seem unsurprising given that it can appear as a hodgepodge of antiquated micromechanical explanations of the causes and symptoms of the passions, psychotherapeutic techniques and underdeveloped ethical claims. It is divided into three parts, the first part of which is concerned primarily with defining the passions, the second with expounding, somewhat tediously, the classification, physiological nature, functions and symptoms of the six principal passions (wonder, love, hatred, desire, joy and sadness) and the third with laying down an account of virtue while making further taxonomical divisions among the secondary passions. In the space of one short book, Descartes grafts together the three principal 'branches' of knowledge described in the preface to the French edition of the *Principles* – medicine, mechanics and morals – without, it seems, any clear strategy for integrating them.

The treatise on the passions seems remote in this regard from the work of the *Meditations*, the root system of Descartes' tree of knowledge, which has an obvious unity and works towards the clearly defined goal of establishing the metaphysical and epistemological foundations for science (AT VII, 17). In a prefatory letter to the *Passions*, Descartes asserts that he intends not to approach the passions as either an orator or moral philosopher but '*en physicien*', as a natural philosopher or physicist (AT XI, 325). Given the ethical turn the treatise takes in the last two parts of the book, this is either a disingenuous claim, or, more charitably, implies that Descartes saw no incongruity between dealing with moral and mechanical matters in an interrelated fashion. Whether such integration is possible is not, however, always obvious to the reader. The passions are defined in Part One (PS, art. 1; 2; 27) by their relationship to the mechanical processes of the body that cause them, and by their being 'referred' to the soul itself. Yet, they are taxonomised throughout the treatise by neither of these relations, but by what Thomists referred to as their formal objects, a normative notion describing the kind of object or situation in which an emotion of a given type is appropriate or even possible.[1] The formal object of regret is the loss of some good; of fear, something threatening; of anger, an injustice, and so on. The enumeration of the passions by reference to their (formal) objects is crucial *inter alia* to Descartes' ethical concerns. Virtue depends on mastery of the passions, and in deciding which passions dispose us to vice and which to virtue, it is imperative to sort out which have as their formal objects things that 'depend only on us', and which do not. By analysing the formal objects of the passions, we can thus see what relationship there is, if any, between our passions and the will, a task that assists the will in trying to master the passions. Although the physiological approach is warranted on its own terms, Descartes' emphasis on it seems strange, therefore, and dissociated prima facie from the overall point of the book, which is to facilitate the pursuit of happiness (*la béatitude*) or the good life.[2]

To appreciate the unity of the *Passions* and the reasons why Descartes claims he must approach the passions *en physicien*, we will, however, have to know a little more about its background, in particular, his correspondence with Princess Elisabeth.

THE CORRESPONDENCE WITH ELISABETH

Elisabeth was a victim of fortune as only someone from a large dispossessed ruling family of Europe in the seventeenth century could be. The

---

[1] According to Anthony Kenny, 'the formal object of øing is the object under that description which must apply to it if it is to be possible to ø it. If only what is P can be ø'd, then 'thing which is P' gives the formal object of øing' (Kenny, 1962: 189). Within the genus of (voluntary) killing, for example, homicide differs from other species of killing in being the killing of a human being, and murder as the killing of an innocent human being (Kenny, 1962: 190–1). If the victim is not human, the act cannot be one of homicide. In the case of emotions, formal objects are still used today to differentiate among emotions and to define their 'appropriateness' conditions. An emotion directed towards an object not perceived as threatening or dangerous to oneself cannot be fear. Anger is reasonable if directed against an injustice and not otherwise. For a recent use of the notion see Ronald de Sousa, 1987: 121–3.

[2] Gueroult argues that by his assertion that he will approach the passions *en physicien*, Descartes did not intend to explicate the passions from a purely physiological point of view but only to claim that he would use the rational method of the sciences appropriate to such a confused and obscure subject matter (Gueroult, 1968/1985: 202). Descartes' approach was that of a *savant* – i.e., someone applying the rational method of examining evidence appropriate to the subject matter of the union of body and soul and the obscure and confused modes the union generates (Gueroult, 1968/1985: 202). Aiming for rigour and an approximation of the scientific method (Gueroult labels it a 'substitute for science' (p.195)) would be sufficient to distinguish Descartes' approach from the popular moralist tradition. Gaukroger (1998) clarifies the point by arguing that Descartes' account of the passions is *grounded* in his natural philosophy, which frees him to use traditional methods for classifying the passions. For further discussion on what's new in Descartes' *Passions*, see chapter 2 and my 1999.

eldest daughter of Elisabeth Stuart, daughter of King James I of England, and the Elector Palatine, Frederick V, the short-reigning 'Winter King' of Bohemia, Elisabeth speaks as one immersed in public life.[3] Her moral and practical dilemmas were not merely hypothetical, and she experienced at first hand both the debilitating and fortifying effects of strong passions. When she asks Descartes in 1645 (13 September) to define the passions, it is with a view to setting passion and reason in accord with one another, and to developing strategies for coping with contingencies that threaten, as she sees it, the very power of reason itself. The search for congruence between reason and passion is the overarching theme of the *Passions,* and the one that unifies it.[4]

Descartes' exchange with Elisabeth begins not with these issues in practical philosophy, however, but with an argument about the metaphysical coherence of his interactionist dualism. From the beginning, Elisabeth urges Descartes to explain how the interaction between an incorporeal soul and a body is compatible with his account of motion, based on the laws of impact and contact between surfaces of bodies (16 May 1643). On 21 May 1643, Descartes responds that to understand the causal interaction between mind and body, one must first understand the union of mind and body, which cannot, however, be further analysed. The notions of mind, body and the union 'are certain primitive notions that are as it were models on the basis of which we form all our other knowledge' (21 May 1643; AT III, 665) More precisely:

For the soul and body together we have only that [notion] of their union on which depends that of the force of the soul for moving the body, and of the body for acting upon the soul by causing its sensations and passions. (AT III, 665)

To say that a notion is primitive is to say that it cannot be analysed in terms of other notions, but also that it is somehow explanatorily basic – that in virtue of which other things are understood and which is not itself understood in terms of other things. Our conception of the union is primitive in the first sense because it is not entailed by the two basic

---

[3] The family was exiled to the Netherlands in 1620. Descartes first mentions Elisabeth in a letter to their mutual friend, Pollot, in October 1642. His correspondence with her dates from May 1643, although it is possible that he may have met her before this.

[4] Lilli Alanen (2003: ch. 6) emphasises the role of Elisabeth's questions to Descartes in the structuring of his thought about the passions. She notes that it is Elisabeth who leads Descartes to consider, on the one hand, the relationship between reason and passion, and on the other hand, the relationship between passion and virtue and happiness.

concepts of Descartes' metaphysics, mind and body, taken separately or conjointly. The conceptions of mind as thinking substance and of body as extended substance entail nothing about how these substances interact or affect one another. Our notion of the union, which is a notion of mind and body interacting, must therefore derive from some source other than our metaphysical concepts of mind and body. It derives instead, Descartes claims, from our 'experience' of moving and being affected by our bodies (AT v, 163). The union is known obscurely through the intellect, but clearly through the senses, which is why those who are immersed in their senses have no doubts about the existence of interaction between mind and body (AT III, 691–2).

Without a clear and distinct idea of the union, Descartes cannot offer Elisabeth a metaphysical account of how interaction between mind and body works, and so what he offers instead is bound to disappoint. He tells Elisabeth that the way in which the mind moves the body (without contact) is no more difficult to understand than the way bodies, on some Scholastic accounts, were thought to move towards the centre of the earth because of their *gravitas* (heaviness) (AT III, 667–8). Descartes does not think that there can be any such quality as *gravitas*, but this is not his point in appealing to the analogy. The point is rather to get Elisabeth to see that her very understanding of this false theory involves an illicit projection of her own experience of moving her body by her thought, an experience of causing motion which does not require contact between the surfaces of two bodies. This experiential understanding of the union is used correctly when it forms part of our understanding of human behaviour, and incorrectly when it is used as a model for understanding how bodies move themselves.

I believe that we use this notion [of force] incorrectly in applying it to weight, which is nothing really distinct from body, as I hope to show in the Physics, and which has been given to us for conceiving the manner in which the soul moves the body. (AT III, 667–8)

As Descartes explains in the *Sixth Replies*, the reason it is incorrect to project the idea we have of our own capacity to move bodies on to bodies themselves through the notion of *gravitas* is that *gravitas* could only cause a body to move in a certain direction if it possessed some kind of cognitive representation (*cognitio*) of the centre of the earth, and where there is no mind, there is no cognition (AT VII, 442). Daniel Garber has emphasised the importance of the analogy in showing Elisabeth that she already has an

understanding of mind–body interaction.[5] Her intuitively clear grasp of
the union will only become confused and obscure through attempting to
explain it further. Moreover, Elisabeth cannot reject the theory of *gravitas*
on Descartes' grounds and claim not to know how the mind and body
interact.

This last point is, however, precisely what Elisabeth claims that she
does not know. She agrees that she knows from experience that the soul
moves the body; what she wants to know is how, if it is immaterial, it does
so. She cannot see the point in arguing from analogy with a false theory,
but in a way her rejection of the argument cuts deeper than that. What she
is rejecting is the possibility of an idea in Descartes' system, and a central
idea at that, based on an *empirical* foundation. We encounter the notion
of the union in our everyday doings and sayings, Descartes writes to her,
when we exercise our senses, creative imagination and will, not by using
our intellect, which can know the union only obscurely (AT III, 691). It is
'only in the use of life and ordinary conversation, in abstaining from
meditating and by studying things that exercise the imagination, that one
learns to conceive the union of the soul and of the body' (28 June 1643,
AT III, 692). It is as if he is saying that Elisabeth knows how the soul
moves the body insofar as she knows how to do things with her body,
converse with others, conjure up images and memories at will and so on,
and that this is genuine knowledge of the union. But for Elisabeth these
practical skills themselves stand in need of reconciliation with Descartes'
dualism, and thus do little more than shift the original problem. Thus she
concludes: 'it would be easier for me to concede matter and extension to
the soul, than the capacity of moving a body and of being moved, to an
immaterial being' (10–20 June 1643, AT III, 685).

Elisabeth's reasons for resisting Descartes' explanation are not the usual
suspects: Leibnizian concerns about the coherence of the conservation
laws given the existence of an incorporeal source of motion, or doubts
about alternative forms of causation based on something other than

---

[5] Garber, 2001: 176. Garber also argues that what Descartes *should* have told Elisabeth is that her
understanding of impact, which she takes to be so clear and distinct, *presupposes* the very understanding of mind–body interaction she claims eludes her (Garber, 2001: 188). The details of Garber's
argument cannot be wholly reproduced here but the basic structure of this interesting argument is
that there cannot be an understanding of how impact works without an understanding of the laws
of motion, in particular the conservation law, which cannot be understood except in relation to
God's immutability and his activity in creating and conserving bodies in motion. But our understanding of God's role as an efficient cause of motion is derived from our experience of the way in
which we move bodies through acts of the will (Garber, 2001: 180–6).

contact between surfaces. Nor is her worry the bald one that exercises most philosophers today of how the immaterial and material per se could interact – hardly a pressing concern for Christians of the seventeenth century. She takes Descartes' point about the union being known through experience and points out the difficulties with it. Her objections raise the spectre that the degree of integration required to explain the experience or phenomenology of the union, of oneness with the body, is incompatible with the real distinction between the mind and the body. She points out something that Descartes would not want to hear – that the roots of the tree are preventing a branch of natural philosophy, the study of human nature, from blooming.

More precisely, Elisabeth presents Descartes with two arguments: let us call the first the *argument from information* and the second, the *argument from the interference of corporeality on rationality*. Both are encapsulated in the following passage:

For if (the soul's moving the body) occurred through *information*, it would have to be that the spirits, which perform the movement, were intelligent, which you accord to nothing corporeal. And although in your metaphysical meditations you show the possibility of (the soul's being moved by the body), it is, however, very difficult to comprehend that a soul, as you have described it, after having had the faculty and habit of reasoning well, can lose all of it through some vapours, and that, although it is able to subsist without the body and has nothing in common with it, is so much ruled by it. (AT III, 685; my emphasis)[6]

The first argument turns the analogy with *gravitas* back against Descartes. To Elisabeth's mind, bodies are no more capable of moving in accordance with a *cognitio* of their end that originates in an immaterial rational soul than they are of being moved by *gravitas*. If the body moves towards a certain end because of instructions given to it by the soul, it must be capable of representing those ends to itself or be sensitive to the informational content of the ideas that move it. But this looks dangerously like thinking, an attribute Descartes denies can belong to bodies.

The second argument points out the conflict in arguing, on the one hand, for the autonomy of the mental, and recognising, on the other hand, the debilitating effects that a body afflicted by strong passions or an imbalance among the humours and spirits can have upon reason. It

---

[6] On the interference of bodily conditions upon thought see also Arnauld's objections to the real distinction argument in the *Fourth Objections* (AT VII, 204).

strikes Elisabeth that a more reasonable explanation of why the mind can move the body and be debilitated by the body is because it is a body itself.

In light of this exchange between Descartes and Elisabeth about mind–body interaction, it is not unreasonable to read the *Passions* as an attempt to articulate the functional integration of mind and body not in such a way as to explain the experience of oneness with the body each of us has, but at least so as to deal with these specific problems, the problem of information and the problem of interference on reason from bodily causes, and thereby to make dualism more palatable to Elisabeth. Given this agenda, approaching the passions *en physicien*, that is, from a micro-mechanical perspective, is not surprising. As will be discussed further in chapter 3, information from the rational soul is not represented or inter-preted by the body-machine, but is encoded in the configurations of animal spirits and processed according to mechanically specifiable proce-dures that in no way presuppose intelligence or cognition. These results, many of which follow through on ideas developed in the *Optics*, are incorporated in the first part of the *Passions* (PS, art. 36).

The second problem, how to reconcile the autonomy of the rational soul with interference from the body, is taken up as one of the central themes of the *Passions*. Descartes must explain the impression of the soul's 'being ruled by the body' and argue against it. The body can in no way rid the soul of its rational powers, but it can limit the materials it has to work with, and distract it from the proper exercise of those powers. It is, therefore, imperative that the rational soul regain its autonomy through mastery of the passions, mastery which consists not in extirpating the passions, for they turn out to be required for the realisation of its autonomy and perfection 'in this life', but in the proper regulation of the passions in accordance with virtue. Self-mastery, as shall be discussed in chapter 8, depends on the cultivation of a master passion, *generosity*, which when habitual is virtue. Generosity depends upon the recognition and value of the absolute freedom of the will, a will that would be compromised, according to Descartes, if Elisabeth's pessimism about the debilitating effects of the body on reason or the materialism to which she inclines were true. It is the fact that the will transcends the determi-nistic realm of matter that enables it to rise above it and gain some degree of control over it.

The early exchange between Elisabeth and Descartes on the interaction problem ends on a disappointing note. When Elisabeth confesses that materialism seems to her the only way to make sense of the interaction between mind and body, Descartes recommends to her that she should feel free to attribute extension and matter to the soul 'for that is nothing but to conceive it as united to the body'. Attributing matter and extension to the soul will cause no confusion so long as she realises that this is not philosophising about the essence of the soul or mind. We are incapable of conceiving distinctly the union of mind and body and their distinction at the same time.[7] Elisabeth responds, however, in a defiantly philosophical mode: extension may not be essential to thought, but since it is not contradictory to it either, she will continue to doubt, using the method Descartes advances that what she cannot sufficiently perceive she will not judge to be so, that the soul is immaterial.[8] Elisabeth has the last word on the subject, following which there is a gap in their correspondence on the question of mind–body union. Stephen Gaukroger surmises that the gap might be indicative of Descartes' engrossment in the dispute with Voetius, but it may also indicate the stalemate Descartes and Elisabeth had reached on the topic of mind–body interaction (Gaukroger, 1995: 387). Descartes and Elisabeth do not return to the problem of interaction once their correspondence resumes.

When their correspondence does resume in May 1645, Descartes is responding to news of Elisabeth's prolonged illness, an illness he attributes to the sadness caused by the state of her household. Their attention turns to the relationship between happiness (contentment of mind) and fortune. Descartes' position on this question, as we shall see, is indebted to certain Stoic ideas. The good that we can attain in this life and the happiness that accompanies it depends entirely upon how we use our wills. But against the Stoics, Descartes asserts that he 'is not one of those cruel philosophers who wish their sage to be insensible' (AT IV, 201–2). Although reason is their 'mistress', passions have a place in the life led wisely.

Until the point at which Elisabeth asks Descartes to define the passions, their exchange follows this practical and moral turn. But there is also a dramatic edge to the exchange, as each correspondent falls into a classical 'humouric' dramatic type. He is sanguine; she is melancholic, and the fact that they are playing out Elisabeth's real world dramas forces Descartes to think about the problems passions pose to human reason and happiness in a concrete way. Elisabeth observes how her misfortune has affected her

---

[7] Letter to Elisabeth, 28 June 1643 (AT III, 691–5).
[8] Letter to Descartes, 1 July 1643 (AT IV, 2).

reason and happiness (despite the fact that she does not equate happiness and fortune). Descartes responds with various psychotherapeutic techniques for calming the heart and facilitating the circulation of the blood. These techniques include distracting the mind with objects which 'bring contentment and joy' as well as recommendations for available medical remedies such as the waters of the Spa.[9] Elisabeth is sceptical of the long-term benefits of psychotherapeutic remedies. She cannot extract herself, she objects, from her senses and imagination; she cannot avoid her obligations, which cause unruly passions; and she cannot put into practice the kind of advice Descartes offers except after the passion has played itself out.[10] Elisabeth's melancholy begins to look characteriological, and while from 1645 onwards their correspondence consists largely of Descartes ministering to her emotional needs, the gloom does not lift.

Nonetheless, it is Elisabeth who, through her questions as much as her outpourings, defines the issues that become central to the *Passions*. Descartes suggests that they read Seneca's *De Beata Vita*, with a view to giving content to his letters, but also with the intention, one suspects, of bringing her round to his views on the independence of *la béatitude* and fortune. He refers to the 'sovereign contentment', which prefigures his discussion of the 'sovereign good' in the letter to Queen Christina of 20 November 1647, which he defines as pursuing only those things, such as wisdom and virtue, which depend upon us. On 4 August 1645, he offers Elisabeth the three rules of his *morale par provision* from the *Discourse on Method*: (1) to try always to make the best possible use of one's mind; (2) to have a 'firm and constant resolution' to do what reason advises and not be led astray by passions (this is virtue); and (3) to limit one's desires as much as possible to things within one's power. In his next letter to her of 18 August 1645, he is careful to distinguish contentment from the sovereign good (using the will well) while noting, however, that the former depends upon the latter. These ideas form the core of the conception of self-mastery developed in the final part of the treatise.

Whether Elisabeth found these reminiscently Stoic exercises helpful is hard to judge. A persisting theme in her criticisms of Descartes' practical philosophy is that contentment in this earthly state cannot be guaranteed without some compliance by external circumstances. Descartes' identification of virtue with a function of the soul – the free exercise of the will – defines the good at a distance from things involving the body. Against

---

[9] Letter to Elisabeth, May or June 1645 (AT IV, 218–22); cf. PS, art. 48.
[10] Letter to Descartes, 22 June 1645 (AT IV, 233–4).

this, Elisabeth raises the characteristically gloomy objection that if the good relies on the autonomy of the will from the body, terminating the union should always be preferable to sustaining it for those seeking virtue.[11]

There is some justice to these criticisms of Descartes' account of the good life, but the view is subtler than Elisabeth supposes. In these early conversations about the passions, Descartes advances the importance of a comprehensive theory of contentment – namely, of the need to understand (1) the bodily causes of discontent, (2) the powers of reason with respect to what comes to it from the body, (3) how the goods of the mind and body are to be ranked against one another, and (4) how the passions distort the value of pleasures and pains stemming from the body.[12] The idea that a proper classification of goods pertaining to the soul and to the body is necessary for defining the good is a recurring theme of the *Passions.* It suggests, furthermore, that Descartes thinks of the happiness of the soul as dependent in some fashion on its relation to the body. As for Elisabeth's suggestion that it is more consistent with his theory of mind that we should desire to end rather than preserve the union, Descartes replies that it is only 'false philosophy' that suggests that this life is worse than the next. Descartes himself can offer no guarantees based on reason that one would enjoy all the felicities of the life after this one.[13] But more to the point, even what we suffer in this life can be a source of inner joy and contentment, and it is not clear that we would be better off in a life that did not provide us with occasions for the joy we experience simply from the fact that, for better or worse, we are being moved. The good for us in this life depends on our capacity for passions, which are the source of our 'sweetest pleasures'.

Elisabeth does not herself endorse the dichotomy between reason and passion she suspects Descartes' metaphysics of entailing, and shows no inclination herself to hurry into the next life. In asking Descartes to define the passions, she notes rather that while many claim that the 'perturbations' of the soul are opposed to reason, she herself has been shown by experience that 'there are passions that carry us to reasonable actions' (AT IV, 290). Descartes' letter of 6 October 1645 contains his first and general definition of the passions. Passions are all the thoughts that are 'excited in the soul without the concurrence of her will, and consequently, without

---

[11] See Elisabeth's letters of 30 September 1645 (AT IV, 302) and 28 October 1645 (AT IV, 323).
[12] Letter to Elisabeth, 1 September 1645 (AT IV, 283–5).
[13] Letter to Elisabeth, 6 October 1645 (AT IV, 315).

any action that comes from her, solely through the impressions in the brain, because that which is not an action is a passion' (AT IV, 310). He goes on to distinguish passions from imaginations that arise from actions of the will, habits or inclinations that dispose one to passions of certain sorts, and from judgements (which also involve the will) about good and evil (AT IV, 160–1). By contrast with judgements, passions in the strict sense have as their proximate causes impressions in the brain. Even if the processes terminating in a passion begin with a judgement or the mind conceiving an object in a certain way, a passion is produced only because of the 'imprinting (of) the image on the brain' (AT IV, 312). At this point, Descartes confesses to having been slowed down by the difficulty of trying to enumerate the particular passions (AT IV, 313). The complexity of the taxonomic project is evident from the exhausting classification of passions undertaken through the *Passions*.[14]

Descartes agrees with Elisabeth that the passions are compatible with reason but stresses that without the involvement of the will the passions will always turn out to have a precarious relationship with reason. Descartes' pragmatism is nowhere more evident than in his account of the passions: if the passions are reasons, then it is important to recognise that they do not always behave as such. If a passion is left unchecked, it can bypass reason and become a direct stimulus to the will to act. Moreover, in being representational modes and exceptionally vivid, passions often appear to be good reasons for acting when they are not.

[The passions] nearly always make the goods as much as the evils they represent to appear considerably larger and more important than they are with the result that they incite us to seek the one and avoid the other with more ardour and care than is appropriate, just as we see also that beasts are overcome by lures and to avoid the little evils they throw themselves into the larger ones. That is why we ought to help ourselves to experience and reason to distinguish good from evil and to know their just value, so that we don't take the one for the other and carry ourselves to nothing with excess. (AT XI, 431)

If Elisabeth's pessimism taught Descartes anything, therefore, it was that the dominance of reason and will over the forces of the body is hard to achieve in practice and unlikely to be achieved through direct confrontation by the will. This idea is encapsulated in article 41 where Descartes asserts that the will has only indirect control over the passions.

---

[14] Enumerating the passions remains a difficulty for modern commentators as well. Ronald de Sousa has argued that unlike beliefs, which uniformly have the True as their 'formal object', each type of emotion is *sui generis*. There is no single formal object for all the passions (de Sousa, 1987: 123).

But if the soul is going to have any influence over the body, it must first have knowledge of the body-machine and a clear demarcation of the functions of the soul and of the body. In light of the concerns that form the focus of Descartes' correspondence with Elisabeth, the natural philosophy which permeates the discussion of the passions is, as Lisa Shapiro has argued, not at all out of place with the normative questions the *Passions* purports to address.[15]

Between May 1645 and the time at which Descartes sends Elisabeth the first draft of the *Passions* (which she acknowledges in a letter of 25 April 1646, AT IV, 404), their correspondence covers a range of additional topics which were incorporated into the 'little treatise'. Elisabeth raises questions concerning how to console oneself about the evils that humans do from free will, and how to measure incommensurable goods, for example, the goods for one's individual soul, like philosophy, and public goods.[16] She also asks whether there are conditions under which excessive passions can be good.[17] Once she had received the first draft of the *Passions* in 1646, she asks how it is possible to distinguish passions by their physiological causes; how we can practice remedies for the passions when we cannot foresee all the contingencies of life; and how we can avoid desiring things which do not depend upon us but are necessary for self-preservation.[18]

The technical question concerning the possibility of physiologically distinguishing the passions makes the taxonomic project all the more pressing. It is only because we can distinguish the passions as thoughts, and because they occur in different combinations, Descartes replies, that it is possible to enumerate them (May 1646, AT IV, 408). Elisabeth's question concerning the possibility of regulating one's passions and desires when circumstances are not in our control leads, finally, to one of the defining aspects of Descartes' theory of virtue: practical wisdom consists in willing what we judge to be best, wisdom which he believes is practically possible, despite the inevitable uncertainty that is part of our embodied existence.

As for the remedies against the excess of the passions, I admit they are difficult to practise, and even that they cannot suffice to prevent the disorders that arrive in the body, but only to make the soul untroubled and to enable her to retain her

---

[15] Shapiro (2003) argues that the physiological story is necessary to show us how we may influence our passions by habituating ourselves to connect different thoughts to the effects of brain motions from those instituted by nature or habit. The principle of habituation is, she claims, the unifying principle of the book.

[16] Letter to Descartes, 30 September 1645 (AT IV, 301–4).

[17] Letter to Descartes, 28 October 1645 (AT IV, 322).

[18] Letter to Descartes, 25 April 1646 (AT IV, 403–6).

free judgement. Nor do I judge that this requires an exact knowledge about the truth of each thing, nor even that one has foreseen in particular all the accidents that can befall one, for undoubtedly that would be impossible; but it is enough to have imagined in general the most annoying accidents, and to be prepared to suffer them. (May 1646, AT IV, 411)

We shall see in chapter 8 how making the will the locus of virtue is problematic, but for the moment it is enough to note that the virtuous use of the will is not conceived of as cut off from the sensitive faculties that depend upon the body. It is necessary to use imagination to prepare oneself for inevitable contingencies, and imagination is a faculty that has its 'seat' in the brain. How these imaginative exercises strengthen the soul is by diminishing opportunities for the soul's being unpleasantly surprised or gripped with a stupefying wonder that prevents appropriate deliberation and action. The artful use of imagination and the directing of wonder in useful ways are important psychotherapeutic techniques for gaining control over the passions. The use of the imagination is crucial for changing the very dispositions of the brain itself, for by imagining difficult situations in which we might find ourselves, we reduce the element of surprise and de-sensitise the brain to incoming images likely to excite the animal spirits.[19]

That the correspondence with Elisabeth defines the central problems Descartes is working through in the *Passions* and illuminates the need to combine mechanistic, medical and moral considerations can be of no doubt. When in November 1647 Descartes sends a revised version of the treatise together with the 'Letter on the Sovereign Good' to Queen Christina through his friend and French Ambassador to the Swedish court, Hector-Pierre Chanut, he notes how he wishes he could include his correspondence with Elisabeth so as to make the treatise 'more accomplished' (AT V, 187–8). In hindsight, we can well appreciate why he would have desired doing so. Their rich philosophical and personal correspondence not only complements the treatise on the passions but also contains our best clues as to why it was written the way it was.

THE INFLUENCE OF THE *MEDITATIONS*

Like the *Meditations, The Passions of the Soul* is a kind of training manual, only this time it is the aspiring sage rather than the aspiring philosopher

[19] I thank one of the referees for suggesting that Descartes' principle of habituation involves changing the structure of the brain by changing the connections between sensory inputs and how the spirits are subsequently channelled. On the mechanism of this restructuring procedure, see chapter 8 and Sutton (1998a; 1998b: 1.3).

who is being put through her paces. Both texts begin with an endorsement of something akin to the Pythian dictum – *Nosce teipsum* ('know thyself'). Be it practical or theoretical, good philosophy begins with a proper understanding of the functions of mind and body, the two essential components of a human being (AT XI, 328; AT VII, 12). The general confusion both texts aim to correct is the tendency to attribute properties and functions to the soul appropriate only to the body (PS, arts. 4–5; AT VII, 26). The *Passions* also carries on the project, begun in the *Sixth Meditation,* of reconceiving the function of sensation from a biological rather than epistemological perspective. The similarities between the two texts are striking and the dissimilarities revealing.

Like sensations generally, passions mislead the soul into false judgements but judgements of a primarily practical and moral kind. Indeed, it is the same weakness in the soul that explains both kinds of error – sensations and passions make their objects salient or vivid to the will, which is thereby disposed to assent to the ideas they propose before reason has considered them adequately. In the theoretical case, as the wax example of the *Second Meditation* demonstrates, the mind is apt to be misled by the vivacity of sensations into thinking that it knows bodies and their qualities more distinctly than any other thing, including the elusive 'I' which does not admit of a corporeal image (AT VII, 29–30). Passions lead a weak soul into 'false opinion' about good and evil – namely, to think that goods that depend on things beyond the control of the will are more desirable or important than those the soul can obtain through its own power (PS, art. 49). It is because passions depend upon events in the brain, tend to exaggerate the value of their objects, vary from person to person, and because conflicting passions (e.g., fear and ambition) can be evoked in the same person by the same situation and pull the will in opposite directions at the same time, that passions are unreliable guides to good and evil (PS, arts. 138, 39, 48). But in the well-ordered soul, passions are more useful than not. The primary function of both sensations and passions is the preservation and perfection of the union of mind and body (PS, art. 40; AT VII, 89).

Having grasped the point that the function of the passions is biological rather than epistemological, the sage-in-training like the meditator turns to the mind itself to ground moral truths. In the practical sphere, this reflective act is not one that can be performed while the existence of one's body is in doubt but is motivated by a passion, *générosité*, which is the noblest kind of self-esteem.

And I notice in us only one thing that is able to give us a just reason for esteeming ourselves: to know the usage of our free will and the command that we have over our volitions. (AT XI, 445)

In both texts, therefore, the exercise of withdrawing ourselves from our senses brings us first and foremost to knowledge of some essential aspect of the soul. The meditator comes face to face with herself as a *res cogitans*, an essentially thinking thing, the sage, the *res volans*. The *Passions* carries the reader to the conclusion that what is known indubitably in the moral domain is the essential freedom of one's own will, and the resolution to use it well becomes the mark of virtue (PS, arts. 153, 156, 148). This is the crowning achievement of the treatise, just as the discovery of the intellectual nature of the soul is a pivotal moment in the *Meditations*. From the discovery that the freedom of the will is the ultimate source of value, true knowledge of the value of other goods, ranked according to the extent to which they depend upon the will or not, is possible.

The identification of what is good for human beings with the good use of the will might seem to preclude the passions from having an indispensable role in the good life. But this is not the case. The passions have a place in the providential order and in the natural life of the sage (PS, art. 145). Descartes' remark, at the very end of the treatise, that 'on the passions alone all the good and evil of this life depends' (PS, art. 212), may seem surprising given that the good is elsewhere defined as the good use of the will (PS, art. 153), and the passions are contrasted with volitions (PS, art. 17). But it is not so strange if we bear in mind that for Descartes our first introduction to good and evil is through the passions, and that the good use of the will in this life is the good use of the will of an embodied agent. The will needs an object, and to meet the needs and ends of the whole human being must be guided by passions. Descartes' account of the place of passions in the good life reinforces the *Sixth Meditation* discussion of the function of sensations in the 'best system that could be devised' (AT VII, 87). When controlled by reason, passions and sensations are our best source of information about circumstances external to the soul, a view which he uses to make the further claim that the tendency of passions to dispose us to certain kinds of error conflicts in no way with the goodness of God (AT VII, 88; AT XI, 438).

The need to classify the passions in relation to their 'formal' objects rather than by their proximal causes in the body can now be better understood. The will of the sage acts autonomously but is bolstered by the passions and, to some extent, guided by them. Many passions direct the will to actions required to preserve the union of body and soul. The representational role of sensations and the passions is discussed in articles 22–4 of the *Passions,* and follows a path laid down by the discussion of sensory representation in the *Meditations* and *Replies.* The passions function by indicating how objects are related to the union, as good or evil, advantageous or disadvantageous, and in what way (past, present or future, surmountable or insurmountable, attainable or unattainable, etc.). An understanding of the passions must therefore take into account the objects upon which action must be taken, as much as their proximal causes. In this function, passions and sensations report the 'truth' much more frequently than falsity (AT VII, 89).

In these respects, the *Passions* complements the project of the *Meditations* in providing an account of the passions compatible with the general rejection of sensations as epistemically foundational. There are, however, significant differences between the two texts. The central metaphysical arguments of the *Meditations* for God's existence and goodness do not appear in the *Passions* but, as we shall see, are presupposed in the weight attached to Providence for controlling desire. The *Passions* is not an exercise in metaphysics, and seems rather to have been deliberately written to keep its subject matter within the purview of natural philosophy, a move that can be read as protecting the metaphysical distinction between mind and body drawn in the *Meditations.*[20] But by far the most significant difference between the two texts is that whereas the *Meditations* recommends withholding assent in *all* theoretical matters which are not clear and distinct, Descartes can make no such demand in the practical sphere. Passions are 'confused and obscure' perceptions, and we should be cautious in submitting to actions they recommend, but we have to act (irresolution is a vice), and we do not always have the luxury of lengthy deliberation when matters are pressing (PS, art. 170).

The epistemic outcomes of the *Meditations* and the *Passions* are thus radically different. Descartes goes so far as to recommend to Elisabeth that when in doubt about how to act, it is best to follow local customs and embrace opinions that are 'most probable', advice reminiscent of that of ancient sceptics and academics.[21] The probabilistic judgements we make

[20] This accords with Descartes' comment to Elisabeth that he did not wish to discuss the union of body and soul in the *Meditations* since its existence, unlike that of the real distinction of mind and body, is not something most people are in doubt about, and that any protracted treatment of the union may have been detrimental to the real distinction argument. See the letters of 21 May 1643 and 28 June 1643.

[21] Letter to Elisabeth, 15 September 1645. Compare Sextus Empiricus' advice to follow the laws of the land and local customs in *Outlines of Pyrrhonism,* 1. 23–4.

in practical and moral affairs compare less favourably than the certain outcomes of Descartes' theoretical meditations, but accord with a distinction he makes elsewhere between moral and metaphysical certainty. Moral certainty is 'sufficient for ordinary life' but lacks the guarantee of necessity that metaphysical certainty carries (AT VIIIA, 327). Whereas the meditator is required to eschew all probabilistic claims, the sage cannot, and is wise precisely because she learns to live well despite uncertainty.

This difference in epistemological outcomes between the projects of the *Passions* and the *Meditations* generates further differences between the two texts and new problems for Descartes' practical philosophy. The combination of finite intellect and infinite will, the limitations of embodiment and the unreliability of the passions, the necessity to act and the 'inevitable evils' of things outside our control, is a volatile mixture (PS, art. 146). Under these conditions, moral and practical errors are inevitable, and the theodicy offered in the *Meditations* begins to look unstable. In light of this outcome that moral error and ignorance are inevitable, Elisabeth is led to question how the sage is supposed to achieve the supreme contentment Descartes insists accompanies virtue. Descartes' metaphysical arguments against the reality of evil and for fate and Providence may impress the meditator, but seem lame against Elisabeth's suspicion that virtue and contentment do not go hand-in-hand.[22]

We should not, therefore, overstate the similarities between the *Meditations* and the *Passions,* but nor should we ignore them. There are enough commonalities to see the *Passions* as a unified work, and one that complements the *Meditations* and extends its project into the practical realm. The overriding aim of the *Passions* is to instruct the reader on how to master the passions so that they will be an indispensable resource for the will in determining right action. To this end, it is necessary for the sage to understand the psychophysical processes undergirding the passions and their effects on the will and on the body. But in the pursuit of virtue, we must be motivated as much by passions arising from the body as by prescriptions from the rational soul. The body is not an impediment to virtue but properly directed, a necessary condition for it.

---

[22] See Elisabeth's letters of June 1645, 16 August 1645, 13 September 1645, and 25 April 1646. Elisabeth asks how the inevitability of error and moral evil can ever be reconciled with God's existence and beneficence (30 September 1645). Descartes' response to the problem of evil is the traditional Augustinian one – 'evil is nothing real but only a privation' – and so not anything caused by God. (To Elisabeth of 6 October 1645, AT IV, 308; See also the *Fourth Meditation,* AT VII, 55.)

CHAPTER 2

Perturbations or sweet pleasures? Descartes' place in two traditions regarding the passions

> Had this excellent Man, Monseiur des Cartes, been half as conver-
> sant in Anatomy, as he seems to have been in Geometry, doubtless
> he would never have lodged so noble a guest as the Rational Soul in
> so incommodious a closet of the brain, as the Glandula Pinealis is;
> the use whereof hath been demonstrated to be no other but to
> receive into its spongy cavities, from two little nerves, a certain
> serous Excrement, and to exonerate the same again into its vein,
> which nature hath therefore made much larger than the artery that
> accompanieth it; and which having no communication with the
> external organs of the senses, cannot with any colour of reason be
> thought the part of the brain wherein the Soul exerciseth her
> principal faculties of judging and commanding.
>
> (Charleton, 1674: preface)

Of the many accusations thrown at Descartes by contemporary philosophers, the strangest is surely the cognitivist's one which holds him
accountable for having reduced emotions to 'mere feelings' or 'the rush
of animal spirits to the brain'.[1] Were it so, *Les passions de l'âme* should
have fallen stillborn from the press, for its principal neuroanatomical
claim – that the pineal gland is the 'seat' of mind–body interaction –
was met with a substantial amount of derision.[2] This is not to say that the
text was not significant as a piece of natural philosophy in its time, but its
influence has more to do with the way questions about the passions were
formed, rather than the particular answers that were given. Descartes was
not the first to conceive of passions as intermediaries of mind–body
union, but his particular conception of the mind as a unified substance

[1] See, for example, Solomon (1988) and Greenspan (1988). For further variations on cognitivism, see
Lyons (1977) and Marks (1982), and for arguments against cognitivism see Griffiths (1989; 1997).
[2] The influential Nicholas Papin, *Docteur en medecin*, argued that the pineal gland was too anato-
mically limited to, as he put it, 'receive all the movements attributed to it' (Papin, 1653: 15). Walter
Charleton added that the gland was too fixed and inflexible to bend in the ways Descartes imagined
it would when the will and the spirits struggled for command over it (Charleton, 1674: preface).

in conjunction with the mechanistic theory of matter forced him to rethink the topic of the passions in radically different ways.

The tendency to view Descartes as a reductionist about emotions is symptomatic of a widespread inability or unwillingness to conceptualise anything in his system as involving mind and body functioning together. It is assumed that the real distinction of mind and body entails a total separation of functions, and thus, if Cartesian passions are bodily processes, they are not 'mental' or 'intentional' phenomena in any sense of those terms, and conversely, if passions are ideas, there is no sense in which they could *depend* upon operations of the body. For those who accept this reasoning, and reject the dualism that gives such conditionals their force, Descartes' account of the passions will seem fundamentally reductionist.

This reasoning is not only false (see chapter 5) but deeply ironic, for if we now think of emotions as ideas, as bearers of intentional content, it is most likely because of Descartes, who, by conceiving of passions as ideas, established the very conceptual foundations modern cognitivists now take for granted. Alternatively, if we think that passions are essentially biological phenomena, we again owe a debt to Descartes, for although he was not the first to synthesise the two pre-existing approaches to the passions, medical and moral-psychological, he was the first to do so in a way compatible with modern scientific perspectives.[3] But we shall not see this except with the hindsight of a little history, a history to which Descartes himself was none too kind.

A POPULAR SUBJECT

That which the ancients have taught [about the passions] is so little to the point and for the most part so little believable that I am unable to have any hope of approaching the truth by following the paths they have followed. (AT XI, 327–8)

---

[3] Treating the passions from both a moral and natural philosophical perspective at the same time was the norm since Galen, and whether one's approach was *en physicien* or as a moral philosopher or rhetorician was typically more a matter of what one took to be fundamental, rather than a way of excluding other perspectives. Gaukroger cites Petrarch's *De remediis*, a compendium of Stoic remedies for the passions, as an example combining medical and moral approaches (Gaukroger, 2002: 224–6). The combination of these two approaches was also evident in those accounts that placed more weight on moral analysis. Aquinas, for example, treats the 'material' component of the passions in accordance with the standard medical view of the humouric system of the body (*Summa Theologiae*, I–II, q. 28, art. 5 and q. 44, art. 1). In his commentary on Aquinas' theory of the passions, *Tractatus quinque ad Primum Secundae D. Thomae Aquinatis*, IV, disp.1, Suarez also advocates natural philosophy as the proper home for discussions on the passions.

Descartes' insinuation that very little of substance had been written about the passions belies the fact that there was an abundance of ancient, medieval and Renaissance texts available on the subject and the extent to which his own account is continuous with those traditions. Interest in perturbations of the soul and abnormal psychological conditions, such as melancholia, was particularly high during the Renaissance. Elisabeth, who we know prompted Descartes to write on the subject, also requested at least one other manuscript on the subject: Edward Reynolds' (1640) *A Treatise of the Passions and Faculties of the Soule of Man* was dedicated to and recommended by her for publication.

Many popular texts which discussed the passions served as general guides for healthy living, the most celebrated being the Salerno doctors' *Regimen Sanitatis Salernitanum* – (initially) 362 rules for daily health – published in over 300 editions 1852. Bartholomaeus Anglicus' *De proprietatibus rerum* included a discussion of the passions and was published in over twenty editions between 1372 and 1601 and in at least five languages. Robert Burton's *The Anatomy of Melancholy,* in three volumes (1621), presented an encyclopaedic study of the causes, symptoms, cures and therapies for that most celebrated disease of the soul, discussed in great and often hilarious detail. (Nothing cures love-melancholy like marriage, but this 'cure' comes last in a long list of remedies of the diet-and-drugs variety, suggesting that it should be undertaken only as a last resort (Burton, 1949: III, 252–5). Timothy Bright's *A Treatise of Melancholy* (1586) was published in three editions by 1613, and Juan de Huarte Navarro's *Examen de Ingenio*s (1594) was published in four editions by 1616. Cureau de la Chambre's *Les caractéres des passions,* the first volume of which Descartes read (though claimed to have derived nothing from doing so), was published in five volumes between 1640 and 1662.[4]

In the moral tradition of writing on the passions in the seventeenth century there were two main centres of influence: Aristotelianism and Stoicism. Nicholas Coeffeteau's *Tableau des Passions* (1630) and Thomas Wright's *The Passions of the Mind in General* (1596/1601), align themselves with the faculty psychology and idea of passions as motions of the sensitive soul of the Aristotelian tradition. The basic orientation of

---

[4] See the letter to Mersenne, 18 January 1641 (AT III, 296). Gaukroger argues that by mixing mechanism and 'a kind of vitalistic naturalism' de la Chambre represented precisely the kind of confusion that arises from attributing functions of the body to the soul which Descartes sought to avoid. The notion of a 'substantial union' can be seen as an alternative to this kind of naturalism on the one hand and occasionalism on the other (Gaukroger, 1995: 390).

Aristotelians was to think that the passions were all by nature good, but in Christian thought the passions were connected with the Fall of humanity, and strict control by reason and the will was required for them to be compatible with virtue. As Wright pontificates: 'the inordinate motions of the passions' are 'thorny briars sprung from the infected root of original sin' (Wright, 1596/1601: 89).

Through a revival of Stoicism in late sixteenth-century France, a number of moral treatises appeared stressing the independence of happiness and fortune. Among Stoic approaches, Anthony Levi has argued that Guillaume du Vair's *De la sainte philosophie* and *La Philosophie morale des Stoïques*, Pierre Charron's *De la sagesse*, Justus Lipsius' *Manuductio as stoicam philosophiam* and *Physiologia stoicorum* and Michel de Montaigne's *Essais*, stand out as bearing obvious similarities to the orientation of *Les passions de l'âme*, and were likely available to Descartes (Levi, 1964). The general influence of Neostoic ideas is evident, according to Levi, from the gradual breakdown of the faculty psychology of Aristotle and his followers, and from a subsequent 'rationalising' of passions as ideas of a unified sensitive and intellectual soul.[5] Juan Luis Vives' *De anima et vita* (1538), with which Descartes was also familiar, also diverged explicitly from the faculty psychology of the Scholastics (Levi, 1964: 26). [6]

Many philosophers prior to Descartes were of the view that the passions were connected with our embodiment and thus contained an involuntary element that would pose an inevitable challenge to the rational soul seeking to perfect itself.[7] For both Plato and Aristotle, passions supply a direct impetus to action, and although passions are typically mediated by some cognition, they are not thereby mediated by reason or deliberation. What a passion *is* on the divergent theories of Plato and Aristotle is difficult to say and well beyond the scope of this book, but it is generally understood that for both passions involve (1) a movement of a sensitive

---

[5] Levi traces this idea to the Florentine Neoplatonist, Marsiglio Ficino (Levi, 1964: 24–5).

[6] The experiments Vives performed to condition certain kinds of behaviour in animals were also known to Descartes, and formed a basis for his ideas about how to 'train' oneself out of vicious emotional habits (e.g., AT XI, 422). See Vives, *De anima et vita*, 1.17, and for discussion, Casini, 2002.

[7] Aristotle's discussion occasionally suggests more than a completely involuntarist notion of passion. In the *Nichomachean Ethics*, 1105b21 Aristotle defines the passions in connection with appetites accompanied by pleasure or pain, but in the *Rhetoric* 2.5 (e.g., 1382a21–2), they are defined in relation to their formal objects, suggesting a connection to belief or judgement. See James, 1997:40–1. Knuuttila (2004, ch. 1. section 4) thinks it fair, therefore, to attribute to Aristotle a 'compositional' theory of emotions, in which an evaluative judgement is a defining constituent of an emotional response.

part of the soul towards or away from some object – i.e., physiological changes and an impulse to certain kinds of behaviour – on the basis of (2) some cognition or evaluation of an object (typically) as it stands in relation to oneself and (3) the feeling or phenomenological awareness of these changes in the soul. For Plato, the emotions belong to the 'spirited' part of the soul (*thumoeides*), and are essentially connected with our self-assessment. (*Republic*, 4.435a-441c). In the disordered soul, emotions are impediments to reason, and the philosopher must strive to rise above them through the independent use of reason. Mastery of the passions on the Platonic view requires the subjugation of emotions to reason, but passions can, nonetheless, be an ally to the rational soul. In his comprehensive study of ancient and medieval theories of the passions, Simo Knuttila argues that the emotions have an even more central place in the Aristotelian conception of the good life (Knuttila, 2004: ch.1). When moderated according to the golden mean, Aristotelian emotions are an essential component of the good life, which requires a significant degree of emotional awareness (through, for example, anger and pity) of the needs of others (*Nichomachean Ethics* 2.6, 1106b18–23; 4.5, 1126a3–8).

In antiquity, the Stoics are distinctive in holding it both desirable and possible to attain a state of complete freedom from (bodily) passions (*apatheia*). The self-centred quality of emotional evaluations meant that there could be neither an objective standard of truth for the emotions, nor a degree of emotionality compatible with virtue. Stoic emotions just *are* species of evaluative judgements, which, because of their inherent tendency to exaggerate the importance of the self in the cosmos and to affirm the appropriateness of giving in to certain forms of distress, are false and vicious. Knuttila argues that it is for this reason that the Stoics opposed any attempt to render the passions virtuous through moderation (Knuttila, 2004: 76–8). There can be no degree of disease or vice compatible with moral health and virtue.[8] Although the Stoics allow as morally acceptable some 'good feelings' (*eupatheiai*) – well–reasoned joy, caution and wishing – these are not emotions or passions in the strict sense. They involve neither a disturbance in the soul nor an attachment to contingent objects or events   (Inwood, 1985: 173–5; Knuttila, 2004: 68–9).

If passions are simply false judgements, it is natural to suppose that they would be eradicated by an appropriate change in belief. But this was

---

[8] See, for example, Seneca, *De ira* 2.9, and Cicero, *Tusculan Disputations*, III.

not thought to be the case. To explain this phenomenon, the Stoics distinguish two components of an emotion: the 'first motion', an involuntary movement of the soul towards or away from some object, and an act of (voluntary) assent to the evaluations suggested by these first motions, such as the evaluation that a situation is good or bad and that one is justified in responding emotionally. What distinguishes the Stoic sage from those who are led by their passions is not freedom from first motions, which are natural, but the act of dissent from the evaluations associated with those motions.[9] Whether we would have the first motions of a passion unless we were already evaluating a situation in a certain way is, however, obscure and points to a tension within the Stoic account of the passions.

The intellectualist character of Stoic passions is clear in Cicero's *Tusculan Disputations* III and IV, in which all 'perturbations' of the soul are defined as the result of judgement and opinion 'so that it may be realised not only how wrong they are but to what extent they are under our control' (343; also, 403). The egocentric quality of these judgements is striking in Cicero's vilification of erotic love in the *Tusculan Disputations*, IV, 35:

Such inconsistency and capriciousness of mind – whom would it not scare away by its very vileness? This characteristic, too, of all disorder must be made clear, namely, that there is no instance where it is not due to belief, due to an act of judgement, due to voluntary choice. For were love a matter of nature all men would love the same object, nor should we find one discouraged by shame, another by reflection, another by satiety. (Trans. King, 1971: 415)

The very idiosyncratic and inconstant character of erotic love – the fact that we do not all love the same objects, the fact that we love something at one time and not at another for reasons unrelated to the virtues of the object – shows how depraved and false this passion is and why we ought to strive for its extirpation.

The illusion of passivity, the experience of feeling victim to one's passions, is explained on the Stoic view by the effects of the involuntary component. The purpose of moral philosophy is to bring us to the recognition that we are agents of our passions. By exercising direct control

---

[9] A classic example is the explanation given by Epictetus of an example from Aulus Gellius' *Attic Nights* 19.1.17–18 of the Stoic during a storm at sea feeling the first motions of fear but not assenting to the proposition that it poses an evil to him. See also Cicero, *Tusculan Disputations*, 3.76; 4.59–63 and Seneca, *De Ira*, 2.2.2–5; 2.3.4–5, and for a useful overview of Stoic detachment, Knuuttila, 2004: 66, 75–8, and Nussbaum, 1994: ch. 10.

over one side of a passion, we may gain control over the whole, and by extension, over our actions. Although most philosophers after the Stoics were keen to distance themselves from this extreme view, believing that the passions were all by nature good, the intellectualist strand in Stoic thought resurfaced in Renaissance accounts. Descartes' own thinking about the passions has distinctively Stoic elements. Although he expresses dissatisfaction with Seneca's *De beata vita,* finding the Stoic idea of the supreme good as 'living in accordance with nature' obscure, and rejecting the conflation of contentment and the supreme good in favour of treating the former as the motivating consequence of the supreme good, Descartes agrees with the Stoics on a number of key points (AT IV, 273–7). The principal task of Cartesian moral philosophy is to use our reason to discriminate what is and what is not within our control, and to regulate desires accordingly, so that our contentment of mind does not depend on what is beyond our power to control (AT IV, 252–3; 263–8). Cartesian passions also have both an intellectual component as ideas and an involuntary bodily component in the motions of the brain that give rise to and sustain them, and even though passions are distinct from judgements, or at least do not entail an act of assent, they are intellectual modes of the soul.[10]

In medical circles, the Stoic influence can be detected in the flourishing of psychotherapeutic (rather than purely medicinal) techniques for controlling the 'diseases of the soul' (Galen, 1963: 53). Galen compared the intemperate with 'wild beasts' that have let themselves be governed by the irrational power of the soul, but it was generally acknowledged that the dependence of passions on bodily processes and uncontrollable external circumstances meant that rational control of the passions would be inevitably indirect.[11] Psychotherapeutic exercises, such as engaging in activities to promote more useful 'contrary' passions on the occasion of an unruly one, or in imaginative exercises designed to limit the effects of unpleasant surprises, were indirect means by which the soul could exercise rational control over its involuntary elements.[12]

---

[10] On the question of whether Cartesian passions are judgements, see chapter 4.

[11] Galen, 1963: pp. 45–6. Since we are not always in the best position to appreciate the irrational side of our nature, Galen recommends asking someone else to check one's irrational passions (p.44.).

[12] Although Descartes disagrees at article 48 with the usefulness of trying to calm the soul by generating conflicting passions, some of his cognitive therapies are similar to those of the Stoics. Through imaginative exercises, Epictetus claimed to show students how to understand situations without distress, and how to use premeditation to prepare them to bear the worst. See Knuuttila, 2004: 78. Descartes' advice to Elisabeth is similar (AT IV, 411).

Aside from his remarks of June 1645 to Elisabeth about the medicinal properties of the spa, Descartes offers little by way of purely medicinal remedies for the passions, proposing instead various psychotherapeutic remedies (PS, arts.50; 211). These include (1) the acquisition of knowledge and forethought (to prevent excessive awe directed at the wrong sorts of things and to prepare us for every eventuality) (PS, art.76; 176); (2) the correct use of reason (PS, arts. 138; 148; 170); (3) reflection upon Divine Providence (PS, art. 145) and (4) the correct understanding and exercise of the will, (PS, art. 156; 161). An important method for obtaining rational control of the body is the correct use of attention, about which more will be said in chapters 3 and 8. Unethical or irrational behaviour is typically a matter of not knowing how to make ourselves do what we know theoretically we ought to, and this lack of practical knowledge is a lack of a 'firm habit of belief', which can only be obtained through a focused attention of the mind (AT IV, 295–6). Cartesian passions are neither voluntary nor subject to direct rational control, but some degree of indirect control is permitted through cognitive exercises aimed at directing attention to connect new thoughts with stimuli received through the senses (AT XI, 369–70).

There is little distinction then for Descartes between the 'cures' for unruly passions and the practice of moral philosophy itself, and this in general explained why it was not uncommon to find during the Renaissance no distinction between treatises on morals and medical treatises on the passions. Pierre de la Primaudaye's *The French Academie,* for example, went so far as to recommend the study of philosophy itself as 'a certain remedy and sound medicine for every vice and passion' (Primaudaye, 1577/1972: 38). Descartes' statement in the *Preface* to the *Passions* that he will approach the passions *en physicien* does not, therefore, indicate that he intends to reduce the passions to physiological processes or ignore their moral status, but nor does it tell us what exactly he thinks he is doing that is so new.

GALENIC PHYSIOLOGY

There will not be mind [*animus*] except through the health of the rational soul [*anima*] nor the health of this [the rational soul] except through the health of the vital and the natural souls, and the health of these two will not be present [*consistit*] except through the health of the body. Nor is there this [the health of the body] except through a balance of the humours. The balance of the humours comes only from a balanced composition [*complexio*], which there will in no way be except through the regimen of the art of medicine, through which there is the maintenance of health in the healthy and its restoration when lost.[13]

It was standard during the Middle Ages to conceive of the passions in accordance with the theory of temperaments, whose great master in antiquity, following Hippocrates, was Galen.[14] According to Galen, the temperament of an individual, and thus her disposition to certain kinds of passions, was the product of the composition of four bodily fluids or 'humours' – blood (hot, moist), phlegm (cold, moist), yellow bile (hot, dry) and black bile (cold, dry) – which themselves were mixtures of the four basic elements: earth, air, fire and water. As the above quote from the tenth-century Persian physician, Abbas, indicates, the dependence of diseases of the mind on humouric imbalances suggested to some that the perfection of reason could only be obtained in the first place through application of the medical arts. Ancient Greek doctors equated health with equilibrium (*eucrasia*) and disease (including emotional distur-bances) with imbalances (*dycrasia*) in this humouric system (Galen, 1928: II, 8). The four classical temperaments – the sanguine, the phleg-matic, the choleric and the melancholic – represented the major forms of *dycrasia*, depending on which humour was predominant (Galen, 1928: II. 9) The theory of temperaments became the cornerstone of medicine during the Middle Ages in both the West and the East. Avicenna attri-butes the strong disposition to joy in a drunken person to a very moist spirit, 'excessively altered by the mixture of the vapours rising there and inundating it and moistening it immoderately'.[15]

The pervasiveness of the theory of temperaments cannot be under-estimated. It infiltrated not just medicine but literary and popular culture generally, as evident from the emergence of the 'humourist' – sixteenth-century literary figures like Ben Jonson and William Shakespeare, who constructed character types from the four classical temperaments (the choleric, the sanguine, the melancholic (famously, Hamlet) and the phlegmatic). At the beginning of the Renaissance, pharmacology was

---

[13] This passage from Haly Abbas, *Regalis dispositio* I *theor.iii* is quoted in Harvey, 1975: 14. See her discussion of the rivalry between medieval doctors and philosophers.

[14] Galen's neuroanatomy was surprisingly sophisticated, especially regarding the functions of the sensory and motor nerves of the spinal cord. He developed a complex theory of localised cerebral lesions and this localisation of functions extended to the discussion of passions. Passions were no longer merely explained by general functions of the brain but by events occurring within the central ventricle of the brain. The idea of cerebral localisation differed from the holism of Hippocratic medicine and persisted beyond the decline of Galenism during the Renaissance.

[15] Avicenna, *De viribus cordis*, I.v.

dominated by the basic principles of Galen's theory of temperaments. The melancholic, for example, suffered an over-abundance of cold and dry (black bile), and required treatment by 'contraries', in this case, medications that moisten and heat the body (Galen, 1928: II, 9).

In antiquity, the four elements were thought to be present in inanimate and animate things alike, and, therefore, some special element was thought necessary to explain sensation and self-motion. The Stoics introduced a new notion – *pneuma* (*spiritus* in the Latin tradition) – that stood for a very fine grade of matter, like a hot breath or fine wind, which permeated the body and accounted for sensation, consciousness and self-motion. Being material, *pneuma* was able to travel through very tiny vessels of the body, such as the arteries and nerves. Galen attributes the origins of this idea and the division between vital pneuma (that which travels through the arteries) and psychic pneuma (that which travels through the nerves) to Erasistratus, one of the founders of the university at Alexandria in the fourth century BC, and who was renowned for being the first to have performed a public dissection of a human body (Galen, 1928: II, 9; Robinson, 1943: 73, 67). Despite his general disapproval of Erasistratus' account of the human body, Galen retained the concept of *pneuma* and the division between vital and psychic pneuma. According to Galen, nourishment digested in the stomach is processed into humours in the liver and then the heart. Vital pneuma originates in the heart and psychic pneuma in the *rete mirabile* – the 'marvellous network' of arteries Galen supposed exists at the base of the brain (Galen, *Opera Omnia*, 1821–33: XIV, 697, 726; Harvey, 1975: 7). The psychic pneuma was the finest grade of matter in the body and accounted for the cognitive, sensory and motor functions of animals. The Latin translation of 'pneuma' – *spiritus* – is the origin of the concept of bodily spirits in Renaissance medical texts, and Descartes' terminology of 'animal spirits' (from *animus*) derives from the notion of psychic pneuma.

Aristotle held that the rational and sensitive soul had its 'seat' or principal organ in the heart. Noting that damage to the brain could affect sensation, intelligence and motion without affecting the functions of the circulatory system or nutritive functions, physicians of the Hippocratic School, notably Galen, shifted the seat of sensation, intelligence and motion to the brain, and placed more weight in explaining these capacities on the functions of psychic pneuma. Influenced by Plato's tripartite division of the soul, Galen also proposed a further division of the animal into three separate but integrated systems or souls centred around the functions of the liver, heart and brain: the vegetative (nutritional and reproductive) system, the animal (cardiovascular) system and the rational (nervous) system. In the Middle Ages, a corresponding division of pneuma or bodily spirits into three (natural, vital and animal) occurred, the natural spirits being connected to the functions of the liver, the vital spirits to the heart and animal spirits to the brain.[16] Later philosophers, seeking to preserve the authority of Aristotle, would attempt to reconcile Aristotle's idea that the seat of sensation was the heart with Galen's account of psychic pneuma, with odd results. Avicenna, for example, held that the brain was the principal seat of sensation and self-motion, but ultimately dependent upon the well-functioning heart.[17] The debate over the seat of the soul was mirrored by a debate over the primacy of psychic or vital pneuma in explaining cognitive functions (Temkin, 1973: 143–4).

'Vitalists' held that the blood contained special properties that 'animated' the flesh of animals and accounted for sensation and locomotion, but since it is the animal spirits that directly affect the brain, it was difficult to see why the blood should be counted among the proximate causes of cognitive functions. For those who followed Galen more closely, the functions of the intellect were no longer bound so intimately with all life-sustaining functions of the body, but were linked to the body only through the operations of the most rarefied bits of bodily matter, the animal spirits.

The dominance of the Galenic theory of temperaments in the history of medicine is staggering. Despite being challenged at various times, Galen remained an authority in medicine in both the East and West until the Renaissance.[18] In 1525, the first editions of Galen's work in Greek were available, and had an immediate impact upon the humanists, including

---

[16] Harvey argues that the tripartite division of the spirits is not evident until the writings of Abbas (Harvey, 1975: fn. 22, p. 64). Temkin claims that Galen was cautious of both vital and natural pneuma, but later texts presenting the Galenic account attribute three spirits to him (Temkin, 1973: 107).

[17] Avicenna, *Canon*, I: 30a62–30b1. See also Aquinas, *Summa Theologiae* I-I.q.83.a.I.

[18] Temkin denies that there was any 'slavish servility' to Galen in either the West or East during the Middle Ages (Temkin, 1973: 118; 123–5). Galenic anatomy was not seriously challenged until the sixteenth century, when Vesalius and Paracelsus criticised it for anatomical inaccuracies. See Neuburger, 1910. The ideas of Galen were available through translations of Arabic medical anthologies, in particular, the *Articella*, which included the *Ars medica* or introduction to medicine by Galen, the *Pantegni*, a selection from the medical encyclopaedia of Abbas which drew heavily on Galen and presented a vitalist conception of emotions, the *Isagoge*, an introduction to the *Ars medica* by Iohannicius, and that exhausting tome of medieval medicine, Avicenna's *Canon*. For discussion of Galen's influence in the latin West, see Temkin, 1973: 100–7, and Knuuttila, 2004: 177–215.

Vives, but advances in anatomy, pathology, and methodology led to a gradual decline in Galen's influence in the medical faculties of European universities.[19] Even after the demise of Galen's authority in anatomy in the sixteenth century, clinical practice remained primarily Galenic until the eighteenth century. Favouring treatment of the diseases of the soul based on a regimen of diet and drugs, Galenic medicine aimed at restoring the 'equilibrium' of the body, and this idea persisted (Temkin, 1973: 165–6).

Descartes' relationship to these historical shifts is complex. He follows Galen on the brain being the 'seat' of sensation and motion, and regards the alternative position, which endows the heart and blood in the arteries with these functions (vitalism), as an opinion 'not worth any consideration' (AT XI, 353; AT XI, 334–5). He retains the terminology of spirits but acknowledges only one kind, the animal spirits, which being the most proximate triggers of sensory and motor functions explain all the movements of animals (e.g., PS, art. 36). Descartes' terminology of 'animal spirits' is, however, divorced from the broader theory of temperaments that defines medieval Galenism. His explanations of differences in temperament no longer invoke the characteristic properties of the four humours (hot, dry, cold and moist), but appeal instead to the 'inequality (in quantity) of spirits', which can be the result of what is ingested or imbibed, as when by drinking too much wine an excessive amount of spirit enters the brain, or which can result from abnormal conditions of the major organs of the body, in particular, the brain and heart (PS, arts. 15, 36, 39). Where the term 'humour' is used, Descartes is quick to establish that there is 'no difference' between the bodily fluids (including what we call 'humours') and those parts of the animal we call solid, beyond the size and rate of motion of the particles of matter of which these parts are constituted (AT XI, 247). In *L'homme*, Descartes compares the way in which the animal spirits produce all the variety of movements in the muscles, depending on the amount of spirits in the nerves and cavities and pores of the brain, to the way in which hydraulically operated machines in the royal gardens are caused to move, play instruments or utter sounds, solely by water flowing into their pipes in varying quantities (AT XI, 130–1). Animal spirits are 'merely bodies', endowed with no other

---

[19] Galen's anatomy was largely based on animal dissections. As postmortem autopsies became available in the later Middle Ages, Galen's account of the *rete mirabile*, the functions of the heart and blood, and division of soul and spirit, were no longer considered viable. See Temkin, 1973: 136–59.

qualities besides the regular modes of extension: size, shape and motion. They are 'extremely small bodies which move very quickly' (PS, art. 10), and as such can pass from the nerves through the tiny pores of the brain and to the nerves again, by means of which they affect all the muscles of the body (PS, art. 16).

If Descartes is indicative of a general trend in medical circles, then it is clear that among the reasons for the decline in Galen's influence during the Renaissance was the fact that the core ideas of Galenic medicine – notably, the idea of three different systems or 'souls', and the three types of bodily fluids or spirits, each possessing its own distinctive properties or 'powers' – clashed with the emerging mechanistic conception of matter. As Oswei Temkin observes, Galen's conception of bodily health is based on an ideal mixture of what would become known, in light of Descartes' devastating critique, as 'secondary qualities' (hot, cold, dry and moist), which were essentially sensible qualities, and thus as Galen claimed, best detected by the skin of the palm of a well-balanced person (*De temperamentis* I, chs. 8 and 9, *Opera Omnia*; Temkin, 1973: 19). As in physics generally, secondary qualities in medicine were replaced by degrees of the same thing – in Descartes' neuroanatomy, by the rate of motion and size of tiny corpuscles of matter (the animal spirits) – which were objectively measurable by emerging mechanical diagnostic devices like the thermometer.[20] It was no longer assumed that the human sensory system was a reliable tool for diagnosing medical problems.

What Descartes likely derives from the paradigm shift in medicine occurring around him is a unitary conception of bodily spirit, with which he must explain all the mental phenomena that depend upon the body, and all the conflicts such dependence produces.[21] But he must also, in the process, reconceive the passions and their relationship to the senses, on the one hand, and reason, on the other, a shift that sets his account apart from two other major authorities on the passions during the Middle Ages, Avicenna and Aquinas.

---

[20] Temkin attributes the invention of the thermometer to Sanctorius Sanctorius (1561–1636), ironically as an attempt to objectively measure imbalances in the humouric system in accordance with Galen's principles (Tempkin, 1973: 160).

[21] The unified conception of soul or spirit was a feature of some naturalist views, such as those of Telesius (1509–88) and Campanella (1568–1639), whose views were likely known to Descartes. I thank Michaela Boenka for discussion on this medical background to Descartes.

THE EMERGENCE OF THE *VIS ESTIMATIVA*

So far we have examined the extent to which Descartes' approach to the passions marks a radical break with traditional methods for examining the passions from the perspective of natural philosophy. But as the conception of a passion had to be adjusted to be congruent with the new conception of matter, so too it had to be developed in ways to fit a changing, non-Aristotelian conception of the soul. As mental phenomena, Cartesian passions and sensations stand in complex relations to other mental phenomena and to the soul itself, which is a simple indivisible substance, at once sensitive, rational and appetitive, and which therefore is unable to be divided against itself. One of the reasons why faculty psychology was attractive was that it offered a simple explanation of psychological conflict. The faculty psychology model explained intrapsychic conflict in terms of conflicts between the sensitive and intellectual parts of the soul. Before we turn to Descartes' solution to the problem of psychic conflict, let us examine the basic elements of the dominant Scholastic conception of the sensitive soul, its functions and its relationship to the rational soul.

If Galen was the master of the theory of temperaments, the eleventh-century Islamic philosopher-physician, Avicenna, was the great medieval master of the theory of internal senses, which defined the functions of the sensitive soul and its relationship to the intellect, on the one hand, and to bodily motion, on the other.[22] The internal senses stored and processed images once they were received into the soul through the external senses, and were crucial to understanding the passions. Avicenna explained internal sensory processing in terms of five powers located in specific cerebral ventricles: *phantasia*, the function of which was to produce images of things not present, located in the front ventricle; *imaginativa*, a power for temporarily storing images (working memory) and combining them into new (e.g., chimerical) formations, located in the middle ventricle; the *Sensus communis*, a faculty for combining distinct images into a more complete image of the object sensed, located in the front ventricles; *memoria* or long-term memory, located in the rear ventricle; and finally, the *vis estimativa*, a power for receiving non-sensible forms of objects which have some utility or disutility for the animal, located in the

---

[22] Knuuttila argues that the sixth book of Avicenna's *Shifa*, available in Latin translation as *De anima* from around 1150, dominated philosophical psychology well into the middle of the thirteenth century, even following the translation of Aristotle's *De anima* (Knuuttila, 2004: 177–8).

central ventricle. It is the estimative power that is essential to the production of a passion. Capable of directing the animal spirits on its own, the estimative faculty could be either the instrument of reason or her chief impediment, as evident in animals lacking the faculty of reason or in humans gripped by unruly passions or dreaming.[23]

The faculty of estimation accounts for the cognitive aspect of an emotion on those theories following Avicenna. It enables an animal to receive non-sensible forms (*intentiones* in the Latin translations) that carry some value for its embodied existence. Since the forms received by an animal when agitated by a passion – for example, the *malicitas* of the wolf for the sheep – are not forms that can be detected by any external sense, a special internal sense was postulated to explain its reception and this was estimation.[24] Some forms are detected by instinct; others are the product of conditioning, for example, when a dog apprehends a stick or brick as dangerous because it has been beaten with such things in the past (*De anima*, IV, 3). Aquinas' influential account of the passions is heavily indebted to Avicenna's theory of the internal senses. Aquinas adopts Avicenna's division among internal senses (collapsing, however, *phantasia* and *imaginativa* into one power) and the role of the *vis estimativa* in explaining passions.[25] Although the theory of the internal senses was developed to apply to both animals and humans, there was a shared concern among its advocates to preserve the pre-eminence of reason in humans. To demarcate the faculty of estimation when it was subordinate to the power of the rational soul, the estimative faculty in humans was referred to as the *vis cogitativa*. The difference between the cogitative faculty in humans and the estimative faculty in animals concerned not their primary function – the detection of *intentiones* – but their different roles in the wider cognitive economy. Estimations in humans are subordinate to universal reason, and passions are second to the will in the order of motive powers, whereas animals are determined to act by the combination of their estimations and passions. Aquinas describes the difference thus:

---

[23] Avicenna held that dreams were the result of the state of the animal spirits in the *virtuus imaginativa*, which, in turn, depended on the state of the bodily humours. Hunger, for example, causes dreams of feasts. The *vis imaginativa* combines images it has either stored itself or from memory and submits them to the *sensus communis*, which perceives them as if they were coming from the sense organs. False dreams arise either from an imbalance in humours or in a body where the senses have not been sufficiently trained to serve reason.

[24] Avicenna, *Liber de anima*, vol. II, p. 39. See also the discussion of estimation in Black, 1993: 219–58.

[25] Aquinas, *Summa Theologiae*, I. q. and Avicenna, *De anima* I.I (26.27–27.36). See also Knuuttila, 2004: 219.

For the sheep, seeing the wolf, judges it a thing to be shunned, from a natural, and not a free judgement, because it judges not from reason, but from natural instinct. And the same thing is to be said of any judgement of brute animals. But a human acts from judgement, because by his apprehensive power he judges that something should be avoided or sought. But because this judgement, in the case of some particular act, is not from a natural instinct, but from some act of combination in reason, therefore he acts from free judgement and retains the power of being inclined to various things.[26]

When fear drives us away from some obstacle, the rational soul can bring to bear general considerations, such as the virtue or utility of courage, and command the body to resist the present evil. Having the power always to act from reason and the will does not mean that one will always exercise it, and those who allow themselves to be guided by their passions have intemperate souls.

Although the functions of the *vis estimativa* are central to the account of how a passion is produced, the passions are not acts of this faculty. Passions are changes in the *vis motiva* of the sensitive appetite caused by changes in the *vis estimativa*. As appetites, they are distinct from and can conflict with the appetites of the will. Aquinas explains the division between these various faculties of the soul, the hierarchical division between intellectual (higher) and sensitive (lower) parts of the soul, and the placement of passions in the sensitive appetite as follows. The soul has two motive powers, will and sensitive appetite, and two apprehensive powers, reason and sensation. The primary principle of division within the soul is the dependence on the body or, more specifically, on a bodily organ for the exercise of the power in question. Sensitive apprehension makes use of the organs of external and internal senses, and an act of the sensitive appetite involves a 'corporeal transmutation', whereas there is no specific organ that the exercise of intellect and will requires.[27] Since a passion in the strictest sense of the term involves a bodily change, either from better to worse or vice versa, a passion belongs in the sensitive part of the soul.[28] Passions in the broader sense indicating the reception of something (like the reception of sensible or intelligible species) into the soul do not involve a change where something is taken away from the body, and hence, exist only in the apprehensive parts of the soul.

Aquinas' second principle of division is what we might refer to in modern semantic parlance as the direction of fit of acts of the soul. Citing

---

[26] Aquinas, *Summa Theologiae* I–I.q.83.a.1.
[27] *Ibid.*, I–II, q.22, a.3.   [28] *Ibid.*, q.22, a.1.

Aristotle (*Metaphysics*.vi.4), Aquinas describes the appetitive power of the soul as having 'an order to things as they are in themselves'.[29] Hence the soul is drawn to some thing because the objects of the appetitive power (good and evil) are in things themselves. The apprehensive power, by contrast, does not draw the soul towards or away from its objects because its act consists in receiving the forms of sensible objects (*intentiones*), and the reception of these forms is sufficient for the act of this power to be complete. This is why truth-values belong to acts of apprehension but not to things, and moral values, like goodness and evil, to things rather than thoughts or perceptions.[30] Passions have the analogue of a world-to-words fit – they seek satisfaction through changing the world (by first moving the soul towards or away from an object) – whereas sensations and estimations have the analogue of a words-to-world fit – their satisfaction depends on changing the soul to fit the world. Desire, for example, is a movement towards an object and is complete only when the object is obtained. Desire cannot merely be the apprehension of a desirable object, for that act is complete once one becomes aware of the object's desirability. The mere apprehension of desirability cannot, in other words, explain on its own why the soul is moved to obtain the object in question. Aquinas concludes that the passions properly speaking belong in the sensitive appetite, and cites approvingly the definition of Damascene:

Passion is a movement of the sensitive appetite when we imagine good or evil: in other words, passion is a movement of the irrational soul when we think of good or evil.[31]

Not only was there thought to be a real distinction between the apprehensive and appetitive parts of the sensitive soul, on views like that of Aquinas, but also a real distinction within each part, a division which was thought necessary to explain some forms of intrapsychic conflict. The sensitive appetite is divided between powers that have good or the avoidance of evil absolutely as their objects (concupiscible appetites) and powers that have objects conceived of as obstacles to good or the avoidance of evil (irascible appetites). Aquinas proposed that there must be a real distinction between concupsicible and irascible powers of the sensitive appetite for the simple reason that the passions interfere with one another. Desire, for example, can be diminished by anger or despair. As Peter King has argued, however, this rationale for divisions within the sensitive appetite was a matter of some dispute, especially among followers of

[29] *Ibid.*, q.22, a.2.   [30] *Ibid.*, q.22, a.3.   [31] *Ibid.*

Aquinas in the sixteenth century. Francisco Suárez argued that the con-cupsicible and irascible powers are not distinct and opposing powers but co-ordinate powers, and all apparent conflict is simply a matter of one power, through its act, 'turning aside' or 'lessening' its other acts. No real distinction between powers of the sensitive soul was required, on this picture, to explain psychic conflict.[32]

The conception of the passions as appetites of a lower part of a divided soul endured throughout medieval and Renaissance accounts of the pas-sions. It is endorsed by Marin Cureau de la Chambre, for example, who also distinguished passions according to whether they were concupiscible or irascible.[33] Descartes' rejection of these divisions within the soul and their rationale shapes his own conception of the passions as ideas of an indivisible mind.

PASSIONS IN AN UNDIVIDED SOUL

The theory of the internal senses, and, in particular, the account of the estimative faculty, was no more compatible with Descartes' physics than was the theory of temperaments or vitalism. The idea of external objects possessing *intentiones* (non-sensible, evaluative forms) propagating them-selves through the medium and passing to the mind is as implausible to Descartes as the idea of sensible or intentional forms generally is. Des-cartes states his general opposition to intentional forms in the *Notae* as follows.

Whoever rightly judges [about] that to which our senses extend themselves and [about] what it is precisely that is able to come to our faculty of thinking from them, ought to agree that no things are exhibited to us by the ideas which we form of them by thought [*cogitatione*]. Therefore, as nothing is in our ideas which was not innate in the mind or the faculty of thinking, excepting only those circumstances which regard experience, we may assuredly judge that these or those ideas which we now have present to our thought may be referred to things posited outside us. And [we may judge this] not because those things send those [ideas] into our mind through the organs of sense, but because they send in something which gives it the occasion, through an innate faculty, to form them at this time more so than at another. Indeed, nothing comes from external objects to our mind from our senses except some corporeal motions... (AT VIIIB, 358–9)

---

[32] King, 2002: 240–1; Suárez, *Tractatus*, v.iv.4, 762b.
[33] See, for example, de la Chambre, 1658: v.ii.225.

In this passage, we get a clear indication that intentional forms are both incompatible with the new theory of matter Descartes is working with and redundant to the explanation of our ideas of sensible objects. But if the idea of forms transmitting themselves from objects to the soul generally was mysterious, the notion of *intentiones* was even more so. *Intentiones* are, by definition, non-sensible features of things and yet a special sense was postulated to receive them. Since, for Descartes, the danger of the wolf is no more transmitted to the soul (be it animal or human) than its colour or shape, there is no need to posit a special faculty of apprehension to receive it.[34] A fear response is explained mechanistically – in terms of an image (understood as nothing but a configuration of animal spirits) becoming associated in memory with an experience of pain and causing both a behavioural response and (in humans) a passion of fear and the idea of danger. The movements of the animal spirits caused by a perception of a wolf are very rapid and cut deep grooves in the surface of the brain, establishing a propensity for the spirits to rush in there and cause in the soul a passion of fear whenever the same or a similar image is formed on the brain (PS, arts. 35–6). No special faculty of the brain is required whose job it is to interpret images. The only judgements the soul makes about danger are posterior to the production of the passion and formed by the intellect.[35] These are not judgements animals devoid of reason can make, and provided there is an alternative explanation for the fear-like responses of animals, couched in terms of the mechanistic processes of their bodies, there is no need to postulate an estimative faculty for them either.

Descartes' rejection of intentional forms goes hand-in-hand with a rejection of the idea that good or evil are 'in things themselves'. He distances himself from this idea when he remarks at article 52 that 'the objects which move the senses do not excite in us diverse passions by reason of all the diversities which are in them, but only by reason of the diverse ways in which they can harm or profit us, or in general be important' (AT XI, 372). Insofar as passions perform this function, they are more often than not 'true'. The sense of 'truth' at work here is mysterious, but whatever it is, it is the same as that described in the *Sixth*

---

[34] The internal senses Descartes acknowledges – imagination, common sense and memory – do not operate by receiving, storing or processing the forms or likenesses (*similitudines*) of external things, but according to the configuration of spirits in the brain. For more details on Descartes' mechanistic theory of sensation, see chapter 3.

[35] On the representational role of passions, see chapter 4.

Meditation passage where Descartes writes that 'all the senses, regarding what is suitable for the body, more frequently indicate truth than falsity' (AT VII, 89). The use of 'truth' and 'falsity' in relation to sensations and passions is not a matter of correspondence to the intrinsic good or evil of external things, but seems rather to be correspondence to the relative value of things for the union. The matter is, however, complicated and we can defer discussion of the truth and falsity of passions until later.[36]

Descartes' attachment to mechanism was not, however, the only source of impetus away from the models which dominated Scholastic philosophy and teaching. As Stephen Gaukroger has argued, treatises according to which the soul was divided against itself offered a fragmented picture of the cognitive functions of the soul and no easy way to reintegrate them (Gaukroger, 1995: 398). This problem was only exacerbated by a widespread, though not universal, commitment among Scholastics to the generality of thought hypothesis.[37] Although both Avicenna and Aquinas reserved the rational soul for intellectual functions, they permitted, as we have seen, a kind of thought or 'judgement' animals make through their estimative faculty. These judgements are restricted to thoughts about individual things – e.g., this (particular) wolf has (a particular) malice – and do not make use of universal concepts.[38] How these judgements were to be used by the intellectual soul of humans in their practical deliberations is puzzling. How is it that the singular propositions formed by the sensitive soul are represented together with universal propositions in the form of practical syllogisms, when there is no common part of the soul that is capable of both general and singular thought? If the intellect is to rationally weigh the singular propositions arrived at by the estimative power against universal maxims, it must be capable of combining them in a single argument. But given the insistence on the generality of thought within the Aristotelian tradition, there is a question how the intellect can ever consider singular propositions. Aquinas attributes to the intellect the power to know singulars only 'indirectly', by turning to the phantasms

---

[36] The complexity is that passions and sensations are often true in the sense of representing external bodies as being suitable or unsuitable for the body while being false in the way in which they represent those bodies. For example, a sensation of cold may be false insofar as bodies do not have such a property but true in representing cold things as potentially harmful to exposed skin. This suggests that Descartes might be working with two standards of truth: correspondence to some real or objective property and utility for the mind–body union. See chapters 4, 7 and 8 for further discussion.

[37] Notable exceptions include William of Ockham and his followers.

[38] See, for example, Aquinas, *Summa Theologiae*, I. 78.4; I. 80–1.

present in the sensitive soul. It is only the senses that are capable of formulating singular thoughts, but the senses are in a part of the soul distinct from the intellect (*De Veritate* I, q.2,6; *Summa Theologiae* I, q.86, 1).[39] Simo Knuuttila surmises that this problem of reintegrating the various faculties of the soul put pressure on theories to establish an over-arching centre of consciousness, a self-conscious 'I' or 'ego', not easily accommodated within the faculty structure.[40] Unity, self-consciousness and 'I'-ness are, of course, the distinguishing marks of the Cartesian mind.

Within the hierarchically structured soul Aristotelian models present, furthermore, it is not obvious that the passions are indispensable. The passions are subordinate to the will, and the estimative faculty is capable on its own of informing the soul of the utility/disutility of external things. These two factors suggest that the ideally rational human being should be able to act virtuously without passions. Indeed, on Christian views like Aquinas', Christ is the model of human rationality, and Christ has only *propassiones* (first motions) and intellectual emotions neither of which are passions in the strict sense.[41] The propensity of Scholastics to view the passions as all by nature good because they are part of God's design sits uncomfortably with the idealisation of dispassionate humanity represented through Christ.

Descartes' conception of the soul as an indivisible, single and integrated cognitive system, the crucial presupposition of the supplementary argument for dualism in the *Sixth Meditation* (AT VII, 86), is in direct opposition to this model of a divided soul. By conceiving of passions as ideas, as representational modes of the intellect, Descartes faces no insuperable obstacle to explaining their accessibility to reason.[42] Since passions, sensations and appetites are the only means by which the soul is informed of the value of external things, and of its union with a particular body, passions are furthermore indispensable to the good in this life. The cost of this unified conception of the soul is, however, that intrapsychic conflict can no longer be explained in terms of interpsychic conflict, conflict between parts of the soul. In response Descartes replaces all

---

[39] I discuss the question of singular knowledge in Aquinas in Brown 2000.
[40] Knuuttila, 2004: 225 and Knuuttila, (unpublished). Knuuttila identifies Avicenna as one of the earliest to handle the co-ordination problems of a divided self, especially the problem of explaining how the appetitive faculties direct themselves to the same objects of the apprehensive powers, by positing a self-conscious subject. See Avicenna, *Kital al-najat*, Bk. II. c. VI; trans. Rahman, 1952: 65–6.
[41] *Summa Theologiae*, III.q.15.a.4.
[42] Descartes' examples often include ideas of particulars, like the sun (AT VII, 102).

psychic conflict with psychosomatic conflict – namely, all apparent oppo-
sitions within the soul are to be explained as conflicts between the will
pushing the pineal gland one way and the spirits pulling it another (PS,
art. 47). When the spirits pull it one way, this is felt in the soul as a
passion, which makes it seem as if it is the soul itself through its passions
and not the spirits that are opposing the will. The passions 'dispose the
soul to want the things for which they prepare the body' and thus can
make it seem sometimes as if the will has two *voluntates* and is thus
divided against itself (PS, art. 40). Although this may seem a somewhat
superficial solution to the problem in that no attempt is made to establish
that all cases of putative intrapsychic conflict can be reduced to cases of
psychosomatic conflict, there is no doubting its ingenuity.[43] The need to
explain psychic conflict was one of the key motivating factors behind the
faculty psychology model, and Descartes offered one way to think about
the problem without imposing divisions within the soul.

FORMAL OBJECTS AND FIRST CAUSES: DESCARTES'
TAXONOMIC PRINCIPLES

A standard way to begin theorizing about the passions was to distinguish
between 'primitive' passions, their subspecies and composites of primitive
passions. It was standard to define the formal objects of primitive passions
in terms of whether they are good or evil and their relationship to other
factors such as time and proximity to the agent. The formal objects of the
passions are the kinds of situations in which it is appropriate (or possible)
to have certain kinds of emotional response. Let us also use the term
'target' to specify the circumstances a passion moves us to create. For
example, the formal object of a fear response is some present danger to the
agent, whereas the target of the fear response is the removal of the threat.
Subspecies of the primitive passions are responses to more refined or
qualified formal objects whereas complex passions involve more than
one primitive passion. Taxonomies of the passions handed down from
antiquity and the Middle Ages diverged from one another on the number
of primitive passions to the point where it is difficult to see what exactly
was to be gained from these lengthy enumerative exercises.[44] The Stoics

---

[43] On the topic of Descartes' idea of psychological unity, see Brown and de Sousa (2003).
[44] Peter King notes that Suarez seems to have been uniquely sensible in this regard. He rejected
attempts to classify the passions on the grounds that any classification was bound to be arbitrary.
Since the passions can be sorted in a variety of ways, depending upon which criteria one chooses,

favoured a fourfold classification of the passions: pleasure (hêdonê) and pain (lupê), relating to the present, and desire (epithumia) and fear (phobos), relating to the future.[45] Aquinas accepts the Stoic classification as the basic one, but proposes eleven primitive passions defined in terms of more specific relationships to objects. Of these eleven, six are concupiscible passions (love, desire, pleasure and their opposites, hatred, aversion and sadness), and five irascible (hope and courage and their opposites, despair and fear, and a passion with no opposite, anger.)[46] Anger is an irascible appetite of approach to a present evil that lacks an opposite because there is no contrary movement of withdrawal from a present or past evil, only sadness, a concupiscible appetite.[47] Descartes' tally is, by comparison, a modest six: wonder, love, hatred, desire, joy and sadness. All other passions are either combinations or species of these six, (PS, art.69).

Descartes shares with his predecessors a commitment to the basic taxonomic principle of the goodness or evil (utility or disutility) of things to which the passions are responses, but rejects, along with Suarez and Vives, the division of passions into concupiscible and irascible. The idea that passions are differentiated according to whether they are responses to good or evil absolutely (concupiscible), or as responses to obstacles which stand in the way of good or evil, and thus are in some sense 'arduous' (irascible), was Platonic in origin (*Republic*, IV), and seems to have been a constant in the tradition, figuring in the works of Galen, Avicenna, Albertus Magnus and Aquinas, although not necessarily in the same form.[48] Descartes rejects the division between concupiscible and irascible powers on two grounds: (1) that it invokes yet a further division within the soul, and (2) that it reduces, falsely, the powers of the soul to two: concupiscence and anger (PS, art. 68). In regard to the first objection, although it seems right to attribute a real

---

there is at most a conceptual distinction among passions, and all taxonomic exercises are of purely instrumental value (Tractatus, IV.disp.I, 12.5; 475b). For a discussion of Suarez' view, see King, 2002: 242–3.

[45] See, for example, Cicero, *Tusculan Disputations*, III, 24–5; Knuuttila, 2002: 51.

[46] *Summa Theologiae*, I–II, q.26; q.40.

[47] *Ibid.*, q.46.

[48] It is a good question when exactly concupiscible and irascible passions began to admit of contraries. Knuuttila argues that for Avicenna the distinction was one between passions whose object was the good (concupiscible passions) and passions whose object was evil (irascible passions) (Avicenna, *De anima*, 1.5, 83.47–52, 4.4, 56.6–57.9; Knuuttila, 2002: 60). Descartes seems to have this kind of division in mind, but it was not Avicenna's but Aquinas' distinction (which permits both good and evil as objects of the irascible faculty and contraries in each category) that was dominant in late Scholastic thought. See King, 2002.

distinction between the concupsicible and irascible powers to Aquinas, later Thomists and Scholastics were, as noted above, more inclined to regard this distinction as merely conceptual.

Concerning the second objection, Descartes writes:

> Since she [the soul] has in the same way the faculties of wonder, love, hope and fear, and in this way the [faculty] to receive in herself every other passion, or to perform the actions to which the passions impel her, I do not see why they have chosen to refer all to concupiscence or anger. (AT XI, 379)

In raising this objection, Descartes could be accused of missing the point of the traditional division between concupiscible and irascible passions. The aim of the distinction was not to reduce all passions to two, concupiscence and anger, but to categorise passions according to whether they move the animal towards a state of rest or are 'terminating' passions once the animal is at rest. The concupiscible appetites draw the soul towards goods taken as absolute and away from evils taken as absolute, and thus lead to states of repose, whether joyful or sad. By seeking to overcome what is arduous, the irascible appetites keep the animal moving towards the ends of the concupiscible passions.[49] The irascible passions thus concern the means to obtaining the ends of the concupiscible passions. To illustrate the integrated functions of the two kinds of passions, Aquinas uses the analogy of fire, which, in seeking to rise higher, seeks also to destroy or resist that which stands in its way.[50]

Aquinas divides the passions according to whether they seek what is useful and avoid what is harmful for the animal, or whether they seek to overcome or avoid that which hinders their obtaining what is useful and avoiding what is harmful. The first principle of division is whether the movement has as its object good or evil. The second principle is whether the movement is one of approach or withdrawal.[51] Assuming that there are no passions that seek evil absolutely or shun good absolutely, the second principle applies only to the irascible appetites. A good considered as arduous may cause the soul to draw away from it. This irascible passion we call despair. An evil considered as an obstacle to good may, alternatively, draw the soul towards it. This produces irascible passions of courage and daring. Every affective series begins and terminates, therefore, in a concupiscible passion.

---

[49] *Summa Theologiae*, 1a–11ae, q.25. a.1.
[50] Ibid., q.23. a.4.   [51] Ibid., q.23. a.1.

Descartes may reject the distinction between concupiscible and irasci- ble passions, but his desire to explain transitions between affective states and to identify terminus points is as great as that of his predecessors. The natural starting point for a series of passions is wonder (*l'admiration*); PS, art. 53). The objects of wonder are novel to our experience or rare and extraordinary.[52] Subsequent investigation of the object of wonder may lead to either esteem (*l'estime*), if one experiences the value of the object as great, or scorn (*le mespris*), if the object turns out to be unworthy (PS, art. 54). From wonder any number of other passions may arise depending upon which impression is created by the object. Esteem, for example, can lead to desire and love. Desire (*le desir*) is the passion that acts directly upon the will, and is thus the last passion prior to action (PS, art. 101). Joy (*la joye*) and sadness (*la tristesse*) are terminating passions (PS. art. 61).

Descartes' taxonomic principles are similar to those used in the tradi- tion. For Aquinas, a passion is categorised according to whether (1) its formal object is good or evil taken absolutely; (2) its object is good or evil taken as arduous; (3) it is a movement towards or away from the object; (4) the good or evil is possessed (present or past) or unpossessed (e.g., future) and (5) whether the good is attainable or unattainable; the evil avoidable or unavoidable.[53] What makes a motion of the sensitive appetite a case of fear is its causal connection with an estimation of the object as dangerous, or more precisely as a not-yet-present evil that stands as an obstacle to good. When an estimation is incorrect – for example, when what we fear is actually harmless to us – there is a mismatch between what we might call the 'evoking situation' and the 'formal object' of the passion. Under these circumstances, the passion does not fulfil its natural function of contributing to the preservation of the animal.

Descartes' own taxonomic criteria are more fine-grained than the Thomistic ones, but share a commitment to the basic principle that passions are responses to the various ways in which objects may be of interest to us. Descartes, however, utilises criteria unrelated to the formal objects of passions, and thus what might not count as a passion in other taxonomies, for example, boredom, counts as a passion in his. The following is a selection of taxonomic criteria culled from Descartes' treatise. Cartesian passions divide according to whether their object:

---

[52] See chapter 6 for a more detailed discussion of this most important passion, *l'admiration*.
[53] Aquinas, *Summa Theologiae*, Ia–IIae, q. 23. a.I.

(1) is good, evil, new or rare, (joy, sadness and wonder);

(2) is great (esteem is for a great good; scorn, for a great evil);

(3) depends on oneself (irresolution, courage and cowardice are directed at goods or evils which depend on oneself);

(4) belongs to oneself or others (jealousy (towards goods one possesses), envy (towards goods others possess), fear (towards evils one possesses); and pity (towards evils others possess));

(5) is deserved or undeserved (mockery, envy and pity);

(6) is caused by oneself or others (self-satisfaction, repentance, anger, pride, vicious humility);

(7) is a response to an action done by others for or to oneself or others (gratitude (a good done for oneself), approval (a good done for others); indignation (an evil done to others) and anger (an evil done to oneself));

(8) is present, past or future (desire (a future good), regret (a past evil), joy (present good) and sadness (present evil));

(9) is attainable or unattainable, surmountable or insurmountable (hope entails seeing a good as attainable or an evil as surmountable; despair, a good unattainable or evil insurmountable).

Other factors include:

(10) the timing or duration of a passion itself – i.e. past, present, future, prolonged or short (prolonged non-intellectual joy might turn into distaste or boredom; a past sadness remembered can produce light-heartedness (relief) or regret);

(11) others' opinion of a good or evil belonging to or caused by oneself (cf. shame and vainglory); and

(12) the intensity or degree of the emotion (excessive and intense wonder is astonishment).

Although Descartes does not use the terminology of formal objects, the notion of 'first causes' of the passions plays a similar role (PS, arts. 51–2). The first causes of the passions are types of distal causes, and it is primarily by reference to these that he differentiates among the passions. As Descartes notes to Elisabeth, since several passions usually occur together, or can have similar physiological roots, the only way of ultimately differentiating them is by understanding their first causes.[54] Thus Descartes distinguishes between different desires solely on the basis of

---

[54] Letter to Elisabeth, 6 October 1645 (AT IV, 310–13).

their different objects (PS, art. 88), and between some complex passions (e.g., virtuous generosity and vicious pride), on the basis of the different judgements that give rise to them (PS, art. 160). Involving exactly the same movement of the spirits, generosity and pride are otherwise identical.

An investigation of Descartes' enumeration of the passions shows that they are anything but defined solely in terms of their physiological causes. Whether we think about Cartesian passions as bodily phenomena with dramatic psychic effects, or as psychic phenomena caused by somatic disturbances, any attempt to approach them from a single point of view would fail to do justice to their dual status. This is as much true today as it was in Descartes' time, and however much he is inclined to locate the study of the passions along a branch of his physics, by resisting reductionism on both sides of the mental–bodily divide, he shows himself in this respect to be a distinctively modern thinker.

CHAPTER 3

The natural integration of reason and passion

As is evident from the forgoing discussion, the standard account of sensation in antiquity and throughout much of the Middle Ages located sensations and thoughts in different parts of the soul and supposed them to have very different relations to the body. For much of the Greek tradition, including Aristotle and the Stoics, there was something divine about thought. Thought was first and foremost about the natures of things. For Aristotle and his successors, it involved reception of the forms of things without matter in the intellect, which, Aristotle suggested and his followers argued, had to be immaterial, and about which the tradition debated its immortality and its relation to God Himself. Sensation, on the other hand, was something we shared with animals and was impossible apart from a body, because it consisted in a modification of the body. Its 'seat' was the sensitive soul, but that should not be understood to suggest anything spiritual or mental – the sensitive soul was nothing distinct from the living organised body. Maintaining a neat separation between thought and sensation proved difficult, and in the struggle to preserve the pre-eminence of reason over the sensitive soul, the passions became an increasingly important focus of historical attention.

In many respects, the separation of thought and sensation in the Aristotelian tradition was superficial. Aristotle in *De anima* modelled thought upon perception and perception in many ways upon sensation, with the result that there were already in the tradition a host of difficult issues about how thought and sensation could be so distinct. Thought and sensation involved the reception in the thinker/sensor of a form, which was in some sense (oft debated) the same as the form that constituted what was perceived or sensed. Exactly how this form got to the intellect in the case of thought was highly controverted, but it was usually agreed that it was in some way related to the 'simpler' case of sensation, in which the form was thought to be propagated through a medium, received in a sense organ in some literal way, and processed by a series of bodily systems which eventually stored it in some part of the body (in the more sophis-ticated Galenist theories, the brain). At the core of this picture lay the sameness of form at every stage of the process. This sameness could be, and was, variously interpreted, but it did seem to commit any inter-pretation at the very least to a literal resemblance among the various items 'in-formed' in the process. Such a view could not countenance a sharp division between what was 'inside' the thinker/sensor and what was without precisely because of this sameness, though it could allow, at least in the case of thought, that the ways in which objects existed inside and outside were radically different.

This picture of sensation and thought was challenged in various ways in the later Middle Ages, but the conservative movements in both philoso-phy and theology that loomed large in Scholastic circles in the fifteenth and sixteenth centuries ensured that it was very much before the minds of those working on the theory of sensation at the beginning of the seven-teenth century. With the abolition of Aristotelian forms under the new science, the Aristotelian theory of sensation and its relationship to thought was no longer tenable, and Descartes, famously, stepped in to reshape the field.

In freeing thought from its dependence on sensation, Descartes also, it seems, freed thought from any dependence on affect in a way that has become the focus of recent criticism. Antonio Damasio writes that:

This is Descartes' error: the abyssal separation between body and mind, between the sizable, dimensioned, mechanically operated, infinitely divisible body stuff, on the one hand, and the unsizable, undimensioned, un-pushable, nondivisible mind stuff; the suggestion that reasoning, and moral judgement, and the suffer-ing that comes from physical pain or emotional upheaval might exist separately from the body. Specifically: the separation of the most refined operations of mind from the structure and operation of a biological organism. (Damasio,1994: 249–50)

In opposition to Descartes' separation of reason and sensation, Dama-sio's studies of patients with prefrontal cortical lesions or injuries suggest that 'certain aspects of the process of emotion and feeling are indispen-sable for rationality'[1] (Damasio, 1994: xiii). When there is extensive

---

[1] Although there is some debate about the viability of 'localising' emotional functions to specific parts of either the left or right hemispheres (Gainotti, 1989; Kinsbourne, 1989), the prefrontal areas of the brain are clearly an important site for the processes whereby signals from the amygdala and somatosensory cortex are consciously registered as emotions or feelings, and where emotions make a direct contribution to decision-making.

damage in the ventromedial sector of the frontal cortex, reasoning and decision-making are impaired along with emotional capacities, and the two sets of functions are interconnected (Damasio, 1994: 61). Marcel Kinsbourne (1989: 25) describes this interdependence of decision-making and bilateral emotional reactions in normal cases in terms of an 'activity cycle', a co-ordinated effort to motivate and sustain the organism in an appropriate action, and to modify actions when the plans of the organism are, by whatever means, interfered with.[2] Subjects with emotional deficits, such as emotional 'numbness' or *anhedonia,* are unable to make decisions in concrete situations, prioritise and follow through on tasks, maintain relationships, judge characters and moderate their behaviour in socially appropriate ways (Damasio, 1994: 46–50; Kinsbourne, 1989: 253; Finset, 1988).

What is striking is that these impairments in decision-making, rationality and social behaviour may exist despite the absence of other neuropsychological deficits – for example, without any impairment of the language module, long-term memory, IQ, logical capacities, knowledge or the ability to conceive of a range of appropriate actions and infer the consequences of each. Deficits in emotional response and decision-making may also occur without a loss of moral and social awareness, or the ability to predict social outcomes or reactions (Damasio, 1994: 46–50). None of this makes sense, Damasio argues, on the Cartesian model of the mind, which has permitted the disintegration of the whole organism, the 'integrated body proper and brain . . . fully interactive with a physical and social environment' (Damasio, 1994: 252). This fragmented view of the human psyche pervades not only philosophy but artificial intelligence and the cognitive sciences generally, which define the functions of the mind in abstraction from an 'organismic' perspective (Damasio, 1994: 248), and neuroscience, which fails to recognise the effects of the physical and social environment on rationality (Damasio, 1994: 250–1).[3]

The deficits that form the core of the evidence Damasio presents against Descartes are principally deficits in practical reasoning, where it makes sense to suppose a tight integration of reason and emotion. But philosophers have also recently begun to question whether theoretical reasoning is possible without the engagement of the whole human being, situated in a world alongside others, without whom the practices of giving

---

[2] See also Kolb and Milner, 1981; Tucker and Newman, 1981.
[3] Joseph LeDoux makes the stronger claim that the whole field of cognitive science has been defined around the exclusion of emotions from the domain of research (LeDoux, 1996: 34–5).

and taking reasons make little sense. Logic may tell us what a valid inference is, but it does not tell us what to believe, what to attend to, or what
we must do when we must do it (Harman, 1977, ch.11; Brandom, 1994;
Dennett, 1987; de Sousa, 1987: 194). The faculty of pure reason unsullied
by emotions or bodily interests, is beginning to look suspiciously like free
banking, something which from the surface grammar seems to make
sense, but turns out to be practically or theoretically impossible.

But is this erroneous notion of reason, detached from the functions of
sense and emotion, Descartes' error or ours in reading him a certain way?[4]
Descartes' argument for the real distinction of mind and body entails
nothing about the extent to which all the functions of the mind could be
replicated by a disembodied mind. And the conjecture that our experience
is compatible with the absence of a body turns out to be completely false.
The argument for the existence of bodies in the *Sixth Meditation* is intended to demonstrate the absolute impossibility (lest God be a deceiver)
of having sensations and passions without having a body (AT VII, 79–80).
Nor does Descartes hold that the mind could make moral judgements or
suffer pains or emotional trauma without having a body. The *Passions*
concludes on the note that 'it is on the passions that all good and evil of
this life depend' and passions are absolutely dependent upon the motions
of the body (PS, aa. 212, 40). But what about the more general accusation
that reasoning is for Descartes, independent of emotion and sensation?

It is tempting from the *Meditations* to read Descartes as subscribing to
characteristically Platonic ideas about the relationship between thought
and the body. Until the mind is reunited with the body in the *Sixth
Meditation*, there is the promise that the mind, reasoning from the
supposition that it might not have a body, would be able to discern ideas
that are clear and distinct from those which are confused and obscure, and
withhold assent from all but the former. In this way, the mind performs
correctly and avoids error (AT VII, 59–60). The success of this project of
establishing the autonomy of the understanding from the body depends,
as John Carriero has shown, on the argument that sense and imagination
are neither necessary for the abstraction of universals nor faculties that
operate independently of the intellect (Carriero, 1990: 220–7). Other texts
support the stronger view that the body is a hindrance to thought, as

---

[4] There is, of course, the highly spurious function-to-form argument, by means of which Descartes
argues that the pineal gland is the 'seat' of the soul, on the grounds that it is the part of the brain in
which bilateral information is united into a single image (AT XI, 352–3; PS, art. 32). But this is
hardly an interesting criticism (Damasio, 1994: 94–5; also Dennett, 1991).

'swamping' the mind from infancy with thoughts about the body (AT V, 150–1; AT III, 424). And although he is reluctant to conjecture about how angels (AT V, 166–7; 356; 402; AT III, 430) and separated souls think, Descartes shows no inclination to disallow the possibility of disembodied thought, and, indeed, acknowledges the existence of intellectual memory, the function of which is to store universals to serve thought that does not involve the body (AT V, 150).

But while there is, undoubtedly, a Platonic strand in Descartes' thinking, there is also the recognition that much of our thought is occupied with matters that require the co-operation of the body, including the practice of experimental science, which relies on our taking note of particular events in the world around us. As we shall see below and in chapter 6, far from being impediments to reason, passions and sensations play an indispensable role in the investigation and navigation of the natural world. The recognition of the dependence of rational action and science on the functions of sense and imagination tempers Descartes' Platonic tendencies.

It is notable, for example, that nowhere in Descartes' corpus is there a pure example of a human mind reasoning *without* sensation, though the texts are rife with admonitions against reasoning *from* sensation.[5] I do not deny the role that an idealised conception of reason autonomous from the faculty of sensation plays in Descartes' philosophy. But this chapter is about his conception of embodied reason naturally integrated with the functions of sensation and passion, and about striking a balance between the strongly Platonist reading, which sees the body as nothing but an obstacle to reason, and a reading which denies the autonomy of reason altogether. This balancing act depends on seeing that although the body has the tendency to swamp the mind with its concerns, it is possible, according to Descartes, to reason well 'in this life', and precisely so because it is possible to use the sensory resources provided by the body as supplements to reason. To get to this point, we will need to understand the mechanistic theory of sensation, and how the rational and sensitive faculties are naturally integrated and mutually supportive. The 'withdrawal from the senses' Descartes advocates in the *Meditations* should, it shall be argued, be taken in its intended epistemically normative sense,

---

[5] There is nothing in Descartes' texts like Avicenna's 'floating man' – a fully formed adult human who comes to exist in a state of complete sensory deprivation, but who, according to Avicenna, is capable of thinking about its own thought and existence. Avicenna, *Liber de anima*, part 1a, ch.1, lines 49–60.

and not as the claim that it is either possible or desirable for human beings to reason well in this life without utilising their sensory and affective faculties.

SENSATION AND MECHANISM

Descartes' rejection of the theory of sensible forms leads him to reject the associated idea that there is any relevant resemblance between sensory images and their external causes, a move which is sufficient to free sensation from any essentially epistemological function. It is important to emphasise 'relevant resemblance' because Descartes does not deny that sensory images ever resemble their causes. What he denies is rather that the intellect relies upon such resemblances to perform its functions. This is the overarching message of the mechanistic account of sensation he offers as a rival to the Aristotelian approach: when sensation is understood from the perspective of mechanics, it cannot play the epistemic role of in-forming thought it was supposed to have on the Aristotelian view.

It is fair to say that the mechanistic account of sensation one finds in the early texts, especially the *Optics* (*La Dioptrique*) and the *Treatise on Human Nature* (*L'Homme*), written between 1629 and 1633, remained more or less constant for Descartes. Readers of the *Principles* and the *Passions* are referred back to the *Optics* as an authoritative text for understanding the mechanism of sensation (AT VIIIA, 15; AT XI, 337–8). The purpose of those early texts is to tell a story about sensation that is compatible with the idea that the physical world is governed by the laws of motion and contact, and is composed only of extension (matter) and its 'modes', principally, size, shape and motion. Every change that occurs within the natural world must be explicable, in principle, in terms of those laws and elementary concepts. Theories with a tendency to animate matter were prime targets for the mechanists. The idea that a form of some material object, a colour or shape, for example, has 'intentional' or 'spiritual' existence in the mind or medium in contrast with its natural mode as the form of a material object is, to Descartes' mind, absurd. But the problem intentional forms purported to solve, the problem of explaining how something corporeal could be a messenger to and from a rational soul, informing the soul of things outside it and carrying its instructions to the body, did not evaporate with the abolition of the form/matter distinction. Descartes must also avoid the dangers of intentionalism – of characterising thought in such a way that presupposes homunculi or 'little souls' capable of reading what happens in the body as signs of things outside it, carrying out the instructions of the soul, setting goals and making decisions. The role of brain images qua images must thus be downplayed lest there be required 'yet again other eyes in our brain with which we could perceive [those images]'[6] (AT VI 130). The messengers of the soul can be nothing other than arrangements of matter to which the machine of the body is constructed to respond according to the principles of mechanics – i.e., in mathematically specifiable ways.

Recall that one of the objections Elisabeth raises against Descartes' dualism is what I earlier referred to as 'the problem of information'. She argues that 'if (the soul's moving the body) occurred through information, it would have to be that the spirits, which perform the movement, were intelligent, which you accord to nothing corporeal' (AT III, 685). Descartes responds by claiming that if Elisabeth wants to attribute matter and extension to the soul, she may do so, provided she bears in mind that this does not make matter thought or thought extended in the sense of having a determinate location or excluding all other bodily extension (AT III, 694). The soul's extension, which just is its union with a body, does not conflict with the strict division between thought and extension. But Elisabeth wants to know how the body is supposed to perform its functions in executing the soul's commands under these conditions. What mechanism mediates the flow of information to and from the soul? Descartes' answer to this was, however, already available in his natural philosophy: there is no flow of information between the soul and the body, only primitive non-symbolic mechanisms of the body geared to respond differentially to movements of the pineal gland produced by volitions. Because these responses depend on movements within the gland that may be produced either by bodily or mental causes, they are capable of creating the illusion of intelligence in, for example, animals and the human body (considered on its own), where there is none. Let us examine these functions of the sensory system a little more closely.

The first stage of sensory processing is the stimulation of the nerves. Different sensations depend on the stimulation of different nerves. There are seven groups of nerves which produce movements of the pineal gland,

---

[6] The significance of Descartes' rejection of images as central to the account of sensation should not be underestimated, or confined to its epistemological consequences. In particular, it enables Descartes to develop a more coherent account of sensory processing. Aside from the absurdity of supposing that there was something in the brain that could somehow interpret images, analysing perception in terms of the perception of mental images would invoke an infinite regress problem.

five connected with the organs of the external senses and two with the heart – the internal senses – which produce what we call passions, and, somewhat misleadingly for Descartes since the term connotes volition, appetites (*Principles* IV, 190; 191; AT VIIIA 316–21). Further differentiation is explained according to differences among the various ways in which the nerves are stimulated. The sensation of light derives from the force with which the optic nerves are stimulated; the perception of colour from the manner in which they are stimulated (AT VI, 130). Each sensation is thus correlated with a dedicated kind and rate of movement of the spirits and the nerves. The nerves themselves are variously described as 'threads' connecting the brain with every region of the body, 'cords' for pulling the muscles and opening pores on the surface of the brain and, by analogy, 'pipes' for conveying the animal spirits that are the 'messengers of the soul' (e.g., AT XI, 130–1; AT XI, 337). As noted in chapter 2, animal spirits are easily excitable and highly rarefied particles of matter in the body, fine enough to move within the nerves and pass through the tiny pores on the folds of the brain[7] (AT XI, 334–5). Contact with the nerve endings creates a movement through the spirits in the nerves in much the same way that one can, by moving one end of a stick or a rope, produce instantaneous movement at the other end (AT VI, 84). The functions of the motor response system are also closely bound with those of the sensory system. Specific movements of the gland produce either muscular contraction, a swelling of the muscle due to an abundance of spirits, or muscular release, a lengthening of the muscle due to the rapid flow of spirits out of the nerves connected to the muscle.

The functions of the spirits in the nervous system are thus intended to be completely consistent with mechanics. External objects create movements among the spirits through pressure on the nerves, which ultimately produce movements in the gland that cause modifications of the soul, on the one hand, and effects on the muscles, on the other hand. Since there is no mechanism straddling both mind and body that could have as its input corporeal motions and as its output ideas, no transducer between the mind and body, there is nothing that converts sensory motions in the

---

[7] Descartes' conception of how the brain is linked to the body is confined to the mechanical push and pull of animal spirits through the nerves. Although the constitution of the bodily humours was thought to affect what happens in the brain, such explanations by the seventeenth century were thought to be subsumable under the general mechanistic framework. The idea of neurochemical connections between brain and body, through what is today principally attributed to the release of hormones and peptides, was neither theoretically available to nor anticipated by Descartes.

body into ideas in the soul.[8] Motions of the pineal gland 'cause' sensations in the soul, but the way they do so is by being responses to incoming motions of the spirits, responses that, on account of the union, are sufficient for a sensory idea to form in the mind.

Because nothing passes between the body and the mind that accounts for the idea the mind forms when stimulated by the senses, Descartes is able to assure Regius of the non-resemblance between sensations and their external causes. Sensory 'images' in the brain are nothing other than the configuration of spirits, which produce certain kinds of responses in the muscles, and in the mind, sensations in the soul.[9] Any resemblance between brain images and their external causes is irrelevant to the theory of how they function. What image is formed depends not just on the kind of external cause that produces it, but also on the structure of the nerves, as well as other stimulations that are occurring at the same time that invariably affect our experience. The number of filaments of the optic nerve limits, for example, the range of colour perception.

If, for example, the object VXY is made up of ten thousand parts which are arranged so as to send rays toward the base of the eye RST in ten thousand different ways, and consequently to make [it] see at the same time ten thousand colours, nonetheless they can only make at most a thousand of them distinct to the soul, if we suppose that there are only a thousand filaments of the optic nerve in the space RST. (AT VI, 133–4)

What an individual perceives will thus be a function of species-specific hardware constraints as much as environmental factors. The quantity of light seen in an object varies in proportion to the size of the pupil and area at the back of the eye occupied with rays coming from each point of the object, as well as by the distance of the object. The objects that stimulate the nerves are small bodies in motion, but because the nerve is composed of fibres, each of which is like a point in a field, the overall effect will depend upon the varying strengths of stimulation to the fibres. Thus a field composed of many colours from a distance appears to have a uniform colour (AT VI, 134). Similarly, strong rays affecting fibres in the centre of the optic nerve can have a spill-over effect on surrounding nerves, giving the impression of an object larger than is actually there (AT VI, 146).

---

[8] On the history of transduction and its demise with Descartes, see King, 1994.
[9] For an account of why the latter counts as genuine causation as opposed to ' occasioning' sensory ideas in the mind, see chapter 5.

The dependence of sensations on proximal causes – the motions of spirits in the nerves and on the internal surface of the pineal gland – means that there is no one-to-one correspondence between a sensation and an external cause. A real-world (as opposed to Demon-world) example adduced in support of this proposal is phantom-limb pain. Since the motions of the spirits in the nerves leading from the site of amputation to the brain are of the same type that normally cause a pain-in-the-hand sensation, the victim of phantom-limb pain experiences the same kind of pain they would if they had an injured hand[10] (AT VIIIA, 319–20). Other examples include pressure on the eyes causing flashes of light and colour, after-images, and passions and appetites caused by imbalances in the bodily humours or spirits (AT VI 131; AT VIIIA, 317–8). But there is another reason for the lack of resemblance between the motions in the nerves and external causes. Since the very same arrangement of matter can cause very different sensations (e.g., of colour or sound or pain, etc.) depending upon which nerves are activated, there is no reason to think that sensations resemble real qualities of the external world.

This same force [which sets the optic nerve fibres in motion causing us to sense a 'violent light'] touching the ears is able to make us hear some sound and touching the body in some other part, is able to make us feel pain. (AT VI, 131)

All this is grist for Descartes' mill on the issue of resemblance and his rejection of intentional forms. No resemblance obtains between a perception of colour or light and the motions of either their proximal or distal causes. Just as words signify things without resembling them, so too the motions of spirits that give rise to sensations produce signals that do not resemble the things of which they are signs (AT VI, 112). Linguistic signification is mediated by convention, sensory signification by the institution of nature, which does not require resemblance in order for the signification to be effective. But we may also draw another moral from this story: the mechanism of the brain is sensitive only to the intrinsic, physical properties of neural signals. It will perform the same functions whether these stimulations have causes external to the body or not.

---

[10] Medical practitioners of Descartes' time worked on the assumption that the stimulation responsible for phantom-limb pain originated at the end of the stump, which was unfortunate since it often led to what were probably unnecessary further amputations. Current theories suggest instead that the stimulation comes from regions in the brain adjacent to those which used to be stimulated by the limb, and which are being stimulated by other parts of the body, like the face. See Ramachandran, *et al.*, (1995; 1998).

The nerves thus conduct 'information' in the form of motions of particles to and from the pineal gland, and the pineal gland responds solely on the basis of the arrangement of matter that acts as a stimulus. What then are the specific functions of the gland itself? Two important sensory faculties have their 'seat' in the gland: the imagination (*phantasia*) and the common sense (*sensus communis*). The common sense solves the binding problem, explaining why sensory experience has a certain unity to it – why we do not, for example, experience the colour and shape of an object separately. The common sense combines the inputs from different nerves in an integrated arrangement, which corresponds in the soul to a unified experience. Descartes not unreasonably supposes that the problem of unified conscious sensory experience is solved spatially, by all the various inputs coming together in one central location in the brain, a view Dennett parodies as the error of 'Cartesian materialism' (Dennett and Kinsbourne, 1972). The prevailing wisdom today is that the binding problem is solved temporally, through the synchronisation of neural activity in both hemispheres (Damasio, 1994: 95 and fn. 4, 277; Dennett, 1991).

If the common sense is crucial to explaining the unified character of our perceptual experiences, the imagination is crucial to our being able to navigate our environment by means of our perceptual systems. It is by means of the imagination that we are able to perceive the relative position and distance of objects, and, by means of that, their size and shape. Even in this domain, however, the role of sensory images is minimal. Spatial imagining does not depend on sensory imaging.

And its (the soul's) knowledge [of position] depends neither upon any image, nor upon any action that comes from the object, but only on the situation of the little parts of the brain where the nerves originate. (AT VI, 134)

Perceiving the position of objects relative to oneself does not require anything like an internal picture resembling these relations. The blind succeed in sensing the position of objects by using a stick, rather than their eyes, and in this case there is no need to suppose that they use an image that preserves the form of the object perceived. The motions in the nerves leading from the hands to the brain caused by the stick touching an object do not resemble the object sensed. Nor is a visual image required to account for visual perception of position (AT VI, 134).[11]

---

[11] Interestingly, Descartes' clinical evidence for rejecting imagistic models of perception is similar to that adduced by contemporary neuropsychologists who argue that spatial imagining does not depend on visual imaging, namely, the representational capacities of congenitally blind patients (see Kerr, 1983; Jeannerod, 1994).

The analysis of distance and position perception is complex, and highly sophisticated for its time. To account for distance perception, Descartes advances a theory based on vergence angles, an idea generally attributed in the vision sciences to Bishop Berkeley (Berkeley, 1709; Logvinenko et al., 2001; Kohly and On, 2002; Logvinenko et al., 2002). As the eyes focus on an object, they turn inwards, altering the angle of the line from the pupil to the object. The perception of distance is then a function of the distance between the pupils, which forms the base of a triangle, and the vergence angles of the eyes. In the *Optics,* Descartes claims that it is the imagination that calculates distance 'as if by a natural geometry', by calculating the distance to the point where the two sides of the triangle converge (AT VI, 137). The brain of the blind man carries out a similar procedure using proprioceptive representations of the distance between his hands and the vergence angles of his sticks. He does not need to know the length of his sticks in order to know how far away the objects are, but he needs some way of representing the distance between his hands and the angles formed as the hands turn inwards when his sticks touch an object. The loss of either a hand or eye (a common experience it seems in the seventeenth century) is no impediment to distance perception. By changing the position of one's body, one is able to supply the imagination with an angle complementary to that of the functioning eye or hand in the original orientation, the magnitude of which is preserved while this operation is performed (AT VI, 137–8).

Whether Descartes was right about distance perception depending on vergence cues or not is irrelevant for our purposes.[12] What is particularly noticeable is the way in which the imagination is described as if it were applying the rules of geometry to calculate the distance of objects. Descartes writes:

And this [calculation of distance is done] by an action of thought [*une action de la pensée*] which being only a wholly simple [act of] imagination does not cease to contain within it a reasoning [*raisonnement*] not unlike that which surveyors use when, by means of two different stations, they measure inaccessible places. (AT VI, 138)

---

[12] This hypothesis was not experimentally tested until 1862 (Wundt, 1862), but the hypothesis that distance perception is a function of vergence eye movements is still a matter of some debate in the vision sciences. Much of the discussion is focused on the question of whether or not the perceived distance of illusory objects (the 'wallpaper illusion') varies with changes in eye vergence (Logvinenko, *et al.*, 2001; 2002; Kohly and On, 2002)

What is it that is doing the 'reasoning' here? It cannot be the brain, lest there be an obvious conflict with the argument for the real distinction of mind and body. That argument rests on the claim that whereas thought is the principle attribute or essence of the mind, extension alone is the principle attribute of body, and hence, the nature of mind and body can be completely understood without attributing either thought (or reasoning) to the body or extension to the mind. There can be no sense in which the body reasons compatible with this argument. It is not the brain per se that calculates distance but the imagination, which is a faculty of the mind that depends for its functions on the functions of the brain. As Descartes writes further along in the *Optics*, it is the soul that sees, but only indirectly by means of the brain (AT VI, 141). But surely the conscious mind is not explicitly aware of the distance between the pupils of the eyes or vergence angles, or the geometrical rules according to which spatial magnitudes are calculated. Further clarification of the position is offered in the *Sixth Replies*, which refers us back to the *Optics* text, and which explicitly attributes the reasoning involved in spatial perception to the intellect (AT VII, 437–8). The fact that we do not notice making these calculations is attributed to the fact that they are often made at great speed and from habits formed in childhood, and thus we mistakenly suppose them to be performed by the senses rather than the intellect (AT VII, 438).

Descartes treats sensations in a way we would now refer to as informationally encapsulated, that is as impervious to influence from other cognitive states such as beliefs or judgements (AT VII, 438–9; AT VIIIA, 317). We see objects through lenses and mirrors as being other than where we judge them to be (AT VI, 142), and suffer emotions contrary to our rational judgements of what is to be desired or shunned (AT VIIIA, 317). In the *Sixth Replies*, the intellect features more prominently in sensory processing than it does in the earlier *Optics*. The stick partially submerged in water looks bent even when we know it is not. How things appear is impervious to judgement, but this does not mean that judgement is neither involved in every sensation nor irrelevant to correcting for sensory misrepresentation (AT VII, 438–9). Between the *Optics* and the *Sixth Replies* Descartes is either inconsistent on whether this reasoning is attributable to the imagination or the intellect, or means in both texts to include the intellect in every act of the imagination. The latter is the more charitable interpretation, but we have still to explain how the conscious mind calculates spatial magnitudes without an explicit grasp of geometry. Were we once conscious of applying these rules, which through habit have become submerged in the mind? Can Descartes allow anything to become submerged in the mind or subconsciously processed? That Descartes is sensitive to the difficulty of answering these questions affirmatively is evident from his assertion that these calculations are performed 'unreflectively'.

> Ordinarily we reach this [conclusion about distance] without reflecting upon it just as when we press some body to our hand we conform [our hand] to the size and the shape of that body and we sense it by this means without any need to think about its movements. (AT VI, 137)

But what is it for the Cartesian intellect to reason unreflectively as opposed to reflectively? One possibility is that unreflective calculating is rule-following that does not depend on the rules of thought being explicitly represented.[13] This may be a contentious answer but it is at least a familiar one in the philosophy of mind and the cognitive sciences generally. The idea that rules of reasoning and language are part of an innate mental structure, rather than a set of learned or acquired propositions which the mind explicitly represents, was, for example, the cornerstone of Noam Chomsky's revolutionary transformational theory of grammar (Chomsky, 1966, 1967). The idea that linguistic competence is essentially rule-governed behaviour, despite the fact that most ordinary speakers are consciously unaware of which rules they are following, has proved explanatorily very powerful in linguistics, and something like this model could be behind Descartes' vague remarks about the processing of spatial information.

The data for these calculations by the imagination-cum-intellect are, however, the outputs of the sensory mechanisms of the body. The same is true for the perception of position, the functions of which are closely interconnected with those of distance perception, and which depends, interestingly, on proprioceptive information that is available to the imagination. The relative position of objects is sensed through an extension of proprioceptive awareness.

> For this situation is instituted by Nature to allow not only that the soul may know in which place is each part of the body it animates with respect to all the others, but also that it be able to transfer its attention to all of the places

---

[13] This is consistent with Descartes' argument in the *Rules for the Direction of the Mind* that the rules of reason cannot be taught, for example, by the method of dialectic popular in the Schools, unless the mind already has innate principles by which to judge, and which such methods can only make explicit (AT X, 372–4).

contained along the straight lines that one is able to imagine drawn from the extremity of each of its parts and prolonged to infinity. (AT VI, 134–5)

In perceiving the position of objects relative to myself, I must first be aware of the position of various parts of my body, particularly my limbs, and be able to imagine lines drawn from my extremities along which objects are positioned with respect to me and each other. Descartes does not specify the form (e.g., visual or kinaesthetic) in which the imagination receives information about the position of parts of its body. But the discussion of the blind man, which immediately follows the discussion in the *Optics*, suggests a lack of visual bias. Although it is not necessary in order to perceive the position of external objects to think of the places one's hands occupy, it seems clear that Descartes thinks of these as one and the same process (AT VI, 135).

Once there is a mechanism for sensing position and distance, the perception of shape and size follow as night, the day. Size is calculated according to the distance of the object and information drawn from the size of the retinal image. For example, we may perceive two ships as of unequal size, even though they cause same-sized retinal images, provided the imagination calculates their distances as being different (AT VI, 140). Sensations of shape are a function of the relative positions of the various parts of an object and not simply of the shape of an image. One may see a circle by means of an elliptical retinal image, because the brain computes that the various parts of the object occupy different positions relative to oneself (AT VI, 140–1).

What follows so far from this discussion of the mechanisms of sensation? It is quite clear that sensations in the soul are a direct function of what happens in the body, and in particular, the central nervous system. The 'mental acts' by which the imagination calculates the distance and position of objects are inconceivable without sensory awareness of the spatial relations between parts of one's own body. The perception of distance and position is, moreover, a central component of other perceptual acts, including, as we have seen, the perception of size and shape. The role of 'body imagining' in perception, if we may so call the proprioceptive awareness we have of our own bodies, may seem anathema to Descartes' account of sensation as that is generally understood to be ontologically independent of the body, but is, as I have tried to argue here, integral to the story. It is difficult to imagine how we would account for the perception of position in a being *not* capable of proprioceptive representation. It is even more difficult to imagine what it would be like to reason about things outside the soul without an awareness of one's own body, as I propose to argue next.

As we learn from the *Sixth Meditation*, the way in which the errors to which the senses lead us can be reconciled with God's goodness is by accepting that their primary function is not to inform us of the natures of material objects but to inform us in ways conducive to our survival as composite beings.[14] The biological advantage of the noxious smell's seeming to be in the food rather than in the nose or the brain or the mind is obvious. It's the food we need to avoid and around which we have to navigate. Similar stories can be told for our perceptions of colour, shape and size, and all the other sensations which enable us to discriminate objects by their surfaces and boundaries. The way sensations in the soul represent objects in this biologically suitable way is, however, a complicated story and one I propose to defer until the next chapter. For the moment, let us consider another problem with Descartes' biological approach to sensation.

To serve as a good answer to the question why an omnibenevolent God would give us sensory systems that incline us to false judgements about the world, the biological account of sensations had better establish an indispensable role for sensations as modes of the mind. The claim that sensory systems have the biological role of preserving the union is fair, and one most modern 'teleological' approaches to sensation would concur with. What is less obvious is why it is biologically essential that the output of these systems include a perception by the soul. The movements of the particles of matter in the sensory system are causally sufficient, on Descartes' view, for appropriate movements of the motor response system, as witnessed in animals. In both our automatic or hard-wired responses and our conditioned or learned responses, the story is much the same. Brain motions are capable of initiating two causal sequences: one to the muscles producing the appropriate behavioural response, and the other to the soul, where conscious sensory perception occurs. Why is this second causal sequence important? It is perhaps useful to have one's bodily disposition to basic survival reinforced by the rational soul, but that seems like overdetermination at best, and, at worse, downright inefficient.

---

[14] See also AT XI, 372.

Although there are a few cases where it is useful to override the behavioural dispositions triggered by sensation, for example, when suffering dropsy, it is unclear that the rational mind would, overall, do a better job of preserving the human body than the body would on its own. Are sensations and passions in the soul mere epiphenomena, by-products of underlying mechanisms of the body that are causally sufficient for preserving the body?

Human beings, on Descartes' view, do not merely react to their environments; they act, and it is in acting that we need to make use of information provided by the senses. It is because I want to do things in my world and by means of my body that I need sensations in the same domain in which I judge things and make decisions. The rational soul needs sensations not only to reinforce the survival-enhancing dispositions already at work in the body but so that it may alter the dispositions of the body to pursue its own ends. Having described the movements of the body-machine by analogy to the movements of a clock or water-driven mill, Descartes, in *L'Homme,* adds the following:

And finally, so that the rational soul will be in this machine, it will have there its principal seat in the brain, and it will be there like a fountain keeper, who ought to be at the sites where all the pipes of his machine go to meet when he wants to get them going or close them off or change in some way their movements. (AT XI, 131)

The metaphor of the fountain keeper may seem an odd choice to portray the relationship between the rational soul and the body. Unlike the fountain keeper, the mind is neither consciously aware of what is going on in its pipes nor capable of producing, preventing or changing, in any direct manner, the movements of the brain (AT V, 221–2; AT XI, 342). The reference to the soul as a fountain- keeper suggests, however, that the function of having sensory information available or accessible to consciousness is somehow connected with rationality. Accessibility to consciousness of sensory information is a precondition for adaptability and creativity in changing circumstances. It is such adaptability and creativity of mind that Descartes claims in the *Discourse* distinguishes 'the dullest of men' from the most superior specimens of other species, and from automata, which might otherwise be able to mimic our behaviour almost perfectly (AT VI, 56–7). But in what way precisely does sensation provide the rational soul with the capacity to direct its body? And what does sensation do for the rational soul that couldn't be done by other means?

Let us grant, for the sake of argument, that sensation is necessary for reasoning as embodied beings, as many critics of Descartes now believe. Establishing that conclusion does not show why sensations have to be experienced by the mind in that form. Why isn't it rationally sufficient in order to pull one's foot out of the fire, for example, to be conscious that there is injury in the foot – why must one also feel pain? Why is it important to be attracted to bright colours, to experience them as blue, green, red and so on, rather than simply register the boundaries and surfaces of different objects?

Using terminology that Ned Block has recently popularised, we may characterise this as the problem of 'phenomenal content'. According to Block and many other contemporary philosophers, sensory states have two kinds of content: representational content, which is conceptual or symbolic, and phenomenal content, which is the *what-it-is-likeness* or *felt* aspect of sensations. A pain state may represent something injurious to the foot, but it also *feels* a certain way, a way that is (perhaps indefinably) different from the state of seeing red or hearing a trumpet. One problem phenomenal content poses is that there seems to be no function that it performs which could not be (and perhaps is) performed by the representational content of a perceptual state, and, *inter alia,* this has led some to believe that phenomenal content is either indistinct from representational content or has no function. In terms of Descartes' theory of sensation, the problem of phenomenal content may seem particularly acute. The claim that rational action depends on available sensory information answers a question about the need for (in Blockspeak) ' access consciousness' of sensory information – the availability of sensory information for use in reasoning, reporting and rationally guiding action – but leaves unanswered any question about the function of ' phenomenal-consciousness' – consciousness of the what-it-is-likeness or felt aspect of sensations (Block, 1997). What do the bitter pains and sweet pleasures that accompany the sensory information used by the rational soul add to the story about the functions of sensation? What indispensable function does the form in which this information is presented play in the life of a rational agent?

THE RATIONAL SIGNIFICANCE OF PHENOMENAL INFORMATION

When we look to the texts for an answer to this last question, a more sophisticated picture of the integration of rational and sensitive functions begins to emerge and the passions take on an increasingly important role. It is a picture that does not distinguish so neatly the functions of phenomenal and access consciousness as contemporary theorists such as Block do. The passions have two important biological functions: they must contribute to the body's giving a quick response to a situation, and they must 'incline' the soul to consent to the movements to which the body is already disposed. In the short term, a person cannot always wait for lengthy deliberation before acting, but her long-term flourishing will often depend upon the outcomes of rational deliberation and decision-making. When circumstances are pressing, being access-conscious of sensory information may only slow down the reaction time, as would any deliberation and decision-making. Phenomenal consciousness is ideally suited for triggering quick responses. The quick adrenalin rush associated with fear can serve as a crude sign of something potentially harmful without being representatively specific and trigger an advantageous 'freezing reaction' (LeDoux, 1996: 163–5). There are advantages in having a fast response system that does not involve much higher-cortical, representational processing, but there are also advantages in being able subsequently to engage in that kind of processing. Bolting off in the opposite direction every time we find ourselves faced with potentially dangerous objects we are not yet in a position to classify limits our choices, to say the least.

What accounts for the ability of Cartesian passions to contribute to fast and effective behavioural responses? If one thinks, for example, about the amount of information one could take in from any particular visual field, the problem is not so much that there seems no obvious reason to represent this information phenomenally rather than in some other way, but simply the sheer bulk of information with which one is confronted. The problem is not so much how to represent this information but what to represent, although answering the how-question may very well be the key to answering the what-question. This problem is reminiscent of the frame problem in artificial intelligence: the problem of designing a system capable, in finite time, of attending to the relevant pieces of information available to it and drawing the relevant inferences while, crucially, ignoring all the irrelevant information and inferences (Haugeland, 1985: 202; Dennett, 1987: 42). Ronald de Sousa has speculated that by controlling patterns of salience and attention, the emotions solve the frame problem for biological organisms (de Sousa, 1987: 195–6). And before de Sousa, Descartes, in the *Passions,* expressed a similar thought:

For it is easy to know, from that which we have said above, that the utility of all the passions consists only in this: that they fortify and make stronger in the soul thoughts which it is good for it to conserve and which would be able easily without them to be effaced. . . (PS, art. 74; AT XI, 383)[15]

---

[15] The downside of this is that all the evil the passions are able to cause is from their sometimes conserving and strengthening thoughts more than is necessary or thoughts that it is not good for the soul to dwell upon at all (PS, art. 74).

One of the principal functions of Cartesian passions is their ability to keep a perception of an object active in working memory. Many passions are the result of perceptions of objects that trigger memories of those or similar objects having produced pleasure or pain in the soul (PS, art. 36). Because of their connections with perception and memory, the passions bring some sensations rather than others to the foreground of the mind's attention, and hold them in working memory long enough for the soul to make a rational decision about how to respond. The passions give to the sensations with which they are connected a special significance, without which the soul would not attend to them or classify them, or alter the dispositions of the body where appropriate. Without the passion of fear or apprehension, the shape of a snake might be no more noticeable or relevant to one's present action than the green of the trees or the chirp of the birds. But how the passions make salient some sensations has to do not so much with their representational content as with the way they present their objects.

Let us return to the much-debated questions of whether there is a real distinction between representational and phenomenal content, and over whether the latter has any irreducible function.[16] Is it because fear has a certain feel associated with it that it captures attention, or because it represents the object as a danger-to-me-here-and-now? For Descartes at least, it looks as if we can say that the phenomenal content of a sensory experience has a functional role irreducible to that of its representational content. Consider the role of wonder (*l'admiration*) in Descartes' account of perception. Wonder is the passion that structures attention, and it does so in the first instance precisely when a perception of an object fails to trigger corporeal memories that would enable the soul to classify the object under perceptual sortals. Wonder is generated by sensations of objects with which we are not familiar, and which we do not, therefore, know how to categorise or evaluate. Wonder is the first of all the passions, and since every other passion presupposes knowledge of the object, the prior effects of wonder are presupposed by every other passion and

---

[16] Block has argued voraciously for a distinction between phenomenal and representational content, and for the claim that phenomenal content is not a functional concept. His worry about phenomenal content having a functional role is that it should then be subject to functional reduction, which would allow it to be duplicated in an artificial system and one that is incapable of feeling or experiencing what it is like to see colours, feel pains, and so on (Block, 1997). The issue hangs on whether there is a difference between something's having a function and its being functionally definable or reducible to its functional role. It is not clear that the former entails the latter, and it is only the former that is required to establish a functional role for the phenomenal content of a state and avoiding a collapse of the two kinds of content.

mode of attention. For this reason, Descartes writes, wonder accompanies all the other passions and augments them (PS, art. 72).

Wonder captures attention through the element of surprise. It is defined as 'a sudden surprise of the soul which makes that it [the soul] carries itself to consider with attention the objects that seem to it rare or extraordinary' (AT XI, 380). This definition suggests that in wondering at something the soul first classifies the object as rare or extraordinary, but we should avoid this construal. It is not because the soul *represents* something as rare or extraordinary that it notices it; rather it comes to think of it as rare or extraordinary because it has noticed it, because of the 'sudden surprise' the object causes. The cause of this surprise is a brain impression that 'represents' the object as unusual and therefore worthy of attention, and the subsequent movement of the spirits, which strengthens the impression and holds the sense organs fixed on the object (PS, art. 70). But the sense in which the brain is capable of 'representing' an object is unclear. Elsewhere, Descartes claims it is appropriate to call an image in the corporeal imagination an 'idea', not on account of its being an impression in the brain but only insofar as it 'gives form to the mind itself' (AT VII, 161). But it is dangerous to suppose that the brain functions by being sensitive to any semantic properties *we* might be prepared to attribute to its impressions. That would sound too much like attributing thought to the body to be tenable on Descartes' account. Luckily, there is an alternative explanation available from article 72 of the *Passions*. The representational properties of the brain impression that causes wonder can be cashed out entirely in terms of the physical effects on the brain of exposure to a novel object. What it means to have an impression of novelty is just for the soft and spongy parts of the brain, not yet trampled by spirits from previous encounters with the object, to be suddenly and strongly affected by rapid movements of the spirits. And it is because of these physical effects that the mind's attention is drawn and it comes to see the object as worthy of further investigation.

Getting the soul to notice something presented to its senses is one function of wonder; keeping its attention is another. It achieves the latter through its effects on specific parts of the brain and on the muscles. These effects include 'strengthening and preserving' an impression in the imagination and memory by fixing the eyes and other muscles of the body on the object in question (PS, art. 70; AT XI, 380–1). The following passage suggests that without the passion of wonder, sensory information would not be stored in memory long enough to become, in Block's terminology, 'access conscious', that is, available for use by the rational faculty:

For when a thing which was unknown to us presents itself anew to our understanding or our senses, we do not retain it at all in our memory unless the idea we have is fortified in our brain by some passion [wonder], or by the application of our understanding that our will determines to one attention and reflection in particular. (AT XI, 384)

Although this passage suggests that attention may have either an active or passive source, the tenor of the discussion is such that the passive source, wonder, is basic. As shall be explored further in chapter 6, the functions of wonder are important not only in practical reasoning but also in applied theoretical reasoning, indeed, to any mental act that requires control over the mechanisms of attention in the body. Although too much wonder (astonishment) is a bad thing, for it renders the body immobile and impedes appropriate action and investigation (PS, arts. 73 and 78), a deficiency of wonder is associated with stupidity (PS, art. 77). It is best to move as quickly as possible beyond a state of wonder, through the acquisition of knowledge and exercise of the will. Nonetheless, the exercise of rationality as embodied beings depends, at least in the interim, on the functions of wonder (PS, art. 76).[17]

Before the soul is moved to judge an object even as novel to its experience, its attention must first be captured. This suggests that the surprise associated with wonder is a preconceptual element and something which explains both the orienting of the soul's attention and its impetus to seek knowledge. Wonder could not perform its function of directing attention and explaining knowledge acquisition if the mind were already access-conscious of its objects. Indeed, it is not clear that one could have information about an object which was access-conscious and wonder about it, at least wonder in this sense which does not presuppose knowledge of the object.[18] To suppose that wonder achieved its effects through representing objects under certain concepts, rather than by the element of surprise would be to suppose that it captured attention by supplying more

[17] Descartes' account of wonder anticipates recent discussions of the role of arousal systems in the brain, the function of which is to make cells in the cortex and the thalamic regions that supply inputs to the cortex more sensitive to incoming signals. Arousal systems contribute to attention, perception, working memory, emotional response and problem-solving (LeDoux, 1996: 289). These systems can be triggered by a stimulus that is novel or by a stimulus with cognitive emotional content. The amygdala, an important seat of emotions on modern theories, contributes to longer-lasting states of arousal than those caused by the perception of a novel stimulus in other sensory systems (LeDoux, 1996: 284–91). Despite the anatomical inaccuracies of his account, Descartes seems to have anticipated some very central psychological points concerning the relationship between affect and attention.

[18] See chapters 6 and 8 for discussion about wonder directed at known but valuable things.

information to the soul. But since the problem was how the soul manages to attend to what, among the vast store of sensory information potentially available to it, is relevant for its needs or purposes, it is hard to see how adding more information is going to help. It is reasonable to conclude that it is primarily by virtue of its phenomenal aspect that wonder captures the attention of the soul.

It is a good question how extensive the role of wonder is in shaping our perceptual experience. Is it the case that what we perceive is a matter of what we notice, or is the scope of perception broader than that of attention? It is easy to slip into thinking that because our experience of ordinary perceptual objects invokes no wonder in us, that it was always the case that wonder is reserved for highly unusual objects. But this is not obvious. To infants just about everything is wondrous (especially if it has buttons). It is not wildly implausible to suppose, therefore, that Descartes' genetic account of perception features wonder extensively and prominently in the early stages, and less so later as perception becomes more and more a matter of perceptual recognition, a function of the impressions laid down in memory, and attention is shaped not just by our natural attraction to novelty but a whole range of cognitive factors which shape our interests, preferences and emotional dispositions.

What then are we to say about Descartes 'abyssal separation of mind and body', of his assumption that reasoning, moral judgement, pains and sensations, can exist apart from the body? The above discussion should cause us to be more cautious in our accusations. Passions and sensations are grounded in bodily processes, and inextricably bound to the processes by which the soul becomes aware of things outside it that are important to its union with the body. This sets the stage for a better understanding of the way in which sensation and reason are naturally integrated, and for appreciating what it is, on Descartes' view, to be a union of mind and body.

THE STATE OF THE UNION

Above I discussed the importance of the body image, or more precisely, body imagining, through proprioception, to the sensory mechanisms that orient us to objects in space.[19] I then argued that the functions of passions and sensations are bound together, principally through wonder and, in

---

[19] Some psychologists today see the body image as depending on our non-discursive abilities to represent the self-movement of parts of our bodies (Van-den-Bos and Jeannerod, 2002). Descartes' conception of the body image is also connected with our experience of agency. See chapter 6.

particular, its phenomenal character, surprise, which solves the problem of attention for Descartes. It's now time to put these ideas together, an exercise that will bring us closer to understanding why it is important for Descartes that even though we are composites of mind and body, we do not experience ourselves as anything other than complete unities.

To see this, let us compare two combinations of mind and body that Descartes thinks are not 'substantial unions'. The first is the example of the helmsman and his ship, which appears in both the *Sixth Meditation* and the following passage from *Part Six* of the *Discourse on Method*.

I have written concerning the rational soul and [argued] that it cannot be extracted from the power of matter, like the other things of which I have written, but that it ought to be expressly created, and how it does not suffice that it be lodged in a human body as a helmsman is in his ship, perhaps just to move its members, but that it is necessary that it be joined and united with it more tightly for it to have, on account of that, sensations [*sentiments*] and appetites like ours and hence to compose a true human. (AT VI, 59)

When the example reappears in the *Sixth Meditation*, the close inter-mingling of mind and body is again argued to be precondition for having sensations, in particular, the sensation of pain (AT VII, 81). The mention of pain in this context is not an arbitrary choice, for it is pain more than any other sensation that makes us acutely aware of our bodies and the relation of their parts to one another.

The second example of a non-substantial union of mind and body is the hypothetical case of an angel united to a human body.

For if an angel were in a human body, it would not sense as we do but would only perceive the motions which are caused by external objects, and by this it would be distinguished from a true human. (AT III, 493)[20]

The case of the angel and human body union is under-described, but presumably the angel is capable of having some information about the state of its body, although not in a sensory form. Unlike the angel in this scenario, we do not 'perceive' the motions in the body caused by external objects, from which we would have to infer their significance, but are immediately aware of the things that impinge on our bodies through sensation. What form these 'perceptions' would have for the angel is obscure, but without sensory content it is reasonable to suppose that they are more like beliefs or intellectual ideas than sensations.

---

[20] See also Descartes to More, August 1649 (AT V, 402).

How much like the helmsman is the angel? When the angel infers damage to its body from perceiving the motions caused by external things, can it initiate an appropriate reaction to the situation? Perhaps. Pre-established harmony, not to mention angelic intelligence, is, after all, a great asset. If the angel is hooked up to a body in such a way that it receives information about the state of its 'vessel', it seems plausible to suppose that it could will effects in its body that are useful for preserving its union with the body. Similarly, when a (modern) ship needs fuel, the helmsman is made aware of this fact by reading the fuel gauge, from which he infers what it needs and acts accordingly. Descartes seems to imply, however, that the lack of sensory awareness of the body/ship in these two cases has consequences for how each acts in the world, which differs in significant ways from that of a human being.

Although both these non-substantial unions are treated alike on the question of what form of information they may have about the state of their vessels, there are significant differences between the two cases that are worth reflecting upon. If we think about how each is able to act, how each is able to move the vessel to which each is joined to achieve certain ends, we find ourselves faced with two radically different pictures. The case of the helmsman and the ship is easier to understand. What enables the helmsman to move his ship is that he is able to locate himself in space with respect to his ship. He knows how to move his ship in part because it is the ship on which he is standing and the parts of which are oriented to him in certain ways, but that presupposes that he is already aware of the boundaries of his own body. One could argue that the reason why the helmsman and his ship could not constitute a substantial union is that the helmsman's ability to move his ship presupposes that he is already a union of mind and body. Any other bodies that he is able to locate with respect to himself are not parts of himself in any literal sense. It would not do, therefore, to require of the helmsman that he locate himself in relation to his body; he simply has no way of locating himself that is different from the way he is aware through sensation of his body and the arrangement of its parts.

The story of how the angel moves its body is more difficult to conceive. How would an angel locate objects, including its body, in relation to itself, so as to move its body in the way the helmsman moves his ship? The angel does not have the kind of primitive awareness of its body we may suppose of the helmsman, and it has no location in and of itself. Two specific problems that militate against the angel's ability to move its body in the way humans do spring to mind. The first problem is that without

sensory information about the location of its body, which on Descartes'
account, I argued above, is presupposed by our processing of spatial
information, it is difficult to imagine how the angel would orient itself
in space so as to be able to move its body through space. What would it
be, for example, for the angel to move its body to the right or to the left?
To the right or left of what? Surely not to the right or left of it, for it has
no perspective from which objects can be right or left. Of its body? But
from which orientation? Front? Back? Which is the front or back of the
angel's body, from the angel's point of view? The second and related
problem is that what the angel lacks, as a result of lacking a sense of the
spatial orientation of its body with respect to other objects, is the kind of
demonstrative knowledge that makes action within the world possible for us.

Consider trying to steer a ship to a particular destination. Knowing the
co-ordinates of the ship and the absolute distance or position of the
destination would not suffice to steer the ship, even if it were possible,
(which, for Descartes, in the absence of absolute space, it isn't), unless that
information can be translated into knowledge about the position and
distance of the ship relative to oneself. I need to know that this information I have about fuel levels, speed, direction, etc., of a ship is information
about this ship, which is positioned with respect to me, my body, in a
certain way. I need to know that the relevant ship is this one here, and no
amount of general knowledge of the kind available to angels can substitute
for this kind of demonstrative knowledge. Nor will having a definite
description of the form 'the ship on which I am presently standing' help
to orient me in relation to the ship, unless I know where I am, and no
amount of general or propositional knowledge will suffice for my knowing that. What enables the helmsman's knowledge to be genuinely working knowledge is that he is aware of his own body in some way other than
by general description and, by extension, aware of the relative position
and distance of the parts of the ship under his control.

I claim that for Descartes sensations ground this demonstrative knowledge, and I strongly suspect that he thought that such knowledge was
impossible without them. There is reason to think that he was right.
Recent discussions of indexicals and demonstratives have suggested that
there is a way of knowing things provided by the use of indexicals and
demonstratives that, while it may not supply propositional knowledge
that could not be supplied in other ways, is nonetheless ineliminable.
Consider David Lewis' example of the two Gods, Yahweh and Zeus, who
know what there is to know, including that there are two gods, Yahweh
and Zeus, one of whom throws thunderbolts and the other manna, but

neither of whom knows which one *he* is. Suppose a situation arises in which it is appropriate to throw a little manna but churlish to throw a thunderbolt. It is Yahweh's turn to act but unless he becomes aware of himself as Yahweh, how is he to act? (Lewis, 1983). In Lewis' example, the two gods are embodied (one sits on Zion, the other on Olympus, one throws this and the other that), but little is made of their embodiment. If we focus on that embodiment, the role of sensation becomes clearer. What is it for Yahweh to become aware of himself as Yahweh, the thrower of manna? Peter Strawson has one suggestion – it is for Yahweh to become aware of himself as a particular material object (this body), to which other things are related in various ways (Strawson, 1959). Strawson insists that such identificatory awareness cannot consist in anything that could be supplied in propositions containing only pure descriptions and general terms. To see that this is so, he invites us to consider a universe in which every object and general relation has an exact duplicate. If this is possible, then Yahweh's grasp that he is this god and not duplicate Yahweh cannot consist in knowing any fact about Yahweh that can be expressed in general terms. Lewis' (and Perry's (1979) and others') suggestion is that it cannot consist in any fact that can be expressed using proper names either since Zeus and Yahweh can each know all of these and still wonder who he is. But if sentences employing demonstratives and indexicals on each occasion of use express a proposition that could be expressed without them – as the standard semantics for such terms has it – then what happens when Yahweh becomes aware of himself as Yahweh cannot be a matter of acquiring a proposition at all. It seems that Descartes would agree. What Yahweh acquires, Descartes would say, is sensation.[21]

Which sensations make salient to us the fact of our embodiment? As Descartes writes to Chanut (1 February 1647), our pre-natal awareness of our bodies occurs first through the passions.

I consider that from the first moment that our soul has been joined to the body, it is likely that it has a sense of joy, and immediately after, of love, and then perhaps also of hate and of sadness, and that the same dispositions of the body that these passions have for their cause are naturally accompanied afterwards by these thoughts. I judge that the first passion was joy because it is not believable that

---

[21] All this accords well with various modern discussions of the phenomenal body as well. Merleau-Ponty argued that the blind person who walks using a stick comes to feel the stick as part of his body and to feel the world at the end of the stick (Merleau-Ponty, 1962). One might doubt whether the stick ever comes to feel entirely part of oneself (though perhaps there could be cases in which it is hard to distinguish the way it feels from the way a paralysed limb feels) but that just shows what it is to feel something as part of oneself.

the soul would have been put into the body except where it has been well-disposed, and where it is thus well-disposed that naturally gives us joy. (AT IV, 604)

Other texts, including the *Sixth Meditation* discussion of why a human being is not like a helmsman and his ship, emphasise the importance of pain in mediating our direct awareness of our bodies. This is compatible with the primitive role assigned to the passions in constituting our prenatal sense of embodiment, which Descartes describes in the letter to Chanut, because of the association between passions and pleasure and pain. Pain is singled out for special attention because, we can now say, of the way in which pain makes us acutely aware of the boundaries of the body and the relations among its parts. Pain is one of the forms in which proprioceptive information is made available to the soul, but wonder is another, and there is generally an element of surprise associated with a painful episode. We do not ordinarily feel the soles of our feet, Descartes observes, because the weight of our bodies accustoms them to hard contact, but, when tickled there, we become immediately aware of them (PS, art. 72; AT XI, 381). New sensations from a region of the body hitherto unnoticed can draw the soul's attention because the motions of spirits undergirding them form new traces on soft parts of the brain.

From the above discussion we again see the importance of phenomenology to Descartes' understanding of the embodied mind. Any non-demonstrative, general, propositional or purely symbolic content of passions and sensations – any content which does not depend essentially on having a body, whatever that content turns out to be – should also be available to the angel, whose ability to operate among bodies located in space is difficult to conceive. We are 'substantial' unions of mind and body because what the capacity for sensation and passion gives us is location, location, location (which some say is everything), or rather, a point of view from which we may have the kind of demonstrative awareness of things that makes our action with respect to them possible.

CONCLUSION

It is not too far-fetched to think that when Descartes turns to the topic of the passions in the last few years of his life, one of the things he is thinking about is how to solve a specific design problem – the problem of specifying the kind of relationship an immaterial mind must have to a body in order to navigate other bodies it shares a space with. Of course, he does not put the problem quite this way, but the problem he faces in the *Sixth Meditation* of accounting for the tendency of sensations to mislead us cuts deeper than the theodicy that is presented there. The question he is addressing is not just why we have sensations that tend to mislead us but why we have sensations at all. Why is it part of the most 'efficient system' that human beings have sensations, passions and appetites? The *Passions* is the culmination of Descartes' thought on this design problem, and brings home the point that the success of our design depends in large measure upon our capacity to feel our embodiment. This way of thinking about the role of Cartesian sensations takes us beyond the standard epistemological obsession with the veracity of Cartesian sensations and typical 'dissociationist' accusations, such as the one noted early on in this chapter, but it also takes us beyond the simplistic answer that sensations are useful for the preservation of the union. What we find instead is a highly integrated account of the rational and sensitive faculties of human beings. Although there is room for disagreement about the nature and extent of this integration, Descartes should at least be credited with having identified the impossibility of reducing the rational action of human beings to the determinations of a 'pure reason', and thus with having been cautious to avoid committing the 'errors' for which he is so often blamed.

CHAPTER 4

Representing and referring

> The medieval theory of perception was realistic; the senses are the
> open gates thronged by the 'species' which emanate by effluence
> from the actual object, and passing into the mind nevertheless
> remain what they were outside it. But if perception is representative,
> the external world, on its entrance to the mind, passes, as it were,
> through a toll-gate of unreality, and its bewildered ghost wanders
> about its new home, for ever doubtful of its own identity.
>
> (Gibson, 1932: 79)

The last chapter argued that the phenomenology of passions is critical
for accounting for the awareness we have of ourselves as embodied beings.
But Descartes repeatedly refers to the passions as representations, often
incorrect or exaggerated, and it is now time to look at the intentionality of
the passions and how, in virtue of their representational content, they
influence thought and judgement. The epistemic and cognitive effects of
the passions depend on their semantic properties, but their status as
representations is problematic for a variety of reasons.

As we know from previous chapters, Cartesian passions and sensations
do not initiate reception by the intellect of the 'bewildered ghosts' of
Aristotelian theories: the sensible and non-sensible forms (*intentiones*) of
material things. Cartesian fear does not represent the *malicitas* of the wolf
by sharing some form, inhering in both the wolf and the sense organs,
albeit in different ways. Descartes wants to insist instead on the capacity of
sensations and passions to misrepresent objects in the normal course of
events, and it is precisely the problem of error that medieval accounts
faithful to Aristotle were so ill-suited to handle. Somehow the forms of
external things were supposed to have made it into the intellect in a
manner sufficient for understanding the natures of material things,
despite whatever degradation of sensory images occurred in the medium.[1]

---

[1] Since it regarded the objects of sensations as real, the traditional Aristotelian picture made no
significant distinction between the ways in which sensible qualities and other qualities or natures

84

Descartes' account of innate ideas departs radically from this Scholastic picture. But although he disparages 'all those little images flitting through the air, called "intentional forms", which exercise so much the imagination of Philosophers' (AT VI, 85), he retains enough of the Scholastic framework that central figures in the development of the modern theory of intentionality, such as Brentano, do not so much as notice a difference (Brentano, 1889/1966: 15–16).[2] In particular, the idea that perception and thought are mediated by intramental entities persisted into Descartes' time, on account of which the status of ideas without objects proved as difficult for him as it was for Aristotelians, albeit for different reasons. A study of how passions and sensations represent can teach us much about Descartes' theory of representation generally, and how he dealt with this problem of 'false' ideas.

OBJECTIVE REALITY AND THE PROBLEM OF ERROR

In arguing for the existence of God, Descartes draws a preliminary distinction between the *formal* reality that ideas have as modes of mind and their *objective reality*. The formal reality of all ideas is the same, but 'insofar as one (idea) represents one thing, another represents another thing', ideas vary in the degree of objective reality they have (AT VII, 40).[3] The objective reality of an idea depends on the degree of formal reality of the thing represented by the idea. Thus, the ideas of a stone, triangularity, a chimaera and God differ in their degree of objective reality according to the degree of (formal) reality these things possess or would possess were they to exist. The idea of a substance has a greater degree of objective reality than the idea of a mode, and the idea of God the greatest degree of objective reality of all.[4]

What then is meant by the notion 'objective reality'? This is an extraordinarily difficult question to answer but for thinkers of Descartes'

were represented. Sensations occupied a place of primary importance in Aristotelian epistemology. Every act of understanding is mediated by and dependent upon an act of sense or imagination (*De anima*, III.7). For an informative discussion of Descartes' notion of objective being in the context of medieval debates in logic and semantics see Normore, 1986.

[2] The idea of intentional forms has persisted into our own time, principally through Brentano's notion of immanent objectivity, a notion that has been appropriated in recent discussions under the name of 'intentional objects' (Brentano, 1973: 88). See my 2000.

[3] This is an inversion of our modern terminology for expressing the contrast between objective and subjective facts. It is the objective reality of an idea which accounts for what we would call meaning.

[4] For Descartes, an idea can have the degree of objective reality corresponding to the degree of reality of the essence of a thing, even if no objects of that kind actually exist. See AT VII, 45.

time, there seemed to be at least two ways of interpreting the notion: one, a deflationary reading, according to which the 'objective reality' of an idea is simply a way of talking about an idea's (extrinsic) relation to an object; the other, a more ontologically loaded sense, in which 'objective reality' and 'formal reality' signify two modes of being things can have. When an idea has objective reality in this second sense, there is some thing that bears an internal relation to the idea, making it to be the very idea it is, and this thing has some being even if it does not actually exist. Although divorced from the theory of intelligible forms or species, the theory of objective reality according to this second interpretation shares an important feature with Aristotelian–Scholastic accounts. Thinking involves the intellect becoming in some literal sense one with the object of thought. Objective reality is, in this sense, reality objectified, the reality of some thing, as it exists in the intellect.[5]

For Suarez and Descartes' Jesuit contemporaries, as represented by Caterus in the *First Objections*, the notion of objective reality implies nothing more than the first, deflationary reading. Objective reality is simply the 'being known' of an object 'as a denomination' (*esse cognitum quoad denominationem*).[6] An extrinsic denomination is a way of referring to something by its relation to something else; in this case a way of referring to an idea by reference to an object really distinct from it. Objective being, on this reading, does not add anything real to the world that would stand in need of explanation, or that would diminish the amount of being in the world if the idea did not exist. Conceiving of the sun produces no additional reality, nor would the sun be diminished in being were it not thought about.

In objecting to this rendering of the notion, Descartes, infamously, endorses something like the stronger reading. Objective reality is a mode of being and not simply an extrinsic denomination. If one has an idea of a triangle or an intricate machine, one is thinking about some thing, and that one is thinking about that thing is not reducible to any extrinsic relation between the idea and the object. If the object of one's

---

[5] Descartes' use of the term accords more with the ontologically robust usage of *esse obiectivuum* among medievals such as Peter Aureol, the early Ockham and the Arab perspectivists. In this tradition, the notion of objective being designates the reality objects have when they are 'seen or judged', and which, for various reasons often having to do with perceptual illusions, cannot be identified with the extramental object. On this history of this notion, see Tachau (1988). I thank John Carriero for helpful discussion on Descartes' use of the term.

[6] See Suárez, *Disputationes Metaphysicae*, vol. XXV, 1, 32; vol. XXV, 908, and AT VII, 92–3.

thought fails to exist, one's thought and its object are not thereby nothing. To object that when the external object of thought does not exist, an idea can still be characterised by an extrinsic relation to an eternal and immutable nature or essence or form of the thing, does not, Descartes argues, answer the question why there should be an idea of it in the mind. If an idea has certain properties, such as the intricacy of a complicated machine or the properties of a triangle which enable one to deduce truths about triangles from it, it cannot be that an idea is a mere label of some object extrinsic to it, regardless of whether the object is an independently existing thing or an eternal essence (AT VII, 104–5).

Appealing to the widely accepted Scholastic principle that there must be at least as much reality in the efficient and total cause as in the effect of that cause, Descartes claims that the objective reality of an idea must also be caused by something that contains, either formally or eminently, all the reality present objectively in the idea (AT VII, 40–1). Something has to account for the properties of the idea, a cause that either contains all those properties itself (a 'formal cause') or something with more reality than that contained objectively in the idea (an 'eminent cause') (AT VII, 41; 79; 104–5; 165). The intricacy in the idea of a complicated machine must thus be produced either by such a machine itself, or our knowledge of mechanics and design, or something greater than either of these (AT VII, 104–5). Although less perfect than the mode of being possessed by objects outside the intellect, objective being is for these reasons 'not on that account plainly nothing' (AT VII, 103).

The epistemological payoffs of this understanding of objective reality are evident from the first argument for God's existence in the *Third Meditation*. The idea of God contains an infinite degree of objective perfection, which, applying the causal principle, leads to the conclusion that it could only come from a source with that much perfection formally or eminently, and, thus, not from any finite substance. And so God necessarily exists (AT VII, 45). But the principle applies to ideas besides the idea of God and supports our judgements about the existence of external things. Axiom v of the geometrical exposition asserts that we are warranted in judging that the sky exists not because we see it, but because our seeing it produces in the mind an idea of it that must have a cause with as much or more reality as the idea contains objectively, and it is reasonable to suppose on that account that the cause is the sky itself (AT VII, 165).

Does all this mean that by merely having an idea we enhance the amount of being in the world? Descartes seems committed to answering this affirmatively. If the reality contained in an idea of an intricate machine is not reducible to the reality of the idea as a mode of mind, then there is being that would not be were the idea not to exist. But this does not, Descartes assures Caterus, mean that the real thing of which it is an idea, for example, the sun itself 'as it exists in the heavens', acquires additional being from being conceived of or would be diminished if there was no idea of it. The following attempt at clarification of the notion of objective being leaves, however, much to be desired.

[T]o be objectively does not signify other than to be in the intellect in the way in which objects are accustomed to be in it. Thus, for example, if someone asks what happens to the sun from its being objectively in my intellect, it should best be responded that nothing happens to it except an extrinsic denomination, namely, that it terminates an operation of the intellect through the mode of an object. If, however, concerning the idea of the sun, it is asked what it is, it should be answered that it is the thing thought inasmuch as it is objectively in the intellect, for no one understands that to be the sun itself inasmuch as that denomination is in it extrinsically, nor will being objectively in the intellect signify that it terminates an operation through the mode of an object, but to be in the intellect in that way in which objects are accustomed to be. Thus, the idea of the sun is the sun itself existing in the intellect not indeed formally as it does in the heavens but objectively, that is, in the way in which objects are accustomed to be in the intellect. (AT VII, 102)

What we learn from this passage is that the idea of the sun is, in some literal but obscure sense, the same thing as the sun itself; it is the sun itself as it exists in the intellect. It is also in some equally literal and obscure sense, not the same thing as the sun itself; it is not the sun itself, as it exists in the heavens. And thus it looks awfully likely that there is no difference between something's being the idea of the sun and the sun's inhering objectively in the intellect. Notice that it is the sun which is objectively in the intellect, just as it was 'the intricacy of design' (AT VII, 105) which was in the idea of the machine, and not merely some degree of being which attaches itself to the idea because of the degree of formal reality these things have or would have were they to exist. It is plausible to suppose, therefore, that the inherence of things in the intellect accounts for what ideas represent, what they are of or about. What distinguishes the idea of the sun from the idea of a machine is that different things are objectively present in each idea. All this creates a metaphysical minefield, but let us try to pick our way a bit further through it.

Michael Ayers has asked in what sense an idea, a mode of mind, could be identical with the thing it represents, for example, a corporeal substance such as the sun.

> Which is the mere distinction of reason, and which the real distinction: (1) the distinction between the idea as mode of thought and the idea as intentional object of thought or (2) the distinction between the latter (i.e., the thing as it exists in the mind) and the real object (the thing as it exists in reality)? It seems clear that, at least on ordinary realist assumptions, there cannot be one thing, the idea, which is really identical *both* to the mode of thought *and* to the real object.
>
> (Ayers, 1998: 1067)

What is disturbing to Ayers is not Descartes' postulation of intentional objects as ways of characterising ideas by their objects, or the distinction between intentional objects and real (extramental) objects, but the obscurity over where to draw the lines between the idea, the intentional object and the real object. If the intentional and the real object are the same thing with two modes of being, then it will not do to identify an idea with this thing, however one characterises its being, because doing so leads to the absurd conclusion that a mode of mind can be strictly identical with a corporeal substance. On the other hand, proposing a representationalist solution, one which draws a real distinction between the thing as it exists objectively and as it exists really or formally, conflicts with Descartes' reply to Caterus, which states unequivocally that the idea of the sun is the sun itself, and which seems to imply something weaker than a real distinction between the two. Positing a real distinction between the sun existing as it does in the intellect and outside the mind also conflicts with our 'anti-individualist' intuitions that lead many philosophers to deny that an idea, like the idea of the sun, could exist and be the very idea it is whether or not the actual sun exists (Putnam, 1975; Burge, 1979, 1982, 1986a, 1986b). But if there is no real distinction between the idea and the thing of which it is an idea, it looks equally impossible that the thing could exist when the idea of it does not, a dangerously idealist conclusion. 'The objective mode of being belongs to ideas by their very nature', Descartes writes, but if the idea and the external thing of which it is an idea are not really distinct, the distinction between two modes of being looks superfluous, or, at best, only useful for characterising ideas about non-existent objects (AT VII, 42).

Unsurprisingly, confusion on this very issue has produced a division within the scholarly community between those who think that Descartes is a representational realist – i.e., someone who thinks the direct objects of thought are immanent or intentional objects from which the mind infers the existence of extramental things – and those who think that he is a direct realist – someone who thinks that the objects of ideas and judgements are the extramental things themselves, by means of their special mode of being in the intellect.[7] Since it has bearing on how we interpret Descartes' whole epistemology, therefore, a lot hangs on how we understand the notion of objective being.

The representationalist reading of Descartes has one extra notch in its belt, or at least so it has seemed. One advantage of thinking that there is a real distinction between the intentional object and the real object of an idea is that there is greater scope for error in the idea.[8] On the representationalist reading, when there is a mismatch between the intentional and real object, an idea may be mistaken and lead to mistaken judgement when we infer from the properties of the intentional object what properties are possessed by the real object, or when we infer from the intentional object that there is a real object when there isn't. But this is too simple an account of error and not what Descartes says anyway. Much of Descartes' discussion about the falsity of ideas can be read as an attempt to account for the content of these ideas while preserving the idea that the thing which has objective reality in the intellect *just is* the thing which actually or possibly exists in reality.

FALSITY: FORMAL AND MATERIAL

It was standard in Descartes' time to attribute truth and falsity to judgements. Whether judgements are thought of as having a sentential or propositional form, or, more loosely, as containing a form or idea which is somehow 'grasped' by the intellect, insofar as judgements involve an act

---

[7] See Kenny's useful discussion (1968: ch.4, sec. 6). For a defence of the representationalist reading of Descartes, see Reid, 1896 and Rorty, 1979: 50–1, and for criticism see Yolton, 1974; 1984, Lennon, 1974, Cook, 1987, Vinci, 1998 and recent discussions in Hoffman, 2002b and Alanen, 2003: ch.5.

[8] Compare causal theories of representational content. If what an idea represents is the object that causes it, then an idea represents whatever causes it, including those things we wouldn't take to be represented by the idea. In contemporary causal theories this is known as the 'disjunction problem', for it leads to the conclusion that an idea represents the disjunction of all its actual and possible causes. The problem with disjunctive content is that it rules out the possibility of error. See Fodor, 1987: ch. 4 and 1990: ch.2.

of assent, they can be described as having succeeded in getting on to the truth, which is the end of judgement, or not, and so being false.[9] When we assent to an idea that isn't clear and distinct, on Descartes' account, we either make a false judgement or arrive at the truth wholly by accident. Judgement that doesn't follow the perceptions of the intellect in accordance with the natural light will always involve an incorrect use of the free will (AT VII, 59–60). The kind of falsity that occurs in judgement is referred to as *formal falsity*, which is falsity strictly speaking, but Descartes reserves a different kind of falsity, *material falsity*, for ideas themselves 'when they represent non-things as things' (*non rem tanquam rem representant*) (AT VII, 43). In his reply to Arnauld's objections to the *Meditations*, Descartes claims that although any idea that provides 'material for false judgement' deserves to be called materially false, the term is appropriate only when the scope for error is great. Confused ideas that are consciously constructed at will provide little scope for error, whereas ideas from the senses, particularly those related to appetite, provide the greatest scope for error, and most deserve being called materially false (AT VII, 233–4).

Certain sensory ideas, those that would later be known as ideas of 'secondary qualities', are singled out as prime candidates for material falsity. The *Third Meditation* cites the idea of cold as an example of an idea that could turn out to be materially false, if cold is nothing but a privation of heat (AT VII, 44). The *Fourth Replies* adds to the idea of cold ideas of colour, 'if it is true, as I have said, that these ideas do not represent anything real' (AT VII, 234). These ideas are drawn from the list that includes all our ideas of 'light and colours, sounds, smells, tastes, heat and cold and other tactile qualities' (AT VII, 43). They are particularly pernicious because, insofar as all ideas are 'as if of things' (AT VII, 44) or 'as if images of things' (French version), they represent non-things as if they were real, and can thus easily mislead the mind into judging that they are real.

Since there can be no ideas which are not as if of things [*nisi tanquam rerum*], if it is true that cold is nothing other than a privation of heat, the idea which represents it to me as something real and positive deserves to be called false; and so on for others of this kind. (AT VII, 44)

---

[9] In the *Second Replies*, Descartes describes the faculty for recognising truth and falsity and judging as tending necessarily towards the truth, provided it is used correctly, that is, when we assent to only that which we clearly and distinctly perceive (AT VII, 144).

Descartes goes on to add that if an idea is materially false, it is true by the natural light that it 'arises from nothing', that it is in me only because of a deficiency of my nature, and hence does not require me to posit a source outside myself. Ideas coming from the senses offer no secure indication of what there is in the world. Even if they are true and represent some reality outside me, it is so slight that I will not be able to distinguish it from a non-thing or have any reason to believe the idea didn't just originate within me (AT VII, 44).

So far it might seem very natural to read Descartes as offering a representationalist account of error. On this reading, materially false ideas are simply those ideas that have intentional objects but no corresponding real object, and of which we are not aware as having been made up at will. They provide subject matter for erroneous judgement because seeming not to depend on the will, they incline us to judge that their objects are real, and because they are so confused and obscure, we cannot tell from them whether their objects are real or not. However, the trouble with this account of material falsity, and the representationalist reading of Descartes that goes along with it, as Arnauld was quick to observe, is that it is completely inconsistent with Descartes' account of objective reality.

Arnauld raises two main objections to Descartes' account of material falsity, each of which is designed to show that it is impossible to hold both that every idea has objective reality and that some ideas are materially false. The first objection deals specifically with the claim that if cold is a privation, the idea of cold is materially false. Arnauld objects that if cold is a privation, there cannot be an idea of it which represents it as a positive being for the following reason.

For what is the idea of cold? Cold itself as it exists objectively in the intellect. But if cold is a privation, it cannot exist objectively in the intellect through an idea of which the objective existence is a positive entity. Therefore, if cold is only a privation, there is never able to be a positive idea of it, and thus none which is materially false. (AT VII, 206)

If, in other words, all ideas have objective reality and objective reality is something, an idea that represents a non-thing must either entail that a non-thing has objective being, which is a contradiction, or that there can be ideas that do not have objective reality, contrary to the original supposition that all ideas have objective reality.

The second objection is that the notion of material falsity is incompatible with the causal principle used to establish the existence of God. Arnauld asks:

Finally, that idea of cold, which you say to be materially false, what does it exhibit to your mind? A privation? Then it is true. A positive being? Then it is not an idea of cold. And besides what is the cause of that positive objective being whence comes the force so that that idea may be materially false? 'I', you say, inasmuch as I am from nothing. Then the positive objective being of some idea is able to be from nothing, which particularly contradicts the fundamental principles of this celebrated man. (AT VII, 207)

Arnauld thus presents Descartes with the following dilemma: either the objective reality of the idea of cold comes from something or it comes from nothing. If it comes from something, it comes either from a privation, in which case it is true, or from something else, in which case it is not the idea of cold. If the objective reality comes from nothing, a 'defect' in my nature, the causal principles used to establish the existence of God are violated.

Arnauld advises Descartes to instead think of all ideas as representing something positive and to restrict falsity to judgement. It is best to do this anyway for the sake of the argument for God's existence, Arnauld recommends, since the force of this argument rests on the intuition that even the atheist cannot deny that the idea of God represents something real and positive (AT VII, 206–7). Alternatively, Descartes could deny that the idea of cold really is the idea of cold, but if he does this, then there is no falsity in the idea, only in the judgement we make about which idea we are having. Either way, Descartes must accept that there cannot be an idea that is materially false (AT VII, 207).[10]

Arnauld's characteristically sensible advice is not, however, taken by Descartes, and it is interesting to speculate why. Why is the category of material falsity so important to Descartes? My sense is that Descartes wants something like a category of vacuous ideas, in which to place at least some ideas coming from the senses, the point being to completely undermine the Scholastics' trust in the senses. If some sensory ideas are materially false, and if all sensory ideas are so confused and obscure that we cannot tell from them which are true and which are false, there would be no reason to trust any of them. But if all ideas regardless of their origins represent something real and positive, then the senses can be trusted, even if only up to a point. If all sensory ideas represent something real, we may still make errors, but these errors would be restricted in ways that pose no threat to empiricism. We might still make errors in judgement when we

---

[10] Later, however, Arnauld endorsed the distinction between true and false ideas. See Arnauld, 1990 and Nelson, 1996.

misapply a sensory idea to objects that lack the sensible quality represented by the idea, but we wouldn't be wrong in thinking that there is or could be such a quality. We might even go wrong in how we define the qualities represented by ideas coming from the senses. It is, after all, compatible with thinking correctly that heat is something real, that I have some false theory about its relationship to matter. By comparison, the claim that some ideas of sensible qualities might represent nothing at all, and do so in a way that makes it seem as if they do represent something real and positive, poses a much deeper threat to Scholastic theories committed to sensation as the basic mode of acquaintance with the natural world.

ON REFERRING

When, however, he [Arnauld] says that the idea of cold is coldness itself as it is objectively in the intellect I think that a distinction is necessary: for it often happens in confused and obscure ideas, among which those of heat and cold are numbered, that they are referred to a thing other than that of which they are ideas. Thus, if cold is only a privation, the idea of cold is not cold itself, as it were objectively in the intellect, but another thing which I take wrongly for that privation; truly, it is the sensation itself which has no being outside the intellect.
(AT VII, 233)

Descartes' reply to Arnauld's first objection is an attempt to secure what Arnauld denies is possible: a coherent notion of material falsity consistent with the claim that all ideas have objective reality. The passage just quoted suggests that materially false ideas like the idea of cold have objective reality, but that this objective reality is not that of a non-being or privation. Then there is this mysterious claim that the objective reality of the idea of cold is something other than cold – the sensation itself – which has no being outside the intellect. A sensation is a mode of mind, and so has some being formally, and in the case of materially false ideas some being objectively. That answers the question of how there could be an idea without objective being. There can't be. Materially false ideas are not counterexamples to the claim that ideas essentially have objective reality. But how is this consistent with the claim that materially false ideas represent non-things as things? If the objective reality of the idea of cold is a sensation, and a sensation, being a mode of mind, is something real and positive, in what sense is the idea materially false?

Descartes' response to Arnauld is perplexing, and many scholars as a result have been inclined to think that Descartes would have been better off to have ditched the notion of material falsity altogether. In her book, *Descartes*, Margaret Dauler Wilson argued that the notion of material falsity does little work in Descartes' theory, and since it disappears from view after the *Replies*, she speculates that he came to see that it wasn't necessary to hang on to it.[11] Her suggestion, like Arnauld's, is that he could have constructed his error theory of sensation from the intuition that sensory ideas are confused and obscure, and from the claim that they produce in us a natural inclination to errors of judgement that are formally false. For reasons I gave earlier having to do with the threat the category of material falsity poses to Scholastic forms of empiricism, I am more inclined to try to make sense of the notion of material falsity. It is not obvious, for example, that the category of confused and obscure ideas is sufficiently precise to capture all the kinds of error to which the senses lead us. Materially false ideas lead us into quite specific kinds of error, and it is important to be able to identify them as such. As Frans Burman records from his conversation with Descartes as late as 1648, there is a kind of error that can occur in connection with certain sensory ideas when we think that they represent real qualities of bodies, which is not like the kinds of error which merely confused and obscure ideas lead us into. In this context, the example offered is an idea of colour.

There is nonetheless occasion for error even if I refer them [sensory ideas] to no things outside me since I am able to err in the very nature of them, as when I consider the idea of colour and say it to be a thing, quality or, more appropriately, colour itself which is represented through that idea, as would be such if I were to say that whiteness is a quality, even if I refer that idea to no thing outside me and I say or suppose no thing to be white. I would be able, however, in the abstract and in the very nature or idea of whiteness itself to err. (AT v, 152)

These errors 'in the abstract' hint strongly at Descartes' notion of material falsity. The cause of our error in judgement in this case is quite specific: it is not because the idea of white is merely confused and obscure, as if I don't know what whiteness really is, or because I think particular bodies are white when they might be some other colour, but because I think whiteness is some real quality insofar as it is represented in the idea.

How then, in light of Descartes' reply to Arnauld, might we make sense of the notion of material falsity? Notice that the passage cited above

[11] Margaret Wilson refers to Descartes' discussion of material falsity as 'confusion confounded' (Wilson, 1978: 110). See also Wilson, 1990 and 1991; Alanen, 1994; Beyssade, 1992; Bolton, 1986; Field, 1993; Hoffman, 1996; MacKenzie, 1990 and 1994; Menn, 1995; Nelson, 1996; and Wells, 1984.

from the *Fourth Replies* (AT VII, 233) does not only assert that the objective reality of the idea of cold is a sensation, but also that the sensation is referred to something other than that of which it is an idea. What work, if any, does this notion of referring do? The *Fourth Replies* does not elaborate, and this is an omission with some consequence. The above passage recorded by Burman uses referring only in regard to judgements that bodies outside me have colours. If referring takes place only in judgements about external bodies; if, for example, in referring the idea of cold to some thing we assent to the idea that certain bodies are cold, an opponent of material falsity like Arnauld can simply object that the only falsity Descartes needs is the formal falsity of judgement. Interestingly, the notion of referring is used extensively in the *Passions* to distinguish between sensations, appetites and passions. Might we glean anything from this discussion to help us understand the notion of material falsity?

At article 27 of the *Passions*, passions are defined as 'perceptions, sensations or emotions of the soul, which are *referred* particularly to it, and which are caused, maintained and strengthened by some movement of the spirits' (PS, art. 27; my emphasis).[12] Passions are distinguished from other sensations and appetites that depend on different nerves through being referred to the soul. At article 22, Descartes writes:

All the perceptions I have not yet explained, come to the soul through the mediation of the nerves, and there exists this difference between them, that we refer some to objects outside us which strike our senses, others to our body or to some of its parts, and finally others to our soul. (AT XI, 345)

What then is it to refer a sensation or passion to some thing?

The following examples of seeing the light of a torch and hearing the sound of a bell suggest that the notion of referring bears some relationship to what we suppose are the causes of our ideas, as well as to what we suppose our ideas to be about or represent.

Because [these external objects] excite two different movements in some of our nerves, and by their means in the brain give to the soul two different sensations which we refer in such a way to the subjects we suppose to be their causes, we think that we see the torch itself and hear the bell and not sense only the movements which came from them. (AT XI, 346)

---

[12] The expression '*se referrer*' was not by any means in the period tied exclusively to acts of judgement. De la Chambre (1658–63: IV.1.439–40; III.2. 105–6) uses the term to express the direction of flow of the animal spirits from the brain to the muscles.

To refer an auditory sensation to some external object, the bell, is the same as thinking that we hear the sound of the bell because (we suppose) the bell is the cause of the idea. Similarly, to refer a pain to a foot is to suppose that the foot is the cause of our idea. The connection between what an idea is referred to and what we suppose the causes of the idea are seems built into the analysis of why passions are referred to the soul. At article 25, Descartes writes that 'the perceptions that are referred to the soul alone are those whose effects are sensed as in the soul itself, and of which we do not know commonly any proximate cause, to which we may refer them' (AT XI, 347).

This explanation has suggested to some interpreters that the soul is the default cause of the passions, and that referring a passion is simply a matter of the soul's making a judgement about itself as the cause of the passions. Paul Hoffman thinks that the causal factor must be worked into the definition of referring.

We refer some sensations, such as the sound of a bell, to external objects that we suppose are their causes in such a way that we think we perceive those external objects. We refer sensations that we feel as in parts of our body, such as hunger, thirst, pain, and heat, to those parts. We refer the passions of the soul to the soul because, Descartes says, we feel their effects as being in the soul itself and because we usually know of no proximate cause to which we can refer them.

(Hoffman, 1991: 160)

As Hoffman is aware, Descartes' explanation at article 25 for why we refer passions to the soul is unsatisfactory. First, Descartes states elsewhere in the text that the effects of the passions are felt as in the heart, not the soul. This is why the mistake about the heart being the 'seat' of the passions is commonly made (PS, art. 33). Second, if Descartes means by 'proximate cause' a brain movement, then the fact that no proximate cause of the passions is known is no more a reason to refer passions to the soul than it is to refer any other sensation there. No proximate causes of *any* sensation are commonly known (AT VII, 436; AT V, 221–2).[13] Hoffman concludes that Descartes has failed to distinguish passions from other perceptions.

---

[13] In a footnote to 'Three Dualist Theories of the Passions', Hoffman toys with other interpretations. His preferred reading is that to refer a perception to some thing is 'to suppose that the perception is in the thing', presumably as a mode of the thing (Hoffman, 1991:196). This comes close to my reading, but what we suppose to be in some thing on the occasion of a sensation is not always what we refer to it, as the case of materially false ideas demonstrates.

In the context where Descartes asserts that the effects of the passions are felt in the heart he presumably is considering only the effects of a passion on the body, which is consistent with there being other effects on the soul, in particular, on the will. This, in turn, is consistent with the idea that we refer a passion to the soul because we experience it as a movement of the will, and so, according to the interpretation under consideration, as originating in the soul. Support for this interpretation is given by Descartes' remark in article 47 that in an undivided soul 'all its appetites are volitions', a confusing comment in light of the distinction drawn between passions and volitions in article 17 (AT XI, 364). But leaving this problem and Hoffman's second observation that the espoused reason for referring passions to the soul - that we do not know their proximal causes – does not distinguish them from any other sensation aside, can it really be the case that, for Descartes, we experience our passions as originating in the soul and, on account of such experiences, we refer them to the soul?

Stephen Voss also interprets the referring function in terms of a judgement about the causes of the passions. As he writes in a footnote to his translation of the *Passions*: 'I propose this hypothesis about Descartes' conception of referring: we "refer" our perception to an object just in case we spontaneously judge that the action causing our perception is within that object' (Voss 1989: 30, n. 23).

Voss' insertion of the adverb 'spontaneously' is illuminating. Descartes is prepared, on other occasions, to acknowledge the habitual and speedy (but essentially intellectual) 'judgements' we make at the 'third grade' of sensory response, and to admit that this is where falsity occurs (AT VII, 437–9). But if it is such judgements that account for the representational content of sensory ideas, it is difficult to know whether Descartes is assuming here that there is an act of assent involved, or whether he is invoking a different sense of judgement. One reason for thinking that the habitual judgements made at the third grade of sensory response are non-volitional is that, given the encapsulation of perception, they do not seem to be ones that we can withhold assent from. The stick partially submerged in water will appear bent no matter how much the intellect resists the conclusion that it is bent (AT VII, 438–9). Is this appearance constituted by a judgement with assent, which the intellect tells us 'not to believe' (AT VII, 439) and so contradicts itself, or by a non-volitional judgement or by something else?[14] The idea that appearances involve

[14] Lilli Alanen (in conversation) thinks that in order to make sense of the discussion of the 'three grades of sensory response' in the *Sixth Replies* (AT VII, 436–8), it is necessary to suppose that

non-volitional judgements is charitable and would not have been out of place in Scholastic theories of perception. Scholars familiar with Aquinas' account of perception would, for example, be used to attributing a rudimentary form of non-volitional judgement to animals exercising their estimative faculties. Either way though, the problem lies not here but with interpreting the referring function as a mode of judgement about the causes of a sensation.

Let us return, then, to consider the suggestion that we refer a passion to the soul because we suppose that it is caused by the soul. To suppose that a passion is caused by the soul would, on Descartes' account of the soul, be to suppose that it arises from some 'action' of the soul. There are only two modes of thought, actions (volitions) and passions, and actions are the analogue of motion in bodies. To suppose my passions are caused by the soul would mean that I experience my passions as ideas that originate within the soul, perhaps because I confuse my passions with moral or practical judgements about my lot in life, or perhaps because what is most salient to me through a passion is the fact that my will is inclined a certain way. This does not necessarily conflict with Descartes' definition of the passions as caused by the body (PS, art. 27), or with his distinction between passions and volitions (PS, art. 17), for I might just be mistaken about what the real causes of my passions are. And it is true that the passions incline the will in determinate ways (PS, arts. 40; 47). But this interpretation suggests something about the phenomenology of the passions that Descartes seems to think is not so – that we experience our passions as originating in our souls rather than feeling ourselves passive subjects of external influences, and it strikes me that it is the latter that gives the true phenomenology of the passions on Descartes' view. This is certainly Elisabeth's experience when she feels that the passions rob her of the very power of her reason, and much of Descartes' correspondence with her on the topic and the moral project of the *Passions* is an attempt to empower Elisabeth and us, his readers, with the recognition that we *can* be masters of our passions (e.g., PS, art. 41).[15] This theme makes little

---

sensations and passions involve a kind of non-volitional judgement. Descartes tells us there that it is only at the 'third grade' of sensory response, which involves judgement, that truth or falsity enters (the first grade being the motions in the brain that give rise to a sensation and the second grade being the immediate effects of those motions on the soul which dispose it to certain judgements). If what he means by 'truth' and 'falsity' in sensory responses is material truth and falsity, Alanen is surely right. An act of assent would suggest formal truth and falsity.

[15] Elisabeth often expresses how the infirmities of her sex afflict her soul (24 May 1645) and maladies deprive her of the power of reasoning (16 August 1645).

sense on the supposition that we falsely experience ourselves as agents of our passions.

Nor is it clear how thinking of ourselves as agents of our passions fits with their function in preserving the union. The biological utility of the passions depends on the fact that they make us think of external objects as affecting us for better or for worse. If the passions are to fulfil their natural function, we must generally regard the causes of the passions as being outside the soul. Perhaps all this is just to say that there is an inconsistency or tension in Descartes' view, but if there is a way to avoid this conclusion while capturing the phenomenology of Cartesian passions as experiences of passivity, then I'd like at least to try and find it.[16]

I propose then a different model for understanding the referring function, one that does not take Descartes' comment at article 25 about our referring passions to the soul because we commonly do not know their proximate causes as definitional. Notice that in the cases of perceptions referred to the body and perceptions referred to external objects, there is a clear link between what the perception is referred to and what it represents. The tinkling sound is referred to the bell and is of the bell. Pain is referred to the foot and represents the foot as afflicted. Is there a general way to capture this representational function of the notion of referring that does not collapse into the idea that a judgement (or more precisely a volitional judgement) is involved?

It is useful at this point to compare the function of 'referring' in Descartes' epistemology to the notion of 'seeing as' in contemporary analyses of perception. Could we say, for example, that to refer a sensation of whiteness to the paper is analogous to seeing the paper as white? To refer pain to the foot is to feel or experience the foot as afflicted. To refer cold to the ice is to experience or feel the ice as cold. Such locutions

---

[16] Alanen provides an interesting and detailed argument that referring a passion to the soul just is to mistakenly think of it as arising from the evaluative judgements of the soul and, therefore, as having some rational basis it in fact lacks (Alanen, 2003:185–90). Alanen argues that this best makes sense of the suggestion in article 25 that we refer passions to the soul because we feel their effects there and know of no proximate cause to which we may otherwise refer them. While interesting in its own right, this does not seem to me to be Descartes' view. It would follow that referring passions to the soul is itself a source of error, because the soul is not the cause of its passions, but the only error Descartes recognises in the passions consists in their tendency to misrepresent or exaggerate the importance of things (PS, art. 138; AT VII, 37). Nor is there any suggestion that the Cartesian sage, knowing the true causes of the passions, would cease to refer her passions to the soul. On the view espoused below, this is because to refer a passion is simply to experience oneself as moved in a certain way and this is true independently of whether one is justified in feeling so moved or not.

represent an object, for example, the ice or the foot, as being modified in a certain way. This suggests two general formulations of the referring function:

(1) To refer a perception A to B is to experience B as modified by A.
(2) To refer a perception A to B is for B to appear as modified by A.

I offer these not as distinct formulations of the referring function but simply two ways of looking at the same experience: one from the point of view of the subject of a perception, and the other from the point of view of the object being perceived. But the second formulation will be useful when we return to the problem of material falsity.

One advantage of the seeing-as talk over talk of judgements is that it enables one to ascribe structured representational content to a perception without collapsing the distinction between perception and belief or judgement. This is useful for accounting for the phenomenology of sensory illusions, like the bent stick illusion of which Descartes speaks in the *Sixth Replies*. We could say that at the third grade of sensory response we see the stick as bent, and that this involves the intellect, perhaps even a judgement, but unless we are small children or idiots we will not assent to this idea or believe that the stick really is bent. When we say that the stick 'appears bent in water because of refraction' what we mean is 'that it appears to us in that mode through which a child would judge that it is bent, and through which even we, following the prejudices which we have become accustomed to accept from our youth, would judge in the same way' (AT VII, 438–9). The way things appear disposes the will to assent to ideas representing those appearances, but falls short of determining the will to assent. The seeing-as locution is preferable, in my view, to the terminology of judgement, for the reason that judgement and acts of assent are generally connected in Descartes' framework, but little hangs of whether we choose to use the language of non-volitional judgement instead (AT VII, 60–1; PS, art. 17).

This interpretation of the notion of referring provides a more plausible rendering of Descartes' assertion that the passions are referred to the soul. It does not, for example, imply that we experience ourselves as agents of our passions. When a passion is referred to the soul, the soul, on this reading, perceives or experiences itself as modified – moved – in a particular way. Just as from a perception of light I see the torch as bright, and from a perception of pain I feel my foot as afflicted, from a perception of fear I am aware of myself or my soul as afraid. As Amelie Rorty has argued, I do not refer the fear outside the soul because it is not external things or my body that appear modified by the passion but my soul (Rorty, 1992: 378).

What then are we to make of the explanation at article 25, which states that passions are referred to the soul because no proximate cause is commonly known, and because their effects are felt there? Whereas perceptions of external things dispose us to think that bodies are modified in certain ways – have colours, sounds, temperatures, etc. – and perceptions of the body dispose us to think our body is affected in specific ways – is in pain, hungry, thirsty, etc. – the passions dispose us to think that our soul is affected – by love, by desire, by anger, etc. It is in this sense of being primarily modes of self- (rather than other-) awareness that the effects of the passions are felt as in the soul. Descartes' second point 'that no proximate causes are commonly known' neither asserts nor implies that we refer our passions to the soul because we think that the soul is the cause of our passions. After having offered his explanation for why passions are referred to the soul, Descartes immediately adds:

> Such are the sensations of joy, anger, and others like them, which are sometimes excited in us *by objects that move our nerves and sometimes also by other causes.*
> (AT XI, 347; my emphasis)

Here Descartes alludes to the fact that unlike other sensations and appetites, passions are not caused by specific types of external events, and are more open to mediation by associated thoughts. Since there is no one type of physical event that provokes anger, it makes more sense to treat anger as a modification of the soul than as a response to a specific type of external cause. We might call the distal causes of anger all 'injustices', but there is no natural kind that these form or supervene upon, nor any definable class of perceptions that would constitute perceptions of injustices and so serve as a natural kind for the proximal causes in the brain of anger.[17] Passions differ in this regard from perceptions of red, or pain, because even though there may well be differences among all the perceptions of red or all experiences of pain, there is more of a chance that these will be differences of degree (differences of shade and hue, or intensity) rather than differences of kind. By comparison, the causes of any given

---

[17] The causes of a passion typically include an individual's past experiences, as preserved in memory, and other cognitive states, as much as the temperament of the brain, and so it is less plausible to suppose a passion could be defined through either its proximal or distal causes. For discussion along these lines, see Amelie Rorty (1992: 379).

kind of passion, both distal and proximal, consist of many different kinds of things, a fact which makes their enumeration especially difficult.

If this reading is correct, the passions of the soul are movements of the will, but they are not ones which originate in the soul or which are experienced as originating in the soul. Passions are not simply perceptions of the good or evil of certain things but wantings or willings that things be a certain way, and thus, if unimpeded, terminate in certain actions. It is in being movements of the will, that it is appropriate to call all the appetites of the soul, including its passions, volitions, even when those volitions are not initiated by the soul itself or with its assent.

On this reading of the referring function, the passions are modes of self-awareness. This idea is useful for explaining the motivational force of the passions. It is because I am afraid that I am inclined to flee. I don't want just to represent to myself some property of external bodies, and then have to figure out the significance of that property for myself.[18] But for the passions to have this biological function, it is not enough that in having a passion I experience my soul as modified in a certain way. I need to represent external events or things as having some bearing on my well-being that requires me to take certain sorts of action. But how, if the passions are all referred to the soul, do they represent external things as important in these ways?

When we refer passions to the soul, we represent not just the soul alone, but the soul as affected in a certain way by some external thing. The soul is afraid but the fear is of the tiger. The soul is envious but the envy is of others' good fortune. One way of explicating this relationship is by saying that it is because I am afraid when a tiger is present, that I experience the tiger as dangerous or think of the tiger as dangerous. The 'because' here is intended in a constitutive sense. What a passion represents is (usually) a complex relation: an external object affecting the union in a certain (good or bad) way. It is not implausible to suppose that a complex relation could be captured by attributing some complex but monadic property (fear-of-the-tiger) to one of the *relata*, the soul. In pre-nineteenth-century theories of relations, defining binary relations as pairs of relatives was fairly standard (see Brown and Normore, 2003). And given that Cartesian passions typically involve other cognitive or sensory modes – e.g., a perception of the tiger, a judgement about another's good fortune – the soul rarely is aware of itself as moved for no good reason. There are,

---

[18] Voss (1989: 31, n.23) also notes the self-referential content of the passions.

however, some exceptions. When, for example, a passion is caused solely by the consistency or rate of movement of the blood, the soul may not be able to identify a 'first cause' of its passion (AT VIIIA, 317). But these are atypical cases. In the normal course of events, a passion is experienced in conjunction with and partly as a response to some impression of an object, to which the passion adds a special significance or value. The passions are, at the same time, modes of self-awareness and modes of awareness of the significance external objects bear to us as unions of mind and body.

MATERIAL FALSITY REDUX

The notions of objective being and material falsity are absent from the text of the *Passions,* but there is no reason to suspect that Descartes had abandoned either notion by 1649. The notion of objective perfection appears in the *Notae in Programma* of 1648, the attack on Regius' 'broadsheet', and the notion of material falsity seems to be lurking in the background of Descartes' conversation with Burman, also of 1648. It is not surprising that the notion of *material falsity* should not arise in the *Passions* for the simple reason that insofar as the passions represent the soul as moved in specific ways, as modified by fear, love, pity, anger, etc., they are all true. If I feel fear, then I am moved by fear, whether or not the external thing I think causes it poses a real threat to me, indeed, whether there is any external cause at all. This accords with Descartes' assertion in the *Third Meditation* that the passions of the soul cannot be false.

No falsity, however, is to be feared in the will or the affections, for even though it is possible to want things which are depraved or non-existent, it is not, therefore, true that I do not want them. (AT VII, 37)

On the reading advanced here, it is because in referring passions to the soul we experience the soul as moved, and cannot be wrong therefore in thinking that the soul is moved in a specific way, that the passions cannot be materially false in the way other sensory ideas can be. Despite their immunity to material falsity, the passions still make their own contributions to false judgements. As shall be explored in chapter 8, the complex relationship between our experience of our passions and our perceptions and judgements of their external or 'first' causes makes us prone to infer from our feelings that external objects and events have certain moral or evaluative qualities which they very often lack.

This reading requires that the soul itself be something that is objectively and subjectively present to itself at the same time. The soul is subjectively present as the thinking substance and objectively present insofar as it is aware of itself as modified in certain ways. This is not a difficult idea to grasp and one with some currency in Descartes' time. At least one of Descartes' sources, Eustachius, thought that this was how the soul's self-awareness was to be understood.[19] And there is some suggestion at the end of the *Second Meditation* that all ideas are modes of self-awareness, whatever else they may represent (AT VII, 33). Perhaps all ideas, insofar as the mind is aware of itself having them, are referred to the soul in a secondary or indirect fashion, but insofar as some are referred primarily outside the mind to bodies, they are not all passions of the soul. If I am aware of seeing the wax because I see and feel it, I may experience my soul in the course of having this idea as modified by a perception, but my perception is directly an experience of the wax as modified in certain ways, as hard, yellow, smelling of clover and so on, and only indirectly an experience of the soul as affected in a certain way by this perception. Passions are, however, on this reading, primarily or directly modes of self-awareness, although they could be indirectly modes of awareness of external things as well. They are explicitly of or about the ways in which the soul is moved or affected by things (for the most part) outside itself. Might we use this analysis of the referring function, drawn from the account given in the *Passions*, to better understand Descartes' solution to the problems surrounding material falsity?

When Descartes replies to Arnauld that the objective reality of the idea of cold is the sensation itself but that the idea is referred to something of which it is not an idea, we may read him, in line with the above formulation of the referring function (1) as saying that that which is a mode of mind, a sensation, is experienced as a mode of body or extended substance. To refer the idea of cold to a body, say, the ice, is to feel or experience the ice as modified by cold. But if the object of the idea is just a

---

[19] Eustachius A Sancto Paulo explicitly makes use of this point to explain how the soul is aware of itself. See *Summa philosophiae quadripartita* (1609) 4.1. d.1.q.2, where he argues that the same thing may be both subjectively in a thing (i.e. in it as in a subject, as dispositions and acts are in the mind) and objectively in the same thing at the same time (i.e. present as an object to the knowing intellect). This does not show that Descartes derived his idea about the objective status of sensations from Eustachius, but it suggests that the idea had some currency in the seventeenth century. Descartes had read Eustachius' text and regarded it as the best abstract of Scholastic philosophy available at the time of writing the *Replies* to the *Meditations*. See his letters to Mersenne of 30 September and 11 November 1640, AT III, 185; AT III, 232.

mode of mind, a sensation, then to refer it to bodies at all is categorically mistaken. Since no mode of mind could modify an extended substance, the idea of cold is not just misapplied but necessarily false.[20] There are no circumstances under which the idea could be attributed to bodies and turn out true. Material falsity, on this reading, involves something like a category mistake rather than a simple error of misapplication in judgement. Material falsity is neither a misapplication of an otherwise true idea (one that represents a real and positive quality), nor a matter of failing to get the nature of a real quality of extended substance right. It is failing to recognise that there is no real and positive quality of bodies corresponding to one's idea.

This analysis does not yet tell us how a materially false idea represents a non-thing as a thing. To say that the idea of cold is false because, in having this idea, we are inclined to refer what is in fact a sensation to some extended substance shows how one thing (a mode of mind) is represented falsely as another (a mode of body), but material falsity was originally defined for ideas that represent non-things as things. It is here that the second formulation of the referring function, (2), comes in handy. To represent a sensation as a mode of body is, at the same time, to represent a body as having some quality that it does not and could not have. Insofar as the idea of cold makes bodies appear to have a quality, coldness, which they do not have, it represents a non-thing (an absence of heat) as a thing.

This last way of formulating the referring function shifts the weight of the analysis from the way we experience our sensations, which suggests something about our minds, to the way bodies present themselves, which suggests something about bodies. A common feature of sensory thought and talk is the ambiguity over whether we are describing a quality of experience or a quality of the object experienced. For example, I might refer to the gritty feeling of sand, and there I seem to be talking about my perceptual awareness, or I might talk about the gritty feel of sand, and now it is less clear that what I am referring to is myself rather than some fact about the sand. Similarly, I can just as easily talk about sensing red-ly (an adverbial construction representing the way the sensation is modified) as of a sensation of red, of a painful feeling or a pain in the foot, a cold sensation or a sensation of cold. Such ambiguities are one potential source of confusion and obscurity in sensory ideas. Where we have an idea representing bodies as having a kind of property they couldn't possibly have, we might well be confusing a quality of

---

[20] Although there are differences between our views, I take my approach here to be in the spirit of Richard Field's excellent 1993 discussion. Field analyses material falsity in terms of second-order ideas that have as their objects sensations, whereas my preference is for an analogue of the seeing-as construction since it does not invoke two orders of ideas.

experience with a quality of the object of experience, and so have a materially false idea.

Ambiguities created by our use of sensory terms are responsible for much strife in modern theories of perception, and reflect our general uncertainty about what exactly is represented by sensations. Statements like 'ripe tomatoes look red', may suggest either that perceivers have a certain type of visual experience when looking at ripe tomatoes, or that ripe tomatoes have a certain kind of property (a red appearance), which some moderns think that it is necessary to posit in order to account for perceptual consciousness.[21] Let us call the first kind of formulation 'subjectivist' – that is, where perceptual experiences are analysed as modes of experience – and the second 'objectivist' formulations – where perceptual experiences are analysed as experiences of modes of bodies. I suspect that, according to Descartes, our natural pre-theoretic inclinations are towards objectivist formulations of our sensory experiences, and that this is what referring a sensation outside the mind comes down to. (Herein lies their biological utility!) But if the discussion of material falsity is any indication, our natural inclination to experience our sensations as modes of awareness of the qualities of bodies does not guarantee that they will in fact represent modes of extension any more than a gritty feeling makes grittiness a real and positive property of sand. This is not to say that referring our sensory ideas to bodies wouldn't on occasion yield a truth. If heat is a real mode of bodies, then referring the sensation of heat to the fire would not produce a false judgement the way that referring the idea of cold does, if cold is a privation. Descartes' point, however, is that such a process is unreliable. If we land on the truth by referring the sensory idea of heat to the fire, it is by accident, and we have no reason to trust our idea or to think that the idea couldn't have originated within us (AT VII, 44).

Why is this ambiguity in the content of our perceptual experience not obvious to us? Descartes suggests in the reply to Arnauld that the reason why materially false ideas lead us into errors of judgement is that sensory ideas are confused and obscure.

For if, he [Arnauld] says, [the idea of cold] exhibits a privation, then it is true, and if [it exhibits] a positive being, therefore, it is not the idea of cold. This is right but on account of this alone I call that [idea] materially false, that since it is obscure and confused, I am not able to judge whether what it exhibits to me is

[21] Gilbert Harman explicitly makes use of the ambiguity of sensory content to explain how *qualia* realists are misled by language into thinking that every act of perception must correspond to some object. See Harman, 1997.

something positive outside my senses or not, and therefore I have an occasion to judge it to be something positive although perhaps it may be only a privation. (AT VII, 234–5)

Being confused and obscure, these ideas do not wear their truth or falsity on their sleeves. It falls to science to inform us whether or not there is more objective reality in a sensory idea than that belonging to the sensation itself.

We are now prepared to understand Descartes' response to Arnauld's second objection, the objection that the account of material falsity violates the causal principle used to establish the existence of God. The objection assumes that if an idea has positive objective being, it cannot be materially false on account of 'arising from nothing', lest there be objective reality that does not have a cause. We do not need to suppose that there can be privative causes to save Descartes from one horn of Arnauld's dilemma only to impale him on another: that if the idea of cold is caused by a privation, it is true. Notice that nowhere in the *Third Meditation* is it asserted that it is the objective reality of a materially false idea that arises from nothing, from a defect in my nature. What arises from nothing is the material falsity of an idea, although it has for its condition the obscurity of the idea. On my reading, the obscurity of a materially false idea arises from the fact that what is just a sensation presents itself as a mode of bodies, and although the sensation is something real and positive with a cause, its falsity is not. Hence, Descartes asserts in his reply to Arnauld:

I do not claim that [an idea] is made *materially false* from some positive being but from that obscurity alone which however has some positive being for its subject namely the very sensation itself. (AT VII, 234, my emphasis)

The claim that material falsity does not need a cause does not stand in opposition to the principle that the objective reality of an idea always needs a cause. My presenting myself as the Queen of France is fraudulent, one might well say 'false', if there is no Queen of France. But there being no Queen of France is not the cause of this false representation; indeed it is no cause at all. Similarly, the fact that cold is a privation does not cause my idea of cold to be false. If the question is why do I have false ideas at all, the answer is that I am not perfect (like God) but not being God is, again, no cause at all. And that's the way it should be. Falsity generally needs no cause, which is not to say that there isn't a cause of the thing that is false.[22]

---

[22] It will be objected that my reading conflicts with Descartes' claim in the *Sixth Meditation* that ideas which come from the activity of the senses must be produced by corporeal substances which contain formally everything which is found objectively in the ideas (AT VII, 55). Since no body can contain formally a sensation, the reality objectively present in a materially false sensory idea cannot

But what makes the idea of cold an idea *of cold*? It is important to see that if we are to preserve the category of materially false ideas, it will not do to reinterpret the objects of sensory experience as something other than the qualities or modes of extended substances. It will not do, for example, to say that our sensory ideas really represent the relative value external objects have for the union, for then they will all turn out true (cf. Simmons, 1999). Nor will it do to treat them as representing 'secondary qualities', if we regard the secondary qualities as mind-relative qualities but no less real for all that. Neither of these alternatives remains faithful to Descartes' account of material falsity. If the idea of cold is materially false, it cannot turn out to be something other than the idea of cold, which might then be a true idea. So what does account for a materially false idea's being the idea it is?

IDENTIFYING IDEAS

Let us come at this last question about the intentionality of materially false ideas by returning to Ayers' question about where to draw the line between the intentional and the real object. We began this chapter by noticing the problems Descartes creates for himself by adopting a strong version of the theory of objective reality. Ayers draws our attention to the following dilemma: either we must identify the idea with the object existing in the intellect, and run the risk of turning Descartes into a representationalist, or we must identify the object existing as it does in the intellect with its real or external object, and run the risk of turning Descartes into an idealist. Is there a way for Descartes to be a direct realist and still maintain his account of material falsity?

On Ayers' own reading, Descartes places the real distinction between the intentional object (the thing objectively existing in the intellect) and

---

be the same as that contained formally in a body. But whether this remark is also intended for ideas that do not have some extramental thing or mode objectively existing is not clear. As Descartes writes in the *Third Meditation*, materially false ideas 'do not require me to posit a source distinct from myself' (AT VII, 44). This leaves open the possibility that the objective reality of materially false ideas is derived from the formal reality of those ideas existing as modes of mind, which are produced by the mind depending on how the sense organs are being affected. In that case the error resides in the mind's passively taking the objects of materially false ideas to be real modifications of bodies. Our knowledge of the existence of bodies would not, however, be undermined by the existence of material falsity. There is no suggestion in Descartes' texts that we might never be able to distinguish the materially true and materially false ideas of sense. But, presumably, our ability to identify the truth contained in our sensory ideas proceeds through the progress of science. Thanks to John Carriero for discussion on these points.

the real extramental object, with the consequence that he turns out to be a representational realist. This is an unfortunate consequence because it means that Descartes' argument for God is immediately destabilised. If 'talk of the sun which is thought of is simply to talk of the thought itself, giving its specific content, direction or "form,"' Ayers argues, '. . . it follows that I cannot think (immediately) about the real sun (or real God!)' (Ayers, 1998: 1068). It is absurd to suppose, however, that an internal relation can exist between a mode of mind and an external object like the sun. Ayers takes Descartes' reference to ideas as 'forms' of thought, in the *Second Replies* (AT VII, 160), as implying an internal relation between an idea and its object, and concludes, therefore, that this object can only be an intentional object. This interpretation seems supported by Descartes' remark to Caterus that if he is asking about what the idea of the sun is 'no one understands this to be the sun itself insofar as this extrinsic denomination belongs to it' (AT VII, 102). Ayers might also have cited Descartes' comment to Arnauld, that if we take ideas as forms of thought, whether cold exists or not does not affect the idea of cold (AT VII, 232). Such passages might seem to imply that ideas are really distinct from their external referents but not their intentional objects and, there-fore, that Descartes is a representationalist. The 'form' of the idea of cold makes it the idea it is.

Ayers interprets Descartes' use of 'form' in this context in a distinctively Scholastic way: the form of a thought specifies the object it represents. Ayers is correct to note that for both Descartes and Aquinas being aware of an object through thought was not to be construed as being directly aware of the thought and only indirectly aware of the object (Ayers, 1998: 1066). As Aquinas puts it: '*Species intelligibilis non est quod intelligitur, sed id quo intelligit intellectus*' (*Summa Theologiae*, I. q. 85. art. 2). Ayers remarks on how difficult it is to get beyond the immediate object in the intellect to the real thing we think directly about. But this Scholastic reading of Descartes' use of the term 'form' in relation to ideas does not sit well with the claim to Arnauld that the form of the idea of cold does not depend on whether cold exists or not. For what Descartes should have said in response to Arnauld, if Ayers is right in attributing this represen-tationalist picture to Descartes, is that the form of the idea does not depend on cold's existing in reality because cold can exist objectively (i.e., as an intentional object), a fact which makes the idea of cold be the idea it is. But Descartes cannot do that because that would be to acknowledge that cold has some being, albeit objective being. Instead, Descartes explicitly denies that cold can exist objectively if it is a privation. In light of this, it does not seem correct to conflate 'form' and 'intentional object' as Ayers understands the latter. Ayers' assumption that Descartes' theory will need to account for the 'status of intentional objects of thoughts which have no real objects' (Ayers, 1998: 1068), begs the question by assuming that there could always be intentional correlates of things which do not exist, and this seems to be precisely what the doctrine of material falsity is intended to deny.

What else might Descartes be doing in referring to the form of an idea? In the *Second Replies*, he defines the form of thought as that 'through the immediate perception of which, I am conscious of the thought' (AT VII, 160). In his reply to Arnauld, Descartes (confusingly) distinguishes between ideas taken in the formal sense, as forms of mind, which are not composed of matter, and ideas taken materially, as operations of the intellect. Taking ideas materially in the latter sense does not make reference to the truth and falsity of their objects, and so it is not this way of taking ideas that leads us to consider them to be true or false, but only in the sense in which they provide 'matter for error' (AT VII, 232). The form of an idea seems clearly connected to what the idea represents, and so to what makes the idea the idea it is, but not, I have argued, to what we would take to be the intentional object of an idea like the idea of cold. It is the form of the idea of cold which remains constant whether or not cold exists, but if cold is a privation, cold is not objectively present in the idea any more than it is formally present in the world. The only other object which could account for the form of a given idea is its real object, whether we are aware from the idea what that object is or not. In the case of the idea of cold, supposing it to be materially false, its form is derived from its object, 'the sensation itself'. It is because of the sensation that we are conscious of our thinking of cold, conscious of having a certain kind of thought, which is not the same as being conscious of some quality, cold. Interpreting Descartes as a direct realist seems to be the only way to make sense of the discussion of material falsity in a way compatible with his account of objective reality.

Denying that Descartes' use of 'form' in this context is a way of referring to the intentional object of an idea is not inconsistent with his use of 'form' in defining idea in the *Second Replies*. The form of a thought contributes to my awareness of it, the thought, not to my awareness of the object, which is accounted for by the notion defined in the following definition (*Definition* III), the objective reality of an idea. Indeed, I may be quite mistaken about which object I am aware of, a fact that undermines the transparency thesis so often attributed to Descartes. This might seem counterintuitive because it implies that, for Descartes, the awareness we have of a thought is logically independent of what we take to be the intentional object of the thought, but how foreign this suggestion is depends on your point of view. If I am right about Descartes' theory of ideas, I can be aware of my thinking of cold, of a chimaera, of nothing, without necessarily being aware of cold, a chimaera, or nothing. Ordinarily, perhaps, I differentiate among my thoughts in the same act of differentiating among their objects, but Descartes' discussion of material falsity suggests that in some cases we may be quite wrong about which object is the object of our thought while quite clear on which thought we are having.

This interpretation of Descartes' use of 'form' as the differentia of thoughts, whatever that turns out to be, enables us to resist positing merely intentional objects as the objects of ideas in cases where there could not be corresponding external objects. This last point is important. When one thinks of a triangle even though no triangles actually exist, it is not the case, for Descartes, that one is thinking of intentional as opposed to real triangles. One is thinking of something real, namely, a triangle, or its eternal and immutable nature, only in an objective mode of being. Existence has very little to do with what one is thinking about, but whether something has a nature or does not. Ayers' additional piece of textual evidence in favour of his reading – Descartes' remark to Caterus that no one will take the idea of the sun to be the sun itself – should not, therefore, be read as a commitment to representationalism. The context in which this is asserted is one in which Descartes is keen to deny the absurd view that the idea of the sun is the real sun, existing in the heavens, with some extraneous label applied to it. It does not follow, however, that Descartes is establishing a real distinction between the idea of the sun and the sun itself, but rather a real distinction between the idea of the sun and the sun in a non-objective mode of being. Descartes' reply to Caterus is compatible with the claim that the idea of the sun is the sun itself (not some bewildered ghost or intentional sun), but the sun in an objective mode of being (AT VII, 102).

Denying that Descartes posits a real distinction between the idea and the thing of which it is an idea saves his account from representationalism, but at what cost? Is the direct realism we have attributed to Descartes simply mad, or indistinguishable from idealism? (cf. Ayers, 1998: 1068). If there is no distinction between the idea of the sun and the sun itself, is it impossible for one to exist without the other? From looking at Descartes' account of material falsity, we can say that the form of direct realism is strong in one direction, but tempered by the account of material falsity. Every idea has an object, and so represents something real or positive (whether actual or possible), but what that object is may be very obscure to us. We may think that we are thinking directly about some mode of bodies when all we are thinking about is a sensation, a mode of mind. Not all forms of direct realism are 'Fido'–Fido theories, and Descartes' is arguably one exception. Nor does it automatically follow that there is no distinction between direct realism and idealism. Here is one way the story could go, which is not to say that Descartes took it in this direction.

Let us suppose that the notion of 'idea' is to be understood as a whole composed of two parts – a mode of mind and the thing it represents, in an objective mode of being. For example, the idea of the sun is a whole consisting of a mode of mind and the sun itself, existing as it does in the intellect. When we think of these parts of the idea as parts of the whole, then the mode of mind is a form of thought and the sun itself is the sun as it exists in the intellect. The idea of the sun could not exist apart from either the mode of mind or the sun itself, anymore than a whole could ever exist apart from its parts. But it is compatible with the conclusion that the idea of the sun (the whole) cannot exist apart from its parts, which includes not existing apart from the sun, that the parts could exist apart from each other. It follows, therefore, that the mode of mind, which is one component of the idea of the sun, could exist apart from the sun itself, at least by an act of God, and, hence, apart from the idea of the sun. Similarly, the sun itself could exist apart from the mode of mind, and hence, the sun could exist even if no idea of it had ever existed. This mereological approach to the relationship between Cartesian ideas and their objects is one way, therefore, to prevent the account collapsing into a form of idealism.

The attraction of this solution is that it enables us (1) to deny that there is a real distinction between the idea and the real object of which it is an idea, (2) to deny that there is a real distinction between the thing existing objectively in the intellect and the thing existing formally outside the intellect, (3) to avoid, therefore, representationalism and (4) to avoid collapsing the distinction between direct realism and idealism. Although this mereological interpretation of Cartesian ideas has these advantages, it leaves unanswered, however, the question of what kind of distinction there is between an idea and its object, between the idea of the sun and the sun itself. It may seem from the above discussion that the distinction is only a distinction of reason. The sun, conceived of objectively, just is the idea of the sun and the idea of the sun is the sun itself existing in the intellect. Descartes' reply to Caterus suggests that he wants something like an internal relationship between ideas and what they represent, but does this reduce the distinction between the two to a mere conceptual distinction? Some readers may find themselves squirming at this suggestion that an idea and its external object are merely conceptually distinct, for the simple reason that conceptual distinctions nowadays do not usually imply that there is more than one thing. No matter what 'mode of being' the sun has in the intellect, isn't it always going to be absurd to suppose that an idea (e.g. the idea of the sun) and a corporeal thing (the sun itself) are numerically one thing?

In the next chapter, I argue against conflating the lack of real distinction with numerical identity. But we may note here that, in terms of Descartes' theory of distinctions, there can be metaphysical (i.e. numerical) distinctions between things that are not really distinct. The modal distinction between a substance and its modes preserves a metaphysical and, hence, numerical distinctness between things that are not really distinct. Similarly, a formal distinction is 'less' than a modal distinction, but greater than a ' distinction of reason *ratiocinantis*' (which has no foundation in reality).[23] And there is even one kind of distinction of reason – *ratiocinatae* – which would ground a metaphysical and, hence, numerical distinction between an idea and its object (AT IV, 349–50).

When applied to an idea and what it represents, any one of these less than real but greater than mere conceptual distinctions with no foundation in reality would ensure some metaphysical and numerical distinction between the idea and its object.

CONCLUSION

The issues raised by Descartes' account of objective reality and material falsity are difficult subjects to treat, and no one who slogs away at them can pretend to come out of the process unscathed or sure of having gotten to the bottom of things. I have argued here that an important key to understanding Descartes' account of representation, and of what it means for an idea to be materially false, is to understand the different ways in which, as laid down in the *Passions,* ideas are referred. With the exception

---

[23] The formal distinction is intended to capture the distinction between special modes of a substance, such as existence, size (in the case of bodies), duration and number, all of which follow from the principal attribute of a substance. Although these modes are distinct from one another modally, because the substance cannot exist without them, they can exist apart neither from the substance of which they are modes nor each other. See the Letter to ***, 1645 or 1646 (AT IV, 349–50).

of the passions, our sensory experiences are not direct experiences of our minds and their contents but experiences of external things as being modified in certain ways. The significance of the referring notion extends, therefore, to the very question of the kind of realism Descartes is advocating. I have argued here for a reading of Descartes as a direct realist that is compatible with his analysis of material falsity, and which doesn't collapse into idealism. Since the *Passions* offers the most detailed explication of the referring function, by ignoring this text, we may find that in treating the parts of Descartes' corpus as distinct from one another, we have missed again something important about the whole.

CHAPTER 5

Action and passion: metaphysical integrationism

> For the soul and the body together, we have only that [primitive notion] of their union, on which depends that of the force by which the soul moves the body, and of the body for acting upon the soul causing in it sensations [*sentimens*] and passions.
>
> (AT III, 665)

When Elisabeth requests from Descartes a definition of the soul 'more particular than in your Metaphysic, that is to say, of its substance separate from its action, thought' in order to explain how 'the soul of a human being is able to determine the spirits of the body to produce voluntary actions' her suspicion is that nothing can move or be moved by a body without being a body itself (6/16 May 1643, AT III, 66). Previously persuaded by Descartes' arguments for a real distinction of mind and body, Elisabeth begins to doubt the coherence of the idea that these two heterogeneous substances might nonetheless interact. As noted in chapter I, Descartes does not address Elisabeth's objection directly, but the *Passions* represents something of an attempt to ground the interaction between mind and body in a way that is, at least, perfectly consistent with his dualism. In light of their exchange, it is not surprising that the *Passions* begins on what would have seemed to be a distinctively metaphysical note. In the first two articles, Descartes invokes the (Aristotelian) categories of action and passion, which specify the conceptual relationship that obtains between substances or within a single substance when a natural change occurs. In the context of changes caused within the mind by the body, and vice versa, the effect of applying these categories is an ingenious but puzzling unity of modes across distinct substances to substitute for the unity of substances Elisabeth suspects is necessary to avoid the fragmentation of the human being. It is not unreasonable to suppose, therefore, that Descartes is here trying to plug a hole Elisabeth thinks prevents the union from being intelligible.

A NEW INTERACTION PROBLEM

Introducing the general notion of a passion, Descartes writes in the first article of the *Passions*:

I consider that all that which is done or which happens anew is generally called by the Philosophers a passion with regard to the subject to which it happens and an action with regard to that which makes it happen. And so, although the agent and the patient are often very different, *the action and the passion do not cease to be always one and the same thing* [*une mesme chose*], which has two names on account of the two different subjects to which one can refer it. (AT XI, 328; my emphasis)

Describing actions and passions as *une mesme chose* might be dismissed as simply two ways of describing a passion of the soul, as something suffered by a soul (a being pushed) and as the result of some activity by an external agent (a pushing), were it not that in the second article, Descartes is careful to specify that the 'action' resides in the agent, the human body.

We never notice that there is any subject that acts more immediately upon our soul than the body to which it is joined and that consequently we ought to think that that which is in the former a passion is commonly in the latter an action. (AT XI, 328)

Putting the first two articles together, we get the striking conclusion that an action in the body, a motion of the pineal gland, just is one and the same thing as a passion in the soul, an idea. But how could a passion of an incorporeal soul be identical with a motion in the body?

Before we tackle this question, however, let us try to come to grips with the basic terminology. What are actions and passions? The two fundamental categories of Descartes' metaphysics are substances and modes. Things that depend on no other (created) thing for their existence are substances, which are known through their 'attributes' or general features. Each substance has a 'principal attribute', which constitutes its nature and essence, and to which all other attributes and modes may be referred (AT VIIIA, 24–5). Extension is the principal attribute of body, and accounts for the fact that bodies have shapes, sizes, are in motion or at rest. Thought is the principal attribute of mind, which explains why minds can think particular thoughts. We use the term 'mode', Descartes writes, when we think of a substance as modified or affected in a certain way, (AT VIIIA, 26). Modes are dependent upon a substance for their existence, and although it is fair to say that a substance must have some modes or other, there is no particular mode it is necessary for a substance to have (AT VIIIA, 29). Since actions of the body (motions of the spirits) and passions of the soul (thoughts) are not things which in themselves can exist independent from substances, it seems reasonable to suppose that they are modes.[1]

The *Passions* is not the first context in which Descartes asserts that actions and passions of distinct substances are 'one and the same', but it is the first text in which actions and passions of distinct *kinds* of substances are claimed to be one and the same thing, and in such a context special problems are bound to arise. If, for example, we suppose that the expression 'one and the same' means ' is (numerically) identical with', it is not clear whether the claims made in the first two articles of the *Passions* are consistent with central tenets of Descartes' metaphysics. For example, do the following propositions form a consistent set?

(1) Action and passion are (numerically) identical (PS, art.1).
(2) The action is in the agent (i.e. is a mode of the body); the passion is in the patient (i.e. is a mode of the mind) (PS, art.2).
(3) Mind and body are really (i.e. numerically) distinct substances (*Sixth Meditation*).
(4) Modes are not really distinct from their substances (*Principles* I, 61).

Consider the following two problems. The first is what appears to be a general failure of transitivity. For any action/passion pair, A and B, which are modes of distinct substances, C and D, it follows that A is identical with B (by 1) and with C (by 2 and 4); similarly, B is identical with A and D; yet C and D are not identical (by 3). If two substances are really distinct and can exist apart, it is natural to assume, given the transitivity of identity, that no mode of one substance can be numerically identical with a mode of a distinct substance. The second problem is specific to cases of interaction within composite entities, such as the union of mind and body. We might call this the problem of incompatible modes. It is one thing to identify modes of distinct substances, like two motions belonging to distinct bodies, as identical, but can a mode of mind, a thought, be identical with a mode of extension, a corporeal motion? What would the nature underlying such a mode be?

AN ARISTOTELIAN IDEA?

The terminology Descartes adopts in identifying actions and passions is, as noted above, Aristotelian. Every natural change for Aristotle involves a

---

[1] See Descartes' *Principles of Philosophy*, I, 51–61, AT VIIIA, 24–30.

motion in the subject undergoing the change, a changing, and a being changed or passion. When an agent causes some change in a patient, between the action and the passion – the cutting and the being cut – there is no real distinction but only a distinction of reason. Every change is an action when referred to the *terminus a quo*, that which brings about the change, and a passion when referred to the *terminus ad quem*, that which undergoes the change or is moved towards a point of fulfilment. In the case of transitive actions, where besides the exercise of a capacity there is a product or result (a being changed), since the change is a transition from potentiality to actuality, it resides in the subject of the change, the patient.

Where, then, the result is something apart from the exercise, the actuality is in the thing that is being made, e.g., the act of building is in the thing that is being built and that of weaving in the thing that is being woven, and similarly, in all other cases, and in general the movement is in the thing that is being moved. . .[2]

Aristotle applies the same reasoning to cases involving a change in the soul. In intransitive actions like perceiving, thinking or understanding, the exercise of the capacity by the agent is the end itself. But in the case of transitive actions like teaching, the end is a change in the patient, for it is the student who undergoes the transition from ignorance to knowledge, not the teacher. Hence the teaching is in the student, and is the same thing as the learning. The activity is teaching only by its relation to the agent (the teacher), who brings about the transition to knowledge.[3] 'Action' and 'passion' are relative terms, different ways of describing the same event.

One interpretation of Descartes' use of this terminology is that he is simply adopting an Aristotelian idea, perhaps without fully understanding it.[4] But there is one crucial difference. Unlike Aristotle, Descartes does not, as we see from the second article of the *Passions*, identify the action and passion as distinct ways of conceiving of some change in the patient, but as modes of distinct substances. The action

---

[2] Aristotle, *Metaphysics*, IX, 1050a, 30–4; *Complete Works*, ed. Barnes, 1984: 1659.
[3] Aristotle, *Metaphysics* IX, 1048b, 18–25.
[4] On the Aristotelian reading, see Des Chene (1996): ch.2 and pp. 257–72. Susan James (1997) also construes the relationship between actions and passions in terms of Aristotle's notions of actuality and potentiality. Denis Kambouchner sees Descartes as departing from the traditional Aristotelian framework but does not go so far as to admit any ontological interdependence between action and passion. Kambouchner is more interested in what he sees as the emergence of a new genre in which the subjects that comprise the union of mind and body are 'empirically interdependent' but ontologically independent, by which I take it he means that an adequate explanation of the functions of sensation and self-movement requires conceiving of the functions of the mind and the body together, despite their real distinction (Kambouchner, 1995: 94–5).

resides not in the patient but in the agent. The same point is made to Regius concerning causal interaction between bodies.

[I]n corporeal things, every action and passion consists in local motion alone and, hence, is called an 'action' when that motion is considered in the mover and a 'passion' when it is considered in the moved. (AT III, 454)

Were Descartes to have adopted the Aristotelian idea that the action and passion are in the moved, things might have been simpler. We could dispense with proposition 2 and the remaining three propositions would have been consistent. Supposing that Descartes did not simply misunderstand the Aristotelian doctrine, we may speculate as to why he does not locate the action in the patient. Paul Hoffman (1990:316) surmises that one motivation might stem from Descartes' general rejection of migrating modes. As Descartes explains to More, a force is nothing but a modal entity, and thus he (More) is correct to deny that it can pass from one body to another (AT V, 404–5). Since modes cannot exist apart from their substances, they cannot be transferred to other substances. Had Descartes thought that the Aristotelian conflation of action and passion presupposed the transfer of qualities from the agent to the patient, he could not have consistently endorsed it in its original form.

Another possible motivation may derive from Descartes' rejection of motion in the soul. The only motion Descartes recognises is local motion, which is a mode of extension. There is an analogue of motion in the soul, namely volitions or the 'actions' of the soul (AT VIIIA, 7; AT II, 24; AT VIIIA, 54). Passions of the soul are thus distinguished from volitions of the soul, even though the latter are also passions in some more general sense because the soul always perceives that it is willing something. At article 17 Descartes distinguishes these two genera of thought, passions and volitions, claiming that all thoughts belong to either of these two categories.

It is easy to know that there remains nothing in us that we ought to attribute to our soul unless it is our thoughts, which are principally of two kinds: namely, the actions of the soul and its passions. Those which I call *actions* are all our volitions because we experience that they come directly from our soul seeming to depend only on it; as, on the contrary, one can generally call *passions* all the sorts of perceptions or awarenesses which are found in us because often it is not our soul which makes them such as they are, and because [the soul] always receives them from things which are represented by them. (AT XI, 342)

This distinction between volitions and passions depends on the motions that produce passions *not* being actions in the soul. What distinguishes a passion of the soul in the strict sense, as defined at article 27, from passions in the more general sense is that the action with which it is 'one and the same' is a mode of the body.

These may be good reasons for a Cartesian not to endorse the full Aristotelian picture, but they do not make it any less mysterious why one would use Aristotle's terminology of actions and passions at all. Lilli Alanen (in conversation) has suggested that what is 'one and the same' is something less specific than modes, a single 'actuality', which, in the *Physics,* is described as the actualisation of some power in the agent and some potentiality in the patient, but which is properly said to happen to the patient. According to Alanen, the phenomenology of Cartesian passions makes this actuality ultimately unanalysable but clearly experienced as a change in the soul and known (through argument) to depend upon the body. Thus, we have two distinct ways of conceiving the passions: one, through confused and obscure experience, and the other, through the natural sciences (Alanen, 2003: 174–8). There is something to this idea, but it does not bring Descartes and Aristotle closer on the analysis of actions and passions. Aristotle's analogies in the *Physics* for the 'single actuality' an action and passion pair constitute – the steep descent being one and the same thing as the steep ascent, the one to two interval being one and the same as the two to one interval – are clear cases of one thing being described in two ways, whereas the 'passion in the mind' and 'action in the body' in Descartes' dualistic system are not.[5] If the latter pair constitute a single thing in Descartes' metaphysics, it is a thing not anticipated by what is generally taken to be the official ontology.[6]

Chances are, however, that the official ontology will need to be revised anyway. Whether we think of Descartes as trying to describe some looser 'actuality' or as doing something metaphysically fancier, such as identifying modes of distinct substances, we have still to tackle the question how anything in the mind can be 'absolutely dependent' (PS, art.41) upon motions in a body from which it is really distinct.

STRADDLING MODES

Paul Hoffman has done more than anyone else to bring the problems associated with Descartes' identification of action and passion to the

---

[5] See, for example, Aristotle's *Physics*, 202a12–20, in *Complete Works*, ed. Barnes, 1984.

[6] It should be noted that Alanen agrees with this. Her reading is consistent with the project of analysing the relationship between actions and passions.

attention of the scholarly community, and deserves, therefore, special mention. Hoffman's idea is that the passages concerning action and passion show that Descartes was committed to the existence of modes that 'straddle' two substances. A straddling mode is 'a mode (token) [which] can simultaneously be a mode of two substances' (Hoffman, 1990: 313). Action and passion are numerically the same mode which, when the soul exists in a union with the body, is a mode of two substances. When we speak of the mode as inhering in the body we refer to it as an action, and when we consider it as a mode of the soul, we call it a passion. Between the action and the passion there is only a distinction of reason. We give it one name when we refer it to the agent (a brain motion), and another name when we refer it to the patient (a passion of the soul) (Hoffman, 1990: 317).

Hoffman has adduced an impressive amount of textual support for his radical thesis of straddling modes. Notable inclusions are Descartes' remarks on the Eucharist and surfaces in the *Replies to the Sixth Objections*. In the case of surfaces, Descartes is prepared to say that when two bodies, A and B, are in contact with each other, the touching surfaces are 'one and the same'. He is also prepared to call surfaces 'modes', and in a move which seems to contradict the conclusion of his argument to More against the possibility of migrating modes, asserts that one and the same surface can remain in existence even though the bodies of which it is a mode are removed, provided they are replaced with bodies of the same dimensions.

When two bodies are mutually touching, the boundary [*extremitas*] of both bodies, which is a part of neither but the same mode of both, is one and the same thing and it can remain although those bodies are removed, provided only that other bodies of exactly the same size and shape succeed them in the same location. (AT VII, 434)

This concession is important for Descartes' account of the Eucharist. What is left when the body of Christ replaces that of the bread, the whiteness and shape of the host, are not 'real accidents', as some Scholastics thought, but simply the surface of the bread. (AT VII, 433–4).

The texts related to surfaces are difficult to interpret but not obviously inconsistent with other aspects of Descartes' metaphysical system. Although in his discussion of surfaces, Descartes seems to commit himself to migrating modes, he is not committed thereby to anything real or subsistent migrating from one body to another. The boundary between two contiguous bodies is, as Descartes points out, 'a part of neither' body, although he is, as we have seen, prepared to call it a mode (AT VII, 433).

Surfaces do not have the same status for Descartes as other modes of extension, like shape and motion. A surface is nothing other than the boundary, 'external place' or limit beyond which there is no more of a particular body, or the beginning of a distinct body, which is why 'it can appropriately be called the boundary of the contained body as much as the containing one' (AT VII, 433). Using contemporary semantic terminology, we might say that expressions like 'the surface of body A' are non-rigid designators, ways of defining a body by its relations to other bodies, rather than names of monadic properties of bodies, about which one might have to worry about their being transferable to other substances or not.[7] 'The surface of body A' might thus refer to something analogous to an office, like 'the Prime Minister of Australia', which can be filled at different times by distinct chunks of matter. Actions and passions, by contrast, seem to have a more robust claim to reality. Whether the discussion of surfaces constitutes evidence for the straddling modes view is thus obscure.[8]

In terms of the above four propositions, Hoffman's strategy is to accept all four as correct interpretations. The chief virtue of his account is that it preserves a natural and literal reading of Descartes' assertion in article 1 that action and passion are 'one and the same'. Each passion is, on Hoffman's reading, token-identical with an action of the body (Hoffman, 1990: 323). In response to the problem of transitivity, Hoffman notes that the token-identity of modes of two substances does not entail the token-identity of those substances, for it does not prevent our clearly and distinctly conceiving thought and extension without each other, and it is the latter which entails that the mind and body can be clearly and distinctly conceived to exist apart (Hoffman, 1990: 317). This seems correct for the following reason: passions and the actions which cause them are non-essential modes of their substances, and thus, for Descartes, the substances of which they are modes are capable of existing apart even if their modes overlap at some time or another. Because substances can

---

[7] See also *Principles of Philosophy*, II, 13 and 15 and my 2006.

[8] Hoffman (1990: 321) claims his is a more convincing interpretation of Descartes' claim in the *Replies to the Second Objections* that ' images in the corporeal imagination are called "ideas" only in so far as they "inform" the mind when turned towards [*conversam*] that part of the brain' (AT VII, 160). Hoffman interprets Descartes as saying that one and the same image is both a mode of mind, relative to which it is an idea (a passion), and a motion of the brain, relative to which it is not an idea. Descartes makes no claim in these passages, however, about the numerical identity between images on the pineal gland and ideas in the soul and it is prudent not to read too much into his being prepared to call corporeal images ideas. He is, after all, also prepared under some circumstances, as we have seen, to call the soul 'extended', but this does not mean that it is extended.

exist apart from their straddling modes, they can exist apart from any other substance their modes straddle.

A harder problem for Hoffman is the problem of incompatible modes. As Hoffman is aware, it is difficult to see how something could be both a way of being extended (a motion) and a way of being non-extended (a thought) (Hoffman, 1990: 318). This would be a problem, however, Hoffman argues, only if the union of mind and body were a simple substance. But given that the union is a composite substance, the attributes of thought and extension are compatible with each other, as attributes of the union (Hoffman, 1990: 318).[9] Hoffman extends an idea which Descartes defends in the *Notae* – namely, that thought and extension can belong in the same subject without contradiction provided the subject is composite – to modes of thought and extension (AT VIIIB, 349–51). But it is not clear how the analogy is supposed to work. Are we to say that a mode can be both a mode of extension and of thought provided it is complex or provided it is a mode of a complex subject? The latter seems to be where Hoffman initially is headed when he draws from the texts in which the union is referred to as a composite substance.[10] But this strategy leads nowhere, for the fact that the union is a composite of mind and body (and so is complex) does nothing to show how a single mode can be both a mode of mind and a mode of body.[11]

Consider now the first option: straddling modes are themselves complex. To keep the case parallel with that of the union, we must say that a straddling mode is itself really a complex of something extended and something non-extended. What could this complex thing be? And in what sense have we preserved the idea that action and passion are 'token-identical', 'one and the same' in a numerical sense? The union is a composite of parts that are token-distinct. By analogy, if actions and passions form a composite, they too should be composed of parts that are numerically distinct. Hoffman admits to an ambiguity in the sense in which straddling modes are complex. A single mode can be complex insofar as it is the subject of extensional and non-extensional 'features' or 'aspects' (Hoffman, 1990: 320). Hoffman considers

---

[9] See also Hoffman, 1986 and 1999.
[10] See Cottingham's argument for 'trialism', 1998: 82–4, and 1985, and Hoffman, 1986.
[11] Because it lacks a principal attribute or essence of its own, the union is arguably not something of which modes can be predicated (Alanen, 2003: 176). One might be tempted to think of an action and a passion as a single mode of the union. But the status of the union as a substance or not is irrelevant to the present problem. If we take an action and a passion to be a single mode of a single substance or third thing, the union, it remains to be shown how one mode can be both a mode of extension and of thought.

four interpretations of the term 'aspects' in this context: aspects are either parts of modes, modes of modes, 'sides' of a mode existing in two subjects at once (Hoffman's preferred view), or nothing but two ways of conceiving of a mode as in the following formulation: 'Straddling modes, even though they exist in two subjects, should not be thought of as complex. Talk of aspects is merely talk of two ways of looking at one simple mode' (Hoffman, 1990: 320).

Since a division into parts implies for Descartes a real distinction (AT VIIIA, 28), the first interpretation is of no help in showing how action and passion can be numerically identical. The second interpretation merely shifts the problem – from explaining how one and the same mode can be both a mode of thought and a mode of extension, to the question how one and the same mode can itself have modes of thought and extension. What 'sides' are is somewhat obscure but, in any case, the third interpretation falters on cases of immanent causation, for example, the spinning top that maintains itself in motion once the whip is removed (or destroyed), for in such cases there are not two substances to sustain different sides of the mode (AT III, 428). By elimination, this leaves the fourth interpretation, which treats action and passion much as Descartes treats motion and rest – as conceptually distinct or relative ways of thinking about the same thing – and as Aristotle treats actions and passions and steep ascents and descents. It is unlikely, however, that for Descartes the difference between a way of being extended and a way of being non-extended is just a difference in the frame of reference. If it were, one would not expect him to be so confident of the real distinction between mind and body. None of these versions of a double-aspect theory adequately addresses the original problem, which was to explain how something that is numerically one could be both a mode of extension and a mode of thought.

The stumbling block in the straddling modes view so far has been the assumption that action and passion are token-identical. This assumption raises other problems besides the incompatibility of modes objection. There is what we might call the inseparability of modes objection. Someone might, for example, reason thus: not even God can separate a thing from itself, hence, if action and passion are token-identical, not even God can make one without the other. But this seems contrary to Descartes' idea of divine power. As Descartes states in the *Replies to the Sixth Objections*:

For to be done naturally is nothing other than to be done through the ordinary power of God, which in no way differs from his extraordinary power; nor does [the ordinary power of God] posit in the world anything other. (AT VII, 435)

In light of this passage, let us add a fifth proposition to our original set: (5) God can do anything any natural cause can do. If we take (5) seriously, we ought to allow that for any mode of the soul which is naturally caused by a motion in the body, God could have caused the one without the other.

Perhaps God's power does extend to separating a thing from itself, at least when that thing is a complex straddling mode. Hoffman points out that in the *First Meditation,* Descartes claims that sensing is a form of thinking, and that we can be certain sensations exist even if there are no bodies producing them (AT VII, 29; Hoffman, 1990: 318–19). By the end of the *Meditations,* however, we learn that God is no deceiver, and hence that we can be certain that our sensations are really caused by external bodies (AT VII, 78–80). While Descartes seems committed to saying that God would not cause our sensations directly (since that would make him a deceiver), Hoffman does not think it follows that God could not do this. The power of God entails that whatever can be brought about naturally could have been brought about directly by God.

On the first three interpretations of the dual-aspect theory, Hoffman thinks an objection like this can easily be met (Hoffman, 1990:322). If aspects are non-essential, a mode can exist without one of its aspects, its extended part, mode or side, and thus be caused by a demon or God (Hoffman, 1990: 325). The fourth reading might be compatible with the possibility of God-caused sensations, provided we take Descartes to be referring to the 'judgements' we make regarding our sensations at the 'third grade of sensory response', which Descartes distinguishes in the *Sixth Set of Replies* from their proximal causes in the body (the first grade) and the immediate effects of those motions on the soul (the second grade) (AT VII, 436–8). The first two grades presuppose the existence of bodies, but the third is described only in terms of the intellect's involvement. If God were to cause our sensations directly there would be third grade or intellectual passions – passions arising only from God's activity upon the soul.

Saying that a straddling mode could exist without one of its aspects (e.g. without its being an action of a body) implies, however, that it could exist without one of the substances of which it is supposedly a mode. This alone violates proposition 4: that modes are not really distinct from the substances of which they are modes. Hoffman's solution at this point depends on the robustness and independence of aspects – on the possibility of an aspect of a mode being non-essential, and thus on the possibility of a mode of mind (just like a surface) existing apart from its substance under unusual circumstances. Or perhaps a mode could come to have a numerically distinct aspect from that which it actually has, were it produced by another agent (Hoffman, 1990: 326).

> So even though a straddling mode is necessarily self-identical, perhaps it is not essential to it that it straddle mind and body. Suppose then that being a sensation is essential to a particular mode, but being a bodily action is not. In that case it would be possible for us to have the very sensations we do even if no bodies existed. (Hoffman, 1990: 325)

What is it exactly that God causes directly in the soul in this counter-factual scenario, and what is it that he is not creating? If being a bodily motion is not essential to a mode's being a sensation, then in what sense is it numerically the same thing as that which God causes in the soul? The distinction between aspects may not, in the end, prove to be a better solution to this puzzle than positing a numerical distinction between actions and passions themselves. At least this is one option we have yet to explore.

ACTION AND PASSION AS TWO MODES

Hoffman's efforts are directed at reconciling proposition (2), the claim that action and passion are modes of two subjects, with proposition (1), the claim that action and passion are numerically identical. Is proposition (1), however, the right way to interpret Descartes' claim that action and passion are *une mesme chose* (or, in the Latin texts, *unam et eandem rem*)? The fact that Descartes refers to the *chose* or *res* that action and passion constitute in the singular does not settle much. For he refers to the union of mind and body also in the singular even though it is a composite of two substances. Calvin Normore and I have argued that the sense in which actions and passions constitute a unity is akin to the way in which the human being is a unity (Brown and Normore, 2003). Like the union of mind and body, there is, on our view, no numerically single metaphysical entity that action and passion constitute, and yet, in some sense, they form a unity.[12]

We propose that the sense in which action and passion are 'one and the same' is that they are not really distinct from each other, but being not really distinct does not entail numerical or 'token' identity. It is not, for

[12] Since Descartes does not recognise primitive relations, we should resist the temptation to say that action and passion constitute a single relation. It wouldn't help anyway. His way of analysing the relation between action and passion – as modes (of distinct substances) that are *une mesme chose* – is precisely what needs explaining.

example, a general principle of Descartes' metaphysics that a lack of real distinction implies numerical identity. Modes are not really distinct from their substances, but there is some distinction between them, a modal distinction, which enables us to count these as numerically distinct (AT viiiA, 29). The original inconsistency in propositions 1-5 can thus be removed by abandoning (1) in favour of the weaker (1)*:

(1)*. Action and passion are not really distinct.

If an action in the body and passion of the soul are numerically distinct but not really distinct, they can be said to be 'one and the same', just as a substance and its modes are one and the same despite being numerically distinct. Although this is not perhaps the most natural way to interpret the claim that action and passion are *une mesme chose*, it has a number of considerable advantages over rival theories. (1)* is compatible with the possibility of some kind of metaphysical distinction (perhaps modal, perhaps formal) between action and passion, and thus with the action being a mode of body, and the passion, a mode of mind.[13] If action and passion are numerically distinct, there is no contradiction in the passion residing in the patient and the action residing in the agent, where patient and agent are distinct substances. With respect to the problem of transitivity, it is important to bear in mind that the lack of a real distinction does not have the features that identity has, such as being symmetrical or being subject to Leibniz' law. A mode is not really distinct from its substance but not conversely, and, in general, what is true for modes is not necessarily true for substances of which they are modes. Could we say that the same is true when a mode is 'absolutely dependent' on another substance and its modes? The fact that a mode of one substance is not really distinct from the substance of which it is a mode and also not really distinct from another substance on which it also depends, does not entail that the two substances on which it depends are not really distinct. Again, if a substance can be clearly and distinctly conceived apart from its modes, including those that depend on other substances, it can be clearly and distinctly conceived apart from any other substance and its modes. The dependence of a mode on the modes of a distinct substance, and hence on another substance, does not threaten to undermine the real distinction between the two substances.

---

[13] By a formal distinction, I do not mean to suggest that actions and passions would belong in the category of attributes, only that they belong in the category of modes that cannot be conceived apart from one another. See AT iv, 349.

The two modes view also preserves the distinction between volitions and passions of the soul. Volitions are not really distinct from the passions that constitute the soul's awareness of its volitions, and the passions of the soul are not really distinct from the actions of the body, but there is some (less than real) distinction between the actions and the passions in each case. Because some distinction is preserved between passions of the soul and motions of the body, there is no need to suppose that there is any other action in the soul besides its volitions.

Since the two modes view does not suppose that a mode of extension is token-identical with a mode of thought, the problem of incompatible modes is not as acute as it is on other interpretations. There is no one thing that has both the nature of a thought and the nature of extension. But if a passion depends absolutely upon the body, such that it is not possible to conceive of a passion without an action of the body, is the passion not, according to the modal distinction, a mode of body? By the same reasoning is not an action in the pineal gland, also a mode of mind? Have we simply substituted one incompatibility problem for another?

One way to approach this last question is to rethink exactly what work the modal distinction is supposed to do. It might be assumed that the relationship of (one-way) dependence characterised by the modal distinction is what defines something as a mode. I am not convinced that this is correct as a general principle, but were it true, it would follow that wherever there is a mode that is not really distinct from a substance, the mode is a mode of that substance. So any sensation or passion that is dependent upon the body for its existence should automatically be considered a mode of body. We have seen the problems that this conclusion generates in discussing Hoffman's view. But there are other problematic cases as well.[14] Our innate ideas are modes of mind that are (eminently) caused by God and so bear a relationship of one-way dependence on God for their being. But innate ideas are not modes of God if, for no other reason than the one Hoffman gives, that God has no modes (*Principles*, I 56; AT VIIIA, 26).[15] My suspicion is that the modal distinction was never intended to define the conditions for something's being a mode, or the conditions under which a mode belongs to a certain kind of substance,

---

[14] If one-way dependence were sufficient for something's being a mode of a substance, and if we take Descartes' comments to Mesland (AT IV, 166–7) about the human body being one and the same through time because of its relationship to the mind, we should conclude that the human body is a mode of mind. Clearly, something is amiss. See my 2006.

[15] Hoffman, 1990: 324.

but to define simply the ontological relationship between those things that are modes and their substances. If this is correct, we should not infer from the dependence of sensations and passions on the body that they are modes of the body as well as of the mind.

Something besides the relationship of one-way dependence is required to explain why something is a mode, but what might that be? I'm not sure that there is a clear answer in the corpus, but here are two speculative answers. The first is that for something to be a mode of a substance it must be of the same ontological category as, or compatible with the principal attribute of, that substance. If God cannot support modes because of His simplicity, then we might just as well say that a body cannot support a passion of the mind because of its extension, and a mind cannot support a motion because of its unextended nature. Provided one has independent reasons for making such claims about the natures of mind and body (which Descartes can at least claim to have from the *Meditations*), this response will not involve any circularity. Determining the compatibility of modes with a given substance is listed as one of the functions of the principal attribute at *Principles* I, 53:

From any attribute whatever the substance is known, but one, however, of each substance is the leading property which constitutes the nature and essence of it and to which all the others are referred. Thus extension in length, breadth and depth constitutes the nature of a corporeal substance, and thinking (*cogitatio*) constitutes the nature of the thinking substance. *Everything else which is able to be attributed to a body presupposes extension and is indeed only a mode of* res extensa, *as all those things which we find in the mind are only diverse modes of thinking.* (AT VIIIA, 25, my emphasis)

Compatibility with the principal attribute of a substance is a necessary but not sufficient condition for something's being a mode of a given substance. And while this restriction rules out straddling modes between distinct kinds of substances, it does not exclude straddling modes between substances of the same ontological type. To be a mode of a substance requires some additional factor besides compatibility with the principal attribute and one-way dependence, something that grounds its inherence. Some notion of inherence certainly seems to be presupposed (although not defined) in Descartes' discussion of the first two kinds of modal distinction.

The first (kind of modal distinction) is known from the fact that we are able to perceive clearly the substance without the mode which we say differs from it, but we are not able, vice versa, to understand that mode without the substance. As figure and motion are distinguished modally from the corporeal substance *in which they inhere,* so also are affirmation and memory from the mind. The second kind of modal distinction is known from the fact that we are able to grasp one mode without the other mode and vice versa but neither, however, without the substance in which they inhere. (AT VIIIA, 29; my emphasis)

The description of the modal distinction in this passage from the *Principles* is intended to define the ontological relationship between modes and substances (and between modes themselves), not to specify the necessary and sufficient conditions under which a mode is a mode of a given substance. If this is correct, then one-way dependence alone will not guarantee the kind of unity that exists between a substance and its modes.

Is there any evidence, however, that the two modes view is what Descartes had in mind when he asserted that every action is one and the same thing as a passion? On the two modes view, what Descartes is trying to define is a relationship of ontological dependence that obtains between modes of distinct substances in such a way that it is impossible to conceive of one completely without the other, and, in general, ontological dependency does not entail numerical identity. The important sources of textual support for this view are those passages in which Descartes conflates a causal relationship with metaphysical dependence, for example, at article 41, where the power of the will is defined with respect to the passions, and it is noted that because passions are 'absolutely dependent' upon the actions in the body which cause them, the will can only indirectly change its passions (AT XI, 359). Another important passage is where in contrasting God and human beings, Descartes observes that even if perception is a perfection of sorts, the fact that it involves being acted upon implies dependency, and hence relative to God's perfections, perception is an imperfection.

And although there may be in us a certain perfection, namely that we sense, because the kind of perfection in every sense is a passion, and to suffer is to depend upon another, in no way is God thought to sense but only to understand and will. (AT VIIIA, 13–4)

Descartes' technical term for the dependency of modes upon substances is the lack of real distinction, not numerical identity. At *Principles* I, 61, where the modal distinction is being defined, Descartes never states that modes and their substances are numerically identical, emphasising instead the metaphysical dependency of modes upon their substances. Why not use this terminology in explaining the dependency that obtains between modes related as actions and passions of distinct substances?

So far, so so. But it might be objected that there is explicit textual evidence against the 'two modes' reading. At *Principles* I, 61, for example, Descartes asserts that the relationship between modes of distinct substances is more properly called a real distinction.

The distinction, however, by which the mode of one substance differs from another substance or from the mode of another substance, as the motion of one body differs from another body or from the mind, and also as motion differs from doubt, seems to be more properly called a real distinction rather than a modal distinction since those modes are not clearly understood apart from the really distinct substances of which they are modes. (AT VIIIA, 29–30)

Notice, however, that the cases under consideration in this passage are precisely cases of independent modes of distinct substances, modes we can clearly and distinctly understand apart from one another but not apart from the really distinct substances of which they are modes. Indeed, the passage suggests a general test for deciding when a real distinction between modes of distinct substances obtains, and thus can be read as allowing, in a roundabout way, real unities between modes of distinct substances. When a mode can be 'clearly understood apart' from either another mode or another substance, then it is really distinct from that mode or substance, and when it cannot be so understood, it follows that it is not really distinct. Descartes is not, at *Principles* I, 61, considering modes of distinct substances related as actions and passions, but compare those of *Principles* I, 48:

we also experience within ourselves certain other things which ought to be referred neither to the mind alone nor to the body alone. These arise . . . from the intimate union of our mind with the body: for example, appetites of hunger, thirst etc.; emotions [*commotiones*] or passions of the mind [*animi pathemata*], *which do not consist of thought alone* [*quae non in sola cogitatione consistunt*], such as the emotion of anger, joy, sadness and love, etc.; and finally, all the sensations, such as of pain, pleasure, light, colour, sound, smell, taste, heat, hardness and of other tactile qualities. (AT VIIIA, 23; my emphasis)

In this passage, Descartes uses the same test we find in *Principles* I, 61 to distinguish modes that we have through the union of mind and body from those that we have from some other source. Because these modes of mind cannot be clearly and distinctly conceived apart from the body, they 'do not consist of thought alone'. For passions and sensations to 'not consist in thought alone' they do not have to straddle mind and body. The single actuality created through the production of a passion isn't a single mode. It is, as we shall see, a much more complex phenomenon.

THE INSEPARABILITY PROBLEM REVISITED

We have now to look at how well the 'two modes' view handles the issues related to God's power to cause a passion directly in the soul. To say that two things are not really distinct would seem to imply that they are inseparable. 'Those things which either are able to be separated by God or are able to be conserved separately are really distinct' (AT VIIIA, 29). Yet, if God is omnipotent and actions and passions are numerically distinct modes, surely God could create a particular passion (for example, this dread of missed deadlines) without any action in the body causing it.

In answering this difficulty, let us draw on the mereological picture of Cartesian ideas advanced in chapter 4 and regard a passion as an idea which is constituted by two parts: a mode of mind and certain motions of the animal spirits. As a whole cannot exist without all its parts, so too a passion, in the strict sense, cannot exist apart from its parts, but just as the parts of a whole can exist separately from each other, so too the mode of mind and motions of the spirits which together constitute a passion could exist apart, if God chooses to separate them. God could make the very mode of mind that, if caused by certain motions in the body, would be a passion, without making those motions in the body, and vice versa. In either case, this would not, however, be making a passion of the soul.[16]

It is crucial to note that it does not follow from this account that the passion of the soul is really distinct from the action of the body. The passion is the whole, which is not really distinct from its parts, the motions of the animal spirits and their effects on the soul, and were we to try to conceive of a passion just in terms of one of its parts, our idea of it would be essentially incomplete. Saying that this whole consists of separable parts is not the same as saying that actions and passions can exist apart. The chief virtue of the mereological picture of the relationship between passions and actions is that it is consistent, therefore, with the claim that actions and passions are *une mesme chose*, while acknowledging God's power to produce any effect in the mind a natural cause can produce.

We can, therefore, agree with Hoffman that what God or the *Malin Genie* of the *First Meditation* could do is cause directly a sensation in the restricted sense of '*seeming* to see, to hear, and to be warmed' (AT VII, 29),

---

[16] This is not to say that God, in making the mode of mind without making a passion of the soul, would not be making an idea. The point is rather that God would not under those circumstances be making *that* idea, which is a passion when naturally caused.

for that is simply to produce a mode of thinking. But the conceivability of this does not entail conceiving of a passion as existing apart from the body that actually gives rise to it. Nothing in the demon hypothesis should be taken as implying a real distinction between or the conceivable separability of passions of the soul and actions of the body.

Thinking of actions and passions as constituting a whole which is made up of events in the body and thoughts in the mind, is as close as we are going to get to the Aristotelian idea that an action and passion constitute a 'single actuality'. Why there should be such strange wholes, composed of distinct kinds of modes, is beyond our understanding because their existence is ultimately tied to that of the union, another piece of forbidden fruit for human understanding. But supposing that these wholes exist is less mysterious than supposing either that actions and passions are token-identical straddling modes or that they are single modes of some third kind of substance besides mind and body, namely, the union.

Does any of this constitute progress against Elisabeth's original objection? Elisabeth is looking for a mechanism to explain interaction, but no mechanism other than the mechanism of the body is required for the soul to move the body if its body-directed volitions are not really distinct from movements of the spirits and, *mutatis mutandis,* nothing else is required for the body to affect the soul if the movements of its spirits are not really distinct from passions of the soul. Has not Descartes here captured the metaphysical relationship required for mind–body interaction in a fashion perfectly consistent with his dualism? In the final analysis, however, the victory may seem hollow, for what exactly is there to distinguish the claim that actions and passions are not really distinct from the claim that there are necessary correlations between modes of mind and body but no real interaction? Little wonder then that interpreters of Descartes in his own time and ours have read his account of mind–body interaction as supporting the doctrine of occasional causes.[17] This is, however, a mistake.

---

[17] Daniel Garber lists many members of the Cartesian school, including Clauberg, Clerselier, Cordemoy, de la Forge, Geulincx and Malebranche, who defended occasionalism (Garber, 2001: 203). Desmond Clarke has recently argued that Descartes is an occasionalist about all types of causal interaction (Clarke, 1999; de la Forge, 1664). See also Nadler, 1995:129–44. Gordon Baker and Katherine Morris see no 'collision' between interactionist and occasionalist readings of mind–body interaction in Descartes, and claim that the occasionalist reading is required to save Descartes from contradiction (Baker and Morris, 1996: 138–42). I confess I don't understand how the 'correlations' they see existing between events in the body and thoughts in the mind, instituted by God, add up to anything richer than parallelism or occasionalism in the traditional sense.

MIND–BODY UNION AND DESCARTES' ANTI-OCCASIONALISM

The above discussion brings to the fore the ways in which the inability to conceive of certain things without making reference to their causes is, for Descartes, evidence of a metaphysical relationship between them. But it may seem objectionable to treat what Descartes is left with as causality in any acceptable sense of the word. Do these relationships between modes of body and mind related as actions and passions constitute genuine efficient causality or something weaker, such as parallelism or occasionalism? I shall here try to dispel this idea by arguing that Descartes' use of the terminology of action and passion is sufficient evidence that he did not subscribe to the doctrine of occasional causes.

Occasionalism is the view that God is the only real cause in the universe; all apparent natural (or 'secondary') causes are simply 'occasions' for God's direct activity.[18] During the Middle Ages, the doctrine of occasionalism was applied by its advocates in all putative causal contexts and was motivated primarily by issues related to divine power. A common belief was that God plays both a productive and sustaining role with respect to substances. Indeed, these two roles are really only two sides of the same power. God's role in sustaining bodies in existence was to some no different from his recreating them in different places at different times, a fact which for occasionalists creates the illusion of their being moved by each other.[19] Descartes too subscribes to the doctrine of divine sustenance and to the conflation of God's sustaining and recreating role, but despite all the attention it still receives in the debate over his alleged occasionalism, the doctrine of divine sustenance is something of a red herring.[20] The focus of medieval concerns about the status of 'secondary causes' was on the question of how consistent Aristotle's account of causality – per se causality – was with divine will, knowledge and power, and only

---

[18] It is possible to restrict one's occasionalism to a particular domain. Daniel Garber holds Descartes to be an occasionalist about body-to-body and body-to-mind causation but not about mind-to-body causation. Garber hesitantly suggests Descartes may have changed his mind, moving towards a more occasionalist picture of body-to-mind causation by the time of the *Notae* of 1648. See Garber, 1993: 9–26; 1992: 299–305; 2001: 205–19. Garber does not, however, rely on the *Passions* in formulating his view.

[19] This is explicitly the case in Louis de la Forge's *Traité de l'esprit de l'homme* (1664: 240). See Garber, 2001: 189–91.

[20] In the context of medieval debates about God's existence and causal role, Descartes' adherence to this doctrine – for example, in the argument for God's existence of the *Third Meditation* (AT VII, 49–50), in his comment to Elisabeth (6 October 1645; AT IV, 314) that God is the 'total cause of everything, and thus nothing can happen without His will', and in his reply to Gassendi that God is the cause of the being (*causa secundum esse*) of created things not merely of their

derivatively with its compatibility with divine sustenance. The conceptual relationship between actions and passions is, for Aristotle, tied up with the account of per se causality, and so, one should expect that to the extent that Descartes follows Aristotle in adhering to the conceptual relationship between actions and passions, he too would be onside with the doctrine of secondary causes. This, at least, is a hypothesis worth exploring.

The debate over occasionalism in the seventeenth century had its roots, therefore, in an earlier debate, and as the debate progressed, the question of conceptual connections between natural causes and effects became pivotal. For the Islamic philosopher, Al-Ghazali, the conceptual connection postulated by Aristotelians between per se or proper causes and their effects, the sculptor and the sculpture, entailed a limitation on divine will, knowledge and power, and the impossibility (without logical contradiction) of miracles.[21] The sculptor is, for Aristotle, a per se cause of the sculpture because that the artefact is produced by a sculptor in a certain way is constitutive of its being a sculpture.[22] The notion of a per se cause contrasts with that of an accidental cause, which bears no internal relationship to the effect. If the sculptor is a musician, we may say that a musician was the cause of the sculpture, but being a musician is only accidentally a cause of a sculpture.[23] Aristotle's account puts an obvious constraint on the adequacy of causal explanations. Causal explanations must be in terms of per se causes. Accidental causation is inexplicable.[24]

The Aristotelian notions of action and passion are ways of expressing this conceptual relationship between per se causes and their effects. The

---

becoming (*causa secundum fieri*; AT VII, 369) – is unremarkable and does not imply a rejection of secondary causes. In particular, it does not distinguish him from a Thomist or Scotist or any other defender of God as a higher-order cause. On the higher-order causality model, God is necessary to explain why a given cause's causing its effect is a causing. God's activity is not however productive of the effect. Nor, for someone like Scotus, is God even a partial cause of the effect. God's causality is of a different order and ratio from natural causes. Contrast the occasionalist, who argues that God directly produces the effect on the occasion of the (finite) cause. It is the finite efficient cause that produces the effect, but it would not be a causing without God's willing it to be so. All this is compatible, so the story goes, with the claim that the finite cause has a genuinely productive role. See John Duns Scotus, *De primo principio* 3.11 (Wolter, 1996: 47) and Calvin Normore's 2003 discussion. Daniel Garber argues against understanding God's conserving role, for Descartes, in terms of His re-creating bodies in different places. He also claims that although Descartes' God is required to sustain substances in existence, this does not mean that those substances cannot affect one another modally (Garber, 2001: 192; 199–202). Of course, insofar as God is the total cause of everything which happens, God *is* required on Descartes' view as a cause of modal changes as much as anything else, particularly if these changes produce new modes of being, but this is consistent with God's being a higher-order cause and a non-occasionalist reading.

[21] Al-Ghazali, *Tahafut-al-falasifa, The Incoherence of the Philosophers* (Marmura's translation, 1997).
[22] Aristotle, *Physics*, II.3; 195a5.   [23] *Ibid.*, II.3; 195a38.   [24] *Ibid.*, II.3; 197a19.

sculptor is a per se cause of the sculpture through her activity, the sculpting, which is at the same time the same thing as the being sculpted, the actualisation of the sculpture. On this picture, the (efficient) cause is the sculptor, the action, the sculpting, and the passion, the being sculpted. Action and passion are two ways of describing the effect, one in relation to the agent and the other in relation to the patient. It was precisely the supposition of a conceptual relationship obtaining between cause and effect that was deemed problematic by occasionalists. Al-Ghazali argues, for example:

On the contrary, it is within divine power to create satiety without eating, to create death without decapitation, to continue life after decapitation, and so on to all connected things. . .we allow the possibility of the occurrence of the contact [with fire] without the burning, and we allow as possible the occurrence of the cotton's transformation into burnt ashes without contact with the fire.[25]

If there can be a sculptor without a sculpture, and vice versa, there is no chance of any conceptual connection, contra Aristotle, between two finite things. Denying that finite causes are necessary to produce certain effects does not, however, exclude their being sufficient causes, but the latter, Al-Ghazali assumes, would make God's causal role redundant. He concludes, therefore, that God's omnipotence entails that He is the direct cause of every natural change, and explains the appearance of secondary causes, in Humean style, in terms of our psychological habits. 'The appearance of conceptual connections between causes and effects is in the meantime explained in terms of the habitual associations we make between successive events.' [26]

The sceptical consequences of Al-Ghazali's position for the possibility of natural science and freely willed actions were not lost on his critics, in particular, Averroes, and the doctrine of higher-order causality, which emerged to account for causality within a divinely ordered universe, was an attempt to relativise the operation of per se causes to what was concurrent with God's will.[27] Even though all natural causes are dependent for their being causes on an external agent, God, whose act is the condition of their activity, it is the natural causes which are productive of their effects, and which are the condition for understanding their effects.

---

[25] *Tahafut al-falasifa*, 17 (1–2), in Marmura, trans. 1997: 170–1.

[26] *Ibid.*, 17 (1), in Marmura, trans. 1997: 170.

[27] See, for example, Averroes' *Tahafut al-Tahafut* (*The Incoherence of the Incoherence of the Philosophers*), 1.4.1, a reply to Al-Ghazali. van den Bergh, 1978.

It is against this background that Descartes' alleged occasionalism must be set. His occasional use of occasionalist language tells us little in the face of his more frequent use of causal terminology.[28] Instead, we must ask whether, for Descartes, there are conceptual connections between finite causes and effects. Consider, for example, how the perceived lack of conceptual connections between finite events motivates Descartes' successor, Nicholas Malebranche, to embrace occasionalism.

As I understand it, a true cause is one in which the mind perceives a necessary connection [*liaison nécessaire*] between the cause and its effect. Now it is only in an infinitely perfect being that one perceives a necessary connection between its will and its effects. Thus God is the only true cause, and only He truly has the power to move bodies.[29]

Since natural causes are not, for Malebranche, perceived by the mind as bearing a necessary connection with their effects, they do not qualify as true causes. The necessity at issue here is conceptual necessity, and it must, therefore, for Malebranche, be knowable a priori or perceived by the mind alone. As noted above, the Cartesian notions of mind and body entail nothing about how they might be sources of motion or affect each other. Where the idea of motion comes from is, for this reason, somewhat mysterious on Descartes' metaphysics and leads Malebranche to conclude that the power and force to move finite substances belongs exclusively to the idea of God.[30]

Malebranche's rejection of per se causality may seem to be part and parcel of the mechanist's rejection of substantial forms, which, for Aristotelians, explain the behaviour and interaction of natural substances. But I take it that by retaining the Aristotelian terminology of action and passion as a means of characterising substances as they are modified by other substances, Descartes is less keen than Malebranche to reject the idea of natural causation. The passions of the soul are essentially caused by motions of the animal spirits, which is why they can be called actions of the body even though they are modes of an incorporeal mind, and

---

[28] Descartes' use of occasionalist language does not indicate a commitment to occasionalism. In response to Regius' assertion that the senses are an adequate source of all our ideas, Descartes replies that we only judge that our sensory ideas refer to real properties because the corresponding motions in the body 'give the mind occasion' to form ideas (AT VIIIB, 359). As Dan Garber points out, however, Descartes' concern here is not with the question of whether or not the body is a real cause of the mind's ideas but with Regius' assumption that ideas resemble their causes (Garber, 1992: 366).

[29] Malebranche, 1980, VI. 2.3; Lennon and Olscamp, 1997.

[30] Malebranche, 1980, VI. 2.3.

voluntarily produced motions of the body are essentially caused by modes of the soul, which is why they can be thought of as actions of the mind and passions of the body. Descartes' account of causality is not, as it is for Aristotle, grounded in the ontology of substantial forms, but this does not make it any less an account of genuine (non-occasionalist) causality. What Malebranche does not seem to realise is the fact that the idea of causality is not a consequence of Descartes' basic ontological categories (mind and body) is epistemologically rather than metaphysically significant. Our knowledge of causality is not based on a priori intuition or deduction.

To understand causality on Descartes' view, we must look not to the metaphysical notions of mind and body but to his third 'primitive' notion, the union of mind and body. Significantly, as we saw earlier, this notion is the product of experience rather than metaphysical reflection. As Descartes writes to Arnauld (29 July 1648):

That the mind, which is incorporeal, would be able to move the body is shown to us not by any reasoning [*ratiocinatio*] or comparison [*comparatio*] with another thing but from a most certain and most evident daily experience. For this one thing is from things *per se* known, which when we wish to explain them [the *per se notae*] by others, we obscure. (AT v, 222)[31]

The kind of certainty we have from the 'primitive' notion of the union and our experience of mind–body interaction is not the kind, therefore, that Malebranche is seeking. It is definitively a posteriori and yet basic to our understanding of causality generally. In a complete inversion of Malebranche's argument, Descartes argues that the idea of God's power is not the primitive idea upon which our understanding of causality is based, but an idea that derives from an understanding of our own power to move bodies. As Descartes explains to More (15 April 1649):

And as it does not disgrace a philosopher to think that God is able to move a body, even though he does not think that God is a body, so also it does not disgrace him to judge something similar concerning other incorporeal substances; and although I think that nothing belongs to God and creatures univocally, I admit, however, that I find in my mind no idea which represents the mode by which God or an angel is able to move matter diverse from that which exhibits to me the mode by which I am, through my thought, conscious that I am able to move my body. (AT v, 347)

Our first exposure to causality is through our consciousness of our own agency – of our ability to move our body and other bodies through our

---

[31] See also the letter to Elisabeth, 28 June 1643 (AT III, 693–4).

volitions. To the extent that we understand the productive role of angels and God, it is dependent upon this basic grasp of our own power to move bodies. Daniel Garber has argued that because we understand God's agency through understanding our own, and through God, the laws of nature, it is ultimately through the experience of our own agency that we understand physics (Garber, 2001: 185–6).[32] If these arguments are correct, our understanding of the union is anything but a peripheral concern in Descartes' corpus.

Descartes' assertion that there are conceptual connections between actions and passions, not just in the mind–body case, suggests a commitment to natural causality in all domains.[33] Even if this kind of conceptual connection is one that we discover through lived experience rather than metaphysical analysis, its status as a certain truth is no less shaky for all that. This is a startling result, for, contrary to what Elisabeth supposes, we have in Descartes' system a kind of certainty that rests on an empirical foundation. It is perhaps for this reason that Descartes warns Elisabeth that we cannot understand the union and the distinction of mind and body at the same time, as if it is impossible to think of something as two and one in a single thought, and why the study of the union is best done outside metaphysical reflection (AT III, 693). Thinking of the mind and body through their a priori concepts sheds no light on how they interact, whereas thinking of the union as one single operating entity is to think of it through an a posteriori concept that inevitably obscures its metaphysical constitution. The two enquiries, the metaphysical one by which we come to know the distinction of mind and body, and the empirical one by which we come to know their union, require different conceptual strategies that cannot be simultaneously employed. Far from being of concern only to the moralist, the concept of the union and our everyday experience of it shows itself, therefore, to be as essential to our understanding of the bumps and grinds of the natural world as it is to our understanding of ourselves.

---

[32] It is surprising then that Garber still thinks of Descartes as committed to a partial form occasionalism. See Garber, 1992: 302–4.

[33] See also Descartes' letter to Hyperaspistes (August 1641) where he asserts that it is absurd to suppose that there can be an action without a passion in the case of a spinning top which sustains itself in motion once its whip has been removed or destroyed (AT III, 428–9).

CHAPTER 6

Wonder and love: extending the boundaries of the Cartesian knower and the Cartesian self

Epistemon: All that is best that one is able to teach you on this subject is that the desire to know, which is common to all men, is a sickness which is scarcely able to be cured, for curiosity increases with learning. . .

Eudoxus: Is it possible, Epistemon, that being learned as you are, that you would be able to persuade yourself, that there is a sickness so universal in nature without there being any remedy to cure it? For my part, it seems to me that just as there are in each land enough fruits and rivers to satisfy the hunger and thirst of everyone, there are enough truths that are able to be known on each matter to satisfy fully the curiosity of orderly souls. The body of the person suffering dropsy is not more removed from its proper temperament than is the mind of someone who is perpetually tormented by an insatiable curiosity. (AT X, 499–500)

The previous chapter was concerned with the role of passions in helping us to understand Descartes' account of causality, in particular, causality between the mind and the body. The relationship between actions and passions is an expression of the experience of unity each of us has with our bodies. That we cannot conceive of passions independently of their causes in the body, and so must attribute them to both the mind and the body, demonstrates the closeness that exists between these metaphysically distinct substances when they form a single system. The union may be accessible only through our experience of these modes and of their inseparability in thought, but the a posteriori quality of this knowledge does not make it less certain. It is now time to look at how the notion of the union might reshape our preconceived opinions about what it is to be an epistemic agent on Descartes' understanding, and about what our being embedded in complex social relations adds to his picture of the mind. This brings us to reconsider the important passion of wonder, and its new ally, love, for these, more than any other passions, are responsible for our ability to acquire knowledge, including knowledge of our selves.

In the unfinished (and difficult to date) dialogue, *The Search for Truth*, the sagacious Eudoxus denounces the 'insatiable curiosity' of his interlocutors as a sign of their ignorance and uncertainty. The thirst for knowledge is like the thirst of the person with dropsy, a disorder of the mind rather than a natural state for human beings. To quench the curiosity of the untutored Polyander ('Everyman'), Eudoxus sets out to examine, in order, the nature of the soul, God's existence, the way the senses receive their objects, what truth and falsity consists in, and then to reveal the 'secrets' behind the works of men which fill us with wonder – 'the most powerful machines, the most rare automatons, the most impressive visions and the most subtle deceptions that artifice is able to invent' – so that we shall 'have the ground no longer to admire at all the works of our hands' (AT x, 505). From there, Eudoxus proposes to pass to the secrets of nature, and then to the elements of science and ethics, dampening Polyander's 'passion for knowledge' as each subject is illuminated by the natural light and nothing remains inaccessible to human understanding.

This denigration of curiosity obscures the essential role wonder (of which curiosity is an extreme) is assigned in the *Passions* of motivating us to knowledge and fixing our attention on what we either don't understand or is in some way important or valuable to us.

One is able to say [of wonder, *l'admiration*] in part that it is useful in that it makes us learn and retain in our memory things we have hitherto ignored, for we wonder only at that which appears to us rare and extraordinary, and something is able to appear thus to us only because we have been ignorant of it or it is different from the things we have known. For it is this difference that makes it that which one calls extraordinary. (AT xi, 384)

If curiosity is a vice, it is because it is a perversion of a natural and useful inclination to wonder about things unfamiliar to us. The idea that wonder has a crucial role in motivating us to acquire knowledge had a long history prior to Descartes, echoing Aristotle's remarks in the *Metaphysics* that wonder is the beginning of philosophy. Aristotle writes:

That it [wisdom: the science of first causes and principles] is not a science of production is clear even from the history of the earliest philosophers. For it is owing to their wonder that men both now begin and at first began to philosophize; they wondered originally at the obvious difficulties, then advanced little by little and stated difficulties about the greater matters, e.g. about the phenomena of the moon and those of the sun and the stars, and about the genesis of the universe. And a man who is puzzled and wonders thinks himself ignorant (whence even the lover of myth is in a sense a lover of wisdom, for myth is composed of wonders); therefore since they philosophized in order to escape from ignorance, evidently they were pursuing science in order to know, and not for any utilitarian end. And this is confirmed by the facts; for it was when almost all the necessities of life and the things that make for comfort and recreation were present, that such knowledge began to be sought. Evidently then we do not seek it for the sake of any other advantage; but as the man is free, we say, who exists for himself and not for another, so we pursue this as the only free science, for it alone exists for itself.[1]

Wonder, for Aristotle, is elevated above the merely utilitarian. The pursuit of knowledge for its own sake is the only legitimate luxury, and being connected with our freedom, is good in itself. Wonder makes us attend first to the obvious difficulties, then to greater things, and is what keeps us on the path to the deepest kind of philosophical understanding.

In the Cartesian system, wonder has the role of motivating us primarily to scientific knowledge, for the objects that cause wonder are extraordinary things the causes of which we do not understand. But the fact that Descartes is inclined to think of curiosity as akin to sickness shows a deep ambivalence on his part towards this passion. There are historical reasons behind this ambivalence. Although many philosophers followed Aristotle in holding wonder to be useful to philosophy, since it is connected with ignorance of the causes of a thing, wonder could not be endorsed without qualification. Augustine, for example, distinguishes between vicious wonder (curiosity) and virtuous wonder. Curiosity is a vice because it is akin to lust (wonderlust?), connected with pride, and evident of a lack of knowledge and self-mastery.[2] It is a vice of the learned, who seek to know

---

[1] Aristotle, *Metaphysics*, I. 2 982b11–28, in *Complete Works*, ed. Barnes, 1984: 1554–5.

[2] Daston and Park (1998: chs. 3 and 8) note that the medieval period is marked by a prevailing suspicion of curiosity, wonder tainted by its connection to ignorance and an insatiable lust for inappropriate knowledge. They argue that among philosophers of the late seventeenth and early eighteenth centuries, wonder and curiosity are realigned with respect to each other through their associations with other passions. Wonder becomes connected with dull stupor, a passion of the vulgar mob rather than the scientific elite, whereas curiosity becomes associated (particularly in Hobbes) with acquisitiveness, an insatiable but laudable desire for knowledge (Daston and Park, 1998: pp. 303–10).

what doesn't concern them, or which it is useless to know, simply for the sake of knowing.[3] Virtuous wonder, by contrast, is a kind of reverential awe – wonder at the marvels of creation that cause us to direct our attention to and humble ourselves before God.[4] There are elements of this view in Descartes' ambivalence towards wonder. Curiosity is an admission of ignorance, but the wonder we experience from contemplation of God is the 'greatest joy which we are able to have in this life' (AT VII, 36), and our awe for the divine within us, the free will, is, as we shall see in chapter 8, central to the moral project of the *Passions*.

In the Middle Ages, wonder was considered a natural response to the 'secrets' of nature, and imperceptible forms or occult qualities were often postulated to fill gaps in explanation. Lorraine Daston and Kathryn Park have argued that the standard Aristotelian apparatus, with its emphasis on universality and orderliness, and its presumption that the behaviour of things can always be explained by reference to their 'specific forms', was ill-equipped to handle a range of phenomena that captured scholarly attention: chance occurrences, unforeseeable effects and divergences from form. Knowledge of specific forms does not enable one to deduce why sapphires are good for eyesight, why the loadstone attracts, why coincidences and chance events occur or why a baby is born with six fingers.[5] As *The Search for Truth* indicates, the kind of wonder we have for the secrets of nature is more a sign of a bad theory than a sign of something truly inexplicable. Such wonder ought to be dissipated by a thorough understanding of mechanics, a scientific method freed from the baggage of specific forms and the doctrinal, non-experimental approach to science.

---

[3] Augustine, 1996–7: 10.35; see Daston and Park, 1998: 120–4.

[4] Augustine, 1957–72, 21.6.

[5] In the *Summa contra gentiles* III.9.9, Aquinas struggles to account for chance or unforeseeable events, like the occurrence of six fingers on a human, as the effects of defects in the agent cause, or of the unsuitable condition of matter, or of an agent with greater strength that changes the natural order. On the Cartesian view, it is the arrangement of matter alone that explains every natural occurrence, and in this framework, the notion of ' defects' has little purchase. Daston and Park (1998: 128–30) argue that although most philosophers in the Scholastic period had a commitment to explain marvels by reference to natural causes, and with minimal recourse to demonic or divine intervention, they were hampered by the fact that the objects of wonder were typically beyond the scope of doctrinal philosophy, which concerned itself exclusively with universal knowledge. They quote the author of the pseudo-Albertine *De mirabilius*: 'One should not deny any marvelous thing because he lacks a reason for it, but should try it out [*experiri*]; for the causes of marvelous things are hidden, and follow from such diverse causes preceding them that human understanding, as Plato says, cannot apprehend them' (Daston and Park, 1998: 129).

The distinction between wonder directed at the seemingly inexplicable and wonder as reverence or awe is reflected in the following ambiguity in the use of 'wonder' in English, (and *admirer* in pre-modern French):

1. I wonder whether (something is the case).
2. It is a wonder that (something is the case).

The first formulation (1), implies ignorance, and when excessive, produces the 'blind curiosity' Descartes disparages. Blind curiosity drives us to seek out rarities, not in order to know their underlying principles, but rather to goggle at them, and this kind of wonder should be extinguished by knowledge (PS, art. 78). Wonder in the second sense (2), however, implies some recognition of the object as worthy of attention, and is compatible with knowledge. Wonder in this sense may persist in the form of either esteem or scorn, depending on whether the value attached to the object of wonder is positive or negative. This second kind of wonder has its uses in promoting self-understanding and self-mastery, as shall be explored later.

Let us proceed, however, by examining more thoroughly the first kind of wonder and its role in motivating our flight from ignorance. In light of the effort expended in the *Meditations* to encourage intellectual habits that are neither dependent on nor impeded by the mind's relationship to a body, it is somewhat perplexing that Descartes should suddenly in the *Passions* announce that it is by a passion that we are (and ought to be!) motivated to investigate the natural world. Why are the intellectual habits the meditator is trained to have without supposing he or she has a body, habits of withholding assent from things not clearly and distinctly understood until they are sufficiently examined, not alone sufficient to motivate the acquisition of scientific knowledge? And why is attention to the extraordinary or exceptional given such a prominent role? What do the marvels of nature teach us that attention to the ordinary truths of Cartesian metaphysics and physics cannot?

DESCARTES' CABINET OF WONDER

God made three marvels: something out of nothing, free will, and God in man.
(*Early Writings*, AT x, 218)

The explosion of interest in ' Cabinets of Wonder' or *Wunderkammern,* and the vast collections of natural and anthropological rarities that sprang up in Europe in the sixteenth and seventeenth centuries, coinciding with the exploration of the New World, has an air of insatiability about it likely to be distasteful to someone like Descartes.[6] There is a fine line between collecting things for the purpose of scientific investigation and collecting things for the sake of having a collection of rare or exotic things and the pleasures of viewing and displaying them. Wonder, the passion, and wonders, the extraordinary things, are useful but not ends in themselves. Excessive wonder or astonishment is harmful, because it produces stupor and impedes appropriate investigation and action (PS, art. 73). But if wonder tends to excess, wouldn't it be better to approach nature with the dispassionate attitude Eudoxus professes to have?

Wonder is introduced in article 53 as 'the first of all passions'. It is the first passion because it occurs before we know whether an object is beneficial or harmful to us and is therefore presupposed by every other passion that attaches some value to an object.

When the first encounter with some object surprises us, and we judge it to be novel, or very different from that which we knew before, or from what we supposed that it ought to be, this makes us wonder at and be astonished by it. And since this may happen before we know whether the object is beneficial to us or not, it seems to me that wonder is the first of all the passions. And it has no contrary, because, if the object that presents itself has nothing that surprises us, we are not moved by it at all, and we consider it without passion. (AT XI, 373)

The primary causes of wonder are things that are novel, unexpected or incongruous – 'not as we supposed them to be'. The element of surprise is critical, which is why wonder is so often connected with laughter (PS, art. 126). Wonder is 'a sudden surprise of the soul which makes it carry itself to consider with attention the objects that seem to it rare or extraordinary' (AT XI, 380). As noted in chapter 3, wonder is caused first by an impression on the brain, which represents the cause as extraordinary, and second by a movement of the spirits which keeps the sense organs fixed on the object and the image preserved in the brain long enough to be examined. Why we are drawn to objects we do not know, and which may, for all we know, turn out to be harmful to us, may seem a bit mysterious, but an explanation for this is given at article 71. The object of wonder is not, strictly speaking, the extraordinary object, the wonder of nature or of human ingenuity, but knowledge, and thus wonder is caused by a disturbance only in the brain, which is the seat of scientific understanding,

---

[6] Collections competed for size, rarity and variety, and were lavishly displayed. See Daston and Park, 1998: pp. 152–5, and chapter 7.

and not the blood or heart. What pulls us towards an object of wonder is not the value of an object, for this we do not yet know, but the knowledge we might obtain of it. We have a natural and passionate inclination to knowledge, and the specific function of wonder is to enable us to learn about new things, to retain what we learn in memory and to keep the mind focused in a state of attention and reflection (PS, art. 75).

Wonder is not unique in performing this attention-and-retention function. Other passions serve to fix and strengthen thoughts about objects, but all these other passions presuppose some knowledge of the object, and hence, presuppose the prior effects of wonder. On account of this order among the passions, wonder is 'customarily found in nearly all the passions and augments them' (PS, art. 72; AT XI, 382). The will is also able to perform the function of fixing attention (PS, art. 76), but not, as Descartes explains to Chanut, without the involvement of an internal emotion – rational love for the knowledge of nature.[7] Insofar as it is not dependent upon any movement of the spirits, however, rational love is not a passion and could exist in a disembodied mind.

All the movements of the will that constitute love, joy, sadness and desire, inasmuch as these are reasonable thoughts and not at all from the passions, could exist in our soul even if she had no body. For example, if she were to perceive that there are many things to be acquainted with in nature that are quite beautiful, her will would carry her infallibly to love the knowledge of these things, that is to say, to consider it as belonging to her. (AT IV, 602)[8]

While our soul is joined to the body, however, this rational love is commonly accompanied by another kind of love, 'which can be called sensual or sensuous' (AT IV, 602). The two kinds of love, rational and sensuous, can exist apart within the human psyche when, for example, the feeling of love is not accompanied by the will to join oneself to some thing because one judges it unworthy or when one judges something most worthwhile and wills to join with it even though one feels no passionate inclination to do so. But normally the two kinds of love go together, the confused thought that is the passion of love disposing the soul to have the clearer thought that is rational love (AT IV, 603). Why is it important

---

[7] Luce Irigaray asks why, if wonder is an attraction to difference, the passions of wonder and love would be separated (Irigaray, 1993:79–80). But wonder initially involves no conception of the first cause of wonder as good or evil. When wonder transforms into esteem, then love is a natural consequence, but not all apprehensions of difference are going to result in esteem, or esteem in love. I think Irigaray is on to something, but in order to see the close connection between these two passions, we need first to articulate the connection between wonder and knowledge.

[8] Letter to Chanut (1 February 1647.)

that the will to know some thing be accompanied usually by rational love bolstered by sensuous love?

Phenomenologically, it seems correct to assign love the function of motivating us, body and soul, to undertake the hard work required to acquire knowledge of difficult subjects, but there are more straightforward reasons for Descartes' choosing this passion to supplement the will in order to know something. As a passion, love is caused by a movement of the spirits that impels the soul to join itself willingly to some object that appears agreeable to it. In the first instance, love impels us to form a kind of cognitive union with an object, to think ourselves part of a whole of which the loved object is the other part, and while we are in such a state, the opportunities for knowledge are greatly enhanced (PS, arts. 79–80). Since love also mimics some of the effects of wonder on the body, it is no surprise that it is able to supplement an act of will to attend to something. In our embodied state, a volition to consider an object must be accompanied by some passion capable of sending the spirits into the muscles to keep the body immobile long enough to attend to it. This passion could be either wonder, which, because of the element of surprise, causes quick reactions in the nerves which, in turn, dilate the orifices of the heart in such a way that fixes attention, or love, which, through its effects on the heart, is capable of keeping the mind engrossed in a subject, preserving an image of the agreeable object, and holding the body in a state of fixed attention (AT IV, 209; AT XI, 417). Since love presupposes some acquaintance with its object, it presupposes the prior effects of wonder (transmuted to esteem), but love can motivate attention once wonder has ceased. Through its effects on the heart, love is connected with joy, and once knowledge is obtained, we are to move beyond it to a calmer joy. The volition to pursue knowledge when knowledge is still being sought and considered good is desire, when complete, is joy, and when incomplete, is sadness (AT IV, 602).

The discussion of the epistemic functions of wonder and love raise a host of interesting questions. The general question we have been considering is why Descartes does not countenance the idea of a purely dispassionate relationship to knowledge, especially in the hypothetical case of a disembodied mind. One simple answer is that since the objects of nature are particular objects of perception, something that is directly capable of holding the body and sense organs fixed and attentive is required, and whether a brute act of will could achieve this when it is continually distracted by external stimuli is obscure. But beyond these practical concerns, there are tantalising suggestions in these passages about the limitations of the human will, and the need, therefore, for something other than the will to initiate knowledge acquisition. Let us begin an examination of these questions by looking at Descartes' official account of the will.

In the *Fourth Meditation*, Descartes defines the will as the ability to do or not do something, to affirm or deny, pursue or avoid something, which the intellect puts forward (AT VII, 57). The will aims at the true and the good, as presented by the understanding, and because, as he writes to Regius, we cannot will without understanding what we will, willing and understanding are simply the activity and passivity of one and the same unified substance (AT III, 372). Descartes' general discussion of the will is set in the context where some knowledge or awareness of the object is taken for granted, where there is an object under consideration and the will's job is to incline us to assent or dissent to some judgement about it, or to pursue or avoid it. But this description does not countenance the context in which we are coming to notice an external object for the first time, and there is something paradoxical in suggesting that the will could determine the mind to notice something it hasn't noticed before, that is, without a prior attending or understanding, so that it might come to know it. The will is blind without an object and cannot, therefore, account for cognising objects for the first time, in light of which Descartes' assigning a passion (wonder) this function is perfectly understandable.

Although the motivation to pursue scientific knowledge may have, therefore, either an active or a passive source, in our embodied state a passion is always involved, at least in the initial stages. The principal utility of wonder is to motivate us to obtain scientific knowledge (PS, art. 76), but one utility of science is that it makes wonder for novelty cease. In *The Search for Truth*, Descartes reserves the name 'science' for a 'doctrine that is so solid and assured enough' (AT X, 513), and he writes to Hogelande that science is 'the skill to solve every problem' in a domain by means of one's own effort and native intelligence (AT III, 722). The sciences, which are 'not anything other than the certain judgements that we base on some preceding understanding [*conoissance*]', enable us to explain 'common things that the whole world understands how to talk about' as well as 'rare and recondite experiments [*experiences*]' (AT X, 503). It is the latter, stock items from nature's *Wunderkammern*, rather than the ordinary facts that he also doesn't understand, that capture Polyander's attention and stimulate his desire for knowledge. Rather than examining each in detail, Eudoxus sets out to equip Polyander with principles to unlock the secrets of any marvellous object he encounters.

I confess, also, that it would be impossible to discuss in detail all of those [rare and recondite things]. For it would be necessary, in the first place, to have researched all the herbs and stones that come from the Indies, it would be necessary to have seen the Phoenix, and in short not to be ignorant of any of the more strange things in nature. But I shall believe that I have sufficiently fulfilled my promise if in explaining to you the truths which can be deduced from ordinary things and things known to each one, I make you capable of discovering for yourself all the others, when it will please you to take the trouble to look for them. (AT x, 503)

A similar point is made in the *Passions* at article 76, where Descartes asserts that there is no other remedy for excessive wonder than 'to acquire the knowledge of many things and to exercise yourself in the considera- tion of all those things which may seem to you most rare and most strange' (AT xi, 385). Wonder motivates us to acquire knowledge, but wonder can also motivate us to overthrow existing theories, which might do better with ordinary facts than with extraordinary ones. Exotic and rare things are singled out, both for their ability to attract and stimulate attention, but also for the challenge they present to received views. The most unusual things are limiting cases for received theories of nature, and when they are explained they no longer grab our attention in quite the same way (PS, art. 76). What remains at the end of science are only the secrets of providence, about which it is impertinent to seek knowledge, or demonstrate that we lack due respect (PS, art.198; AT iv, 415). The works of God leave us in awe but not wonderstruck.

Wonder is thus particularly useful in freeing us from bad theories, like the theory of specific forms, and the test of a good theory is how well it unlocks the secrets and marvels of nature and frees us from wonder. But until we are certain we have the right theory, it is appropriate to keep wondering. Hence, a general deficiency of wonder is not associated with the most able minds but with those too dull and stupid to wonder about things (PS, art. 77). Those naturally inclined to wonder, like Polyander, are not necessarily possessed with the best minds, but with 'excellent common sense' and 'no high opinion of their abilities' (AT xi, 386). This is not a priori science. It is our experience of the world that motivates us to pursue knowledge and question accepted models of explanation in the sciences. Grabbing our attention is, however, only a first step, and as the wax example from the *Second Meditation* illustrates, knowledge depends on the intellect stepping in to unlock the essence of matter and the laws of nature, so that we may we see that all ' marvels of nature' are simply the consequence of the arrangement of tiny particles of matter.

SELF-WONDER AND SELF-KNOWLEDGE

We are ourselves marvels of nature and wonder has a role to play in unlocking the secrets of human nature, as well as revealing to each individual that he or she is a particular person. When we consider self-knowledge from the perspective of an embodied investigator, a very different picture emerges than the one commonly supposed to be 'Cartesian'. In particular, understanding one's self is not a matter of performing the *cogito*, of turning one's own mind back on itself, but is based on the experience each of us has of being an agent in the world.

Contemporary puzzles associated with self-knowledge are often said to have Cartesian roots insofar as Descartes is said to have subscribed to two related ideas: (1) the transparency of the mind to itself, and (2) the method of knowing oneself by direct introspection. One problem that follows from these two ideas is the problem of the elusive self. When we introspect we are not directly acquainted with any persisting substance but only our thoughts. That our minds are essentially thinking substances has struck many of Descartes' critics as neither a transparent nor directly introspectible fact. Another problem concerns the supposed first-person authority of the Cartesian mind. This is the problem of how to reconcile the transparency principle, that each of us knows what we are thinking, with ' externalist' intuitions about the contents of our thoughts. On the externalist picture, what makes our ideas the ideas they are – what we are thinking of or about – is, at some fundamental level, fixed by factors about which we may have only partial knowledge, the causal history of our ideas and the social context in which those ideas are expressed and shaped through language (Putnam, 1975; Burge, 1979; 1982; 1986a-b; 1988; Davidson, 1987). It seems intuitively very plausible to us that our access to our minds is privileged, at least to the extent that it doesn't depend upon inferences from perceptions of our bodies or behaviour, and is thus very different from our knowledge of other minds. And yet it seems equally implausible to suppose that our bodily existence is simply irrelevant to the understanding we have of ourselves.

Both these ideas, the transparency principle and the principle of direct access, are overstated in contemporary debates. A study of the *Passions* tells us that there is much about the mind that is neither introspectible nor transparent to the mind. We are often confused about what type of thought (a passion or a volition?) we are experiencing, and whether the soul or something 'external' produced it. And it is our individual histories as much as our individual temperaments that shape our emotional dispositions and the effects of our history may be quite opaque to us. But there is also Descartes' emphasis that a correct understanding of the human body is a necessary precondition for understanding the soul and nature generally.

Let us consider the question of self-knowledge from the point of view of an embodied mind. Performing this exercise will not supplant the *cogito* as an account of the mind's knowledge of its essence or the epistemologically foundational role it plays in Descartes' system, but it will provide a richer account of what self-knowledge is for Descartes.[9] Let us consider first the role that knowledge of the human body plays in Descartes' analysis of the human being and its self-knowledge, and then the role that knowledge of our own agency plays in constituting our knowledge of ourselves as individual persons. The passion of wonder is involved in both these forms of self-discovery.

Applying mechanical principles to understand the human body plays a number of important epistemic roles for Descartes. On a scientific level, it enables him to explain phenomena that were perplexing to Scholastic physicists but manageable on newer approaches in medicine. In Descartes' time the human body was full of secrets and, occasionally, subject to monstrous defects that fascinated physicians and natural philosophers.[10] Descartes himself is not above being intrigued by the monstrous and bizarre. Although the claim that being bitten by a mad dog will cause the dog's image to appear in one's urine is dismissed as a fable, more serious attention is given to the possible causes of birth defects and birthmarks (AT I, 153). Descartes' initial scepticism that the cravings, injuries, dietary or other practices of pregnant women can cause anomalies in infants, gives way to a robust explanation consistent with mechanics (AT I, 153). When the mother 'transforms the effects of her imagination to the correspond-ing part of the baby' through the close correspondence of those parts, birth defects and birthmarks may appear 'as may be proved by reasoning based on mechanics' (AT III, 120–1; see also AT III, 20–1). Again, the test of a good theory is how well it handles the strange, the inexplicable and the extraordinary, as well as the ordinary facts. In general, applying mechan-ical principles to explain the normal functioning of the human body without recourse to 'vital spirits' or the secondary qualities of Galenic

---

[9] The *cogito* argument yields the principle that our soul exists, which is the 'first' principle of Descartes' system, because it is easily known and from it we may move to the existence of God and created substances (AT IV, 444–5).

[10] On the fascination with monsters during the Middle Ages and Renaissance, see Daston and Park, 1998: ch.5.

medicine, enables Descartes to endorse new developments in medicine in a way consistent with his physics and metaphysics.[11]

At the metaphysical level, knowledge of the human body plays a critical (and hitherto largely ignored) role in the real distinction argument. The embodied self is a self aware of the union of its mind with its body. But the idea the mind has of the union is confused and obscure, and disposes it to think of the soul as something corporeal. In the *Second Meditation,* the tendency to attribute matter to the soul is attributed to a profound ignorance of what the soul is.

It occurs to me that I am nourished, that I walk, that I sense and that I think, which actions indeed I used to refer to the soul. But what this soul was I either did not notice or do not know scarcely what image I was imagining, of a wind or fire or ether, which was infused into the coarser parts of me. (AT VII, 26)

To correct this tendency, we must not only examine what the soul is essentially, but also, and at the same time, what the human body is and how it is able to move itself. In the *Description of the Human Body,* Descartes attributes our ignorance in thinking that the soul is the principle responsible for all bodily movements to our experience of moving our bodies by our wills, and to our ignorance of anatomy and mechanics (AT XI, 223–4). In this context, acquiring a better 'acquaintance with oneself' is not a matter of performing the *cogito,* but a matter of acquiring a better understanding of the human body, knowledge that is useful for both morals and medicine.

There is nothing to which one is able to attend more fruitfully than to touch on one's own acquaintance with oneself and the utility which one ought to hope from this acquaintance does not regard only morals, so that it seems just the first of several, but particularly also medicine in which I believe that one would be able to find many very certain precepts, as much for curing sicknesses as for preventing them, and even also to slow down the course of ageing, if one were sufficiently learned to be acquainted with the nature of our body and one had not at all attributed to the soul the functions that depend only on it (the body) and the disposition of its organs. (AT XI, 221–2)

How does our experience of moving our bodies by our wills contribute to our mistaken view of the soul? The answer given is that we infer

---

[11] A concise example of mechanics applied to the human body can be found in the letter to Vorstius, 19 June 1643. Natural and vital spirits are nothing other than the blood, and the differences between all the so-called 'spirits' and their functions are simply the result of refinement of the matter and the degree of agitation in the spirits and the vessels (e.g. arteries or nerves) in which they travel (AT III, 687–9).

(incorrectly) from our experience of willing our bodies to move that the self-motion of human and animal bodies can be explained only through the concept of the soul and not through the concept of body, which is simply the concept of whatever is determinable in shape and location and occupies space in such a way as to exclude other bodies (AT VII, 26). The sceptical arguments of the *Meditations* force the reader out of this way of thinking about the soul, but there is another source of motivation behind Descartes' conversion to the view of the soul as simply *res cogitans*, and that is his astonishment (a species of wonder) that the self-motion of the body could be explained without reference to thought.

As for having the power to move itself, as of the power of sensing or of thinking, I judged that this in no way pertains to the nature of body. Indeed, I am *astonished* [*mirabar*] that such faculties [of self-movement] are to be found in bodies. (AT VII, 26; my emphasis)

Through an understanding of mechanics, the ordinary motions of the body become, temporarily at least, extraordinary. These are motions that depend neither upon external forces nor upon the soul. This wonder is useful insofar as it frees us to re-examine both the nature of the soul and of the body, and, thus, human nature generally. Indeed, one could argue that without Descartes' investigations in natural philosophy, which enable him to explain the functions of the living human body without reference to thought, the real distinction argument for dualism and the *cogito* argument would not be as compelling as they are. For although the sceptical arguments (putatively) show that the intellect can exist without the body – (as any Thomist might have agreed) – they do not thereby show that the human body could function as it does without a soul (as no Thomist would have agreed).

Insofar as this knowledge of the human body is scientific, it must be motivated by wonder or the will conjoined with love. Wonder directed at the capacity of matter, in certain formations, for self-motion, without the 'animating' effects of an Aristotelian soul or vital spirits, motivates Descartes to re-examine the nature of the soul, and its relationship to matter, and is thus in good measure responsible for the paradigm shift in thinking about the self the *Meditations* seeks to bring about.

What should we say then about the self in Cartesian philosophy? It is generally identified with the mind, the *res cogitans*, but the *Sixth Meditation* brings us back to ourselves as unions of mind and body, at least for the duration of this life. What happens to the self is not that it comes to see that it 'has' a body, as Ryle famously supposed, but that it *is* a body as well as a mind (Ryle, 1949: ch.1).

. . . and so from the fact that some of these perceptions are agreeable to me while others are not, it is plain that my body, *or more properly me wholly in as much as I am composed from a body and a mind,* is able to be affected by various beneficial and harmful things from surrounding bodies. (AT VII, 81; my emphasis)

Descartes' whole self cannot be grasped by means of direct introspection, nor is it transparent to the mind. His coming to understand what kind of being he is is as much dependent on his scientific understanding of the human body, and the wonder that presupposes, as on his direct awareness of his thought and the existence of his mind.

INDIVIDUAL SELF-KNOWLEDGE

The account of self-knowledge offered so far has focused on general or scientific knowledge of the embodied self and its relationship to the process by which we can come to accept the 'first principle' of knowledge, that the soul is a thinking thing. But what can we say about individual self-knowledge, the knowledge I have of my particular 'whole' self? Does it consist simply in my grasping the *cogito*?

The soul's first thoughts of its particular union with matter are its passions: joy, at the pre-natal moment of union, love for its acquisition of new matter, hatred and sadness for its lack of new matter or suffering from a bad condition (AT IV, 604–5). These passions all presuppose an element of wonder: something new or a change in the disposition of the body has occurred that makes the soul aware of its union with the body. When a change occurs in the brain, the soul's attention is drawn to some thing. Because of the element of surprise, any movement accompanied by wonder will have a greater effect both on the mind and on the body. This is so, as Descartes explains to Elisabeth (May 1646), even though wonder originates in the brain and would seem, therefore, to have a lesser effect than those passions that arise from the composition of the blood (AT IV, 409–10). The cognitive link we have to the union is mediated, however, both by the actions we perform through the body and sensation.

Each person finds always in himself without Philosophy the knowledge that he is one sole person, who has together a body and thought that are of such a nature that this thought is able to move the body and sense the accidents which occur to it. (AT III, 694)

We need to examine this claim carefully, for it is unclear that Descartes is entitled to make it. On Margaret Wilson's reading, for example, what my mind is aware of directly when I will to move my body is only the volition, which is just a thought. Similarly, what I am aware of are not 'the accidents which occur' to my body but the sensations those accidents produce, which are also thoughts. On Wilson's reading, all Descartes is entitled to claim is that each of us is aware of 'one side of the equation' (Wilson, 1978a: 216). The argument for the existence of bodies in the *Sixth Meditation* is an argument that the only possible source of those ideas is the body, but arguably that is an inference to the best explanation and not the experience Descartes claims we each find within us of our embodiment (AT VII, 79–80). Wilson's concern is reasonable, and the following passage from Descartes' letter to Arnauld (29 July 1648) seems only to reinforce the idea that it is only the mind and its contents that are directly known.

It is true, however, that we are not conscious of that mode by which our mind sends the animal spirits into these or those nerves; for that mode does not depend on the mind alone but on the union of mind and body. We are conscious, however, of every action through which the mind moves the nerves, in as much as such an action is in the mind, indeed, in which it is nothing other than an inclination of the will towards this or that motion. (AT V, 221–2)

Notice, however, that Descartes immediately follows this remark by asserting that the fact that the mind can set the body in motion is shown to us not by reasoning or comparison with other matters, but 'by the most certain and plainest everyday experience' (AT V, 222). What is this experience we have of moving the body that is not to be confused with an argument to the conclusion that our minds stand in some relation to bodies?

My own inclination is to think that for Descartes our awareness of our own free will as unions of mind and body, and the goodness of it, are not simply matters of knowing one side of the (mind–body) equation. I can will to enlarge my pupils and be aware of my volition, but I cannot thereby make my pupils enlarge, although I can by an act of will look at a distant object that has the effect of enlarging my pupils (PS, art. 44). If there is any difference between the experience of trying to move one's body but failing and the experience of succeeding, it is not a difference in awareness of anything belonging just to the mind.

The experience I have of moving my body depends on my receiving some feedback from my body that is phenomenologically marked as not originating in my mind – as not a matter of what I will although connected in some way with my will. It is, I suspect, the combination of a volition to move the body together with a passion, which is the effect of the movement produced in the body, which constitutes my awareness of successfully moving my body. These are both thoughts, but only one, the volition, is a mode of mind we can attribute to the soul alone, as Descartes says at *Principles* I, 48, and the effect of these together constitutes my sense of myself as an embodied agent. An example of the kind of feedback system I have in mind, one in which the effects of a volition on the body are felt through a passion as part of a single process, can be found in the following passage, where Descartes is attempting to describe the difference between a habit or disposition towards a certain passion and a passion itself. Habits are formed when, through their effects on the body, judgements and passions reinforce each other. A judgement that a town is about to be besieged affects the spirits in such a way as to produce the passion of fear, which, in turn, keeps the soul focused on this thought. The loops are so tight and so fast that the soul experiences the connection between its judgements and passions as a 'single operation'.

By the same means [the soul] determines the spirits which go from the brain by the nerves into the muscles to enter into those which serve to close the openings of the heart and retard the circulation of the blood, following which the whole body becomes pale and cold and trembling, and the new spirits which come from the heart towards the brain are agitated in such a way that they are not able to help form there any images other than those which excite in the soul the passion of fear, all of which follows so closely one upon the other that it seems as if they are a single operation. (AT IV, 313)

When I attempt to move my body but fail, it is precisely the feedback provided through a passion that is missing. The phenomenological differences between experiencing one side of the mind–body equation and experiencing a unity of mind and body through one's conscious awareness of one's own agency account for the experience each of us has of being a particular unity of mind and body.

What then are the passions that are central to this experience of unity? We might find an answer to this question by looking at those passions that are closely connected with our use of the will in our embodied state. These are passions involving some form of self-assessment, principally, self-esteem and self-contempt, which are, in turn, species of wonder. Esteem is the soul's inclination to represent to itself the value of some object (PS, art. 149). When these passions relate to ourselves, when we consider our own merit or demerit, we are told that it is only 'the knowledge of how to use our free will and the empire we have over our volitions' for which we may be reasonably praised and thus esteem ourselves (PS, art. 152; AT XI, 445). Insofar as they involve an appraisal of one's own actions as successful or unsuccessful, these passions either sustain the soul in the action it deems good for it (and dispose it to such actions again) or deter it from ones it deems bad (PS, arts. 177, 190, 191). Self-esteem and self-contempt are the basic forms of our self-assessment as embodied beings; more complex forms of feedback include self-satisfaction, self-pity, repentance and remorse (PS, arts. 177, 190, 191, 200).

Wonder at the things I do by my own volitions is the kind of self-wonder that is always available to me so long as I act. It is contrasted with the kind of wonder those have who wonder at themselves whenever something new happens to them, and thus vacillate between esteem or contempt for themselves, depending on whether they view what happens as advantageous or not (AT XI, 452). Depending on a movement of the spirits, self-esteem connected with the use of one's will is not the kind that can be derived from within the mind alone. It involves some kind of appraisal, but there is no need to think of these appraisals as intellectually or morally loaded. There is no reason to deny that infants experience moving their bodies in the way they want, and the wonder and joy that accompanies it. The 'I moved that!' look of delight on an infant's face expresses as much self-wonder as the self-satisfaction of adults. My sense of me-ness comes first from experiencing the effects of my will on my body and it is only philosophy which much later enables me to focus on my mind alone and raise doubts about my embodiment.

Because they constitute modes of awareness of our wills in action in the world, these various species of self-directed wonder open the way for forms of self-assessment (of successful versus unsuccessful action) to become part of the process by which each of us identifies herself or himself as a particular person. This makes embodied self-knowledge a distinctively normative exercise for Descartes, and one that opens the way for others and their assessments to become part of the same process by which each of us develops a sense of individuality. The experience of embodiment thus brings to mind most immediately the fact that each of us inhabits a world in which we act and that we share with others.

OTHER MINDS

Within the practical sphere, our free will is revealed through our actions, and our knowledge of the latter, Descartes seems to suggest, is dependent upon passions like self-esteem. Not only does this account for the experience of ourselves as individual unions of mind and body, but it enables others to mediate the process through their judgements about or reactions to our actions. There are complex interplays between our own passions and those of others, which affect our conception of our own agency, and make us attuned to other minds. When I look out the window and see bodies in hats and coats, I may wonder whether all I see are automata. But when others cause me to feel pride or shame, grateful or indignant, I cannot be disposed to think of them as anything less than persons, other moral and rational agents whose actions and reactions matter to me and to them. The passions that are caused by others' negative or positive reactions to one's actions include virtuous humility (PS, art. 155), shame (PS, art. 205), vicious humility or abjectness (PS, art. 159), vanity (PS, art. 157) and pride (PS, art. 204). Others are based on one's own assessments of others' actions: scorn (PS, art. 163), derision (PS, art. 178), gratitude and vicious ingratitude (PS, arts. 193–4), indignation (PS, art. 195) and anger (PS, art. 199). It is passions such as these that inform me most immediately of the existence of other minds, even if it takes the intellect to prove it.

Why it is the case, however, that we care what others think? As we are told at article 40 of the *Passions*, the principal utility of the passions is to dispose the soul to thoughts useful for the preservation of the union. This has suggested to some that Descartes might be some kind of egoist with regard to the passions; that their primary purpose is, as Patrick Frierson describes this view, 'the furthering of one's own good, especially the good of the body' (Frierson, 2002: 316; also Wee, 2002). One passion in particular plays an important role in countering this impression – love. Love explains why it is we form various kinds of non-substantial (but no less real for all that) unities – families, groups, communities – and why it is, therefore, that what others think about us matters and contributes to our forming particular conceptions of our selves as whole persons.[12]

LOVE

In the letter to Elisabeth of 15 September 1645, written just prior to the preparation of the first draft of the *Passions*, Descartes argues that in order to judge well it is necessary to bear in mind that, among other truths, one is always part of a whole that is greater than any of its parts.

After one has then recognised the goodness of God, the immortality of our souls and the grandeur of the universe, there is still one truth the knowledge of which seems to me especially useful and that is that although each of us is a person

---

[12] Compare Frierson, 2002: 325–6.

separated from others, and whose interests consequently are in some fashion distinct from those of the rest of the world, one ought always to think that one could not subsist alone and that one is, in effect, one of the parts of the universe, and more particularly still, one of the parts of this earth, and of this state, of this society and of this family, to which one is joined by one's domicile, one's solemn oath, and by birth. And it is necessary to prefer always the interests of a whole of which one is a part to those of his person in particular, though always with measure and discretion, for one would do wrong to expose oneself to a great evil to procure only a little good for his parents or his country. (AT IV 293)

Our link to these greater unions is forged through love. The noblest form of love, where duty and virtue combine with love, involves a preference for the interests of others in the union, as the good father demonstrates when he puts his children's interests before his own (PS, art. 82).

Love is defined at article 79 as an 'excitation of the soul. . .which incites it to join itself in volition to the objects that appear to be suitable to it' (AT XI, 387).[13] Like other passions, the function of love is to preserve the union or render it in some way more perfect (PS, art. 137; AT XI, 430). Among the passions, love is 'extremely good', because, by joining us to real goods, 'it makes us to that extent more perfect' (PS, art. 139; AT XI, 432). Excessive love for real goods is never bad because it makes us apply ourselves to them as well as to ourselves (PS, art. 139), nor does love corrupt us as much as hatred, the object of which is evil (AT IV, 613–14). Excessive love for the wrong object is, however, always bad, and when conjoined with desire, it uses all the spirits of the brain to keep the image representing the object present before the mind, preventing all other motions of the pineal gland that would be more useful for it to have (PS, art. 120).

The conceptualisation of others through love as part of one's self is reminiscent of Aristotle's account of friendship in books VIII and IX of the *Nichomachean Ethics,* and the ethical implications are somewhat similar. By identifying with others as part of one's extended self, one is rationally motivated to act for their sake. The account also inherits some of the philosophical problems associated with Aristotle's view. Descartes needs an argument to show that the demands of friendship or community are not in conflict with the pursuit of other goods, such as knowledge, happiness or justice. Elisabeth is sceptical of Descartes' confidence that the demands of public life do not conflict with private interests and concerns. She questions the feasibility of reconciling individual and public

[13] See also the letter to Chanut, 1 February 1647, AT IV, 602–5.

interests simply by conceiving of oneself as part of a whole (30 September 1645, AT IV, 303–4). Nor is she prepared to grant Descartes the assumption that, by working for oneself, one cannot fail also to work for others (30 November 1645, AT IV, 336–7). What lies behind Elisabeth's scepticism is a general worry that goods are incommensurable. How is it possible to weigh the public good my actions may bring about against the pains I would have to endure, or to measure the relative worth of my interests against others'? Would not the very distinctness of the idea of private pain from the idea of a public good make the former seem much greater in my mind and deter me from right action?[14] Thus she writes to Descartes on 13 September 1645:

> It is true that the custom of estimating goods according as they are able to contribute to contentment, of measuring this contentment according to the perfections that they make, to give birth to pleasure, and to judge without passions of these perfections and of these pleasures, would safeguard them from a quantity of faults. But to estimate goods thus it is necessary to know them perfectly, and to know all those things among which one is constrained to choose in an active life, it would be necessary to possess an infinite science. (AT IV, 288–9)

Some bond is needed to get one to act for the sake of others, particularly when doing so incurs some cost to oneself, and, if Elisabeth is right, it is not a bond that can be forged by the intellect in the absence of an infinite science. Descartes would seem to agree: it is not the intellect but passions like love that make altruism possible.

Descartes distinguishes love and its opposite, hatred, which are passions and depend upon some movement of the spirits, from judgements, which can have the same effect as these passions in bringing the soul to join itself 'in volition' to, or separate itself from, other things, and from the 'internal emotions' which accompany such judgements. The phrase 'in volition' is glossed at article 80 as implying not desire but the assent by which we consider ourselves as joined to another thing in such a way that we imagine a whole of which we are a part. Hate makes us consider ourselves alone as a whole separated entirely from other things. This suggests that love is a complex psychological attitude involving the will's assent to its unification with another thing in conjunction with an idea of oneself as part of some larger whole fostered by the imagination. It is the role of the imagination that distinguishes the passion of love, or 'sensuous love', as Descartes describes it in the letter to Chanut (1 February 1647; AT IV, 602–7), from judgements, or rational love, which also involves an act of

---

[14] See Elisabeth's letter to Descartes of 30 September 1645 (AT IV, 301–4).

assent to union with other things. The imagination is brought in not simply to imagine the lovable qualities of the beloved. Indeed, conceptualisation of lovable qualities may proceed from love rather than precede it, when, for example, love causes the soul 'to imagine lovable qualities in objects where she would see only faults on another occasion' (AT IV, 603). What seems crucial is rather the capacity of the imagination to present to the will for its consent an idea of the self in union with another. In the case of sexual unions, the imagination causes us to think of ourselves as deficient in that we are one half of a whole, and to imagine the acquisition of this other half as the greatest of all goods (PS, art. 90; AT XI, 396). Although the name 'love' is given (by romanticists and poets) to this inclination, Descartes prefers to think of the principal passion involved in sexual unions as desire arising from attraction (PS, art. 90). Love differs from desire, according to Descartes, in not having possession of the object as part of its *telos,* and whereas erotic desire remains unfulfilled unless there is reciprocity, love is not so constrained. In both cases, however, the principal cause of the passion uniting us to others is an imaginative representation of union with the object as good or agreeable, from which it follows that sensuous love for God is impossible (AT IV, 607).

There is nothing in God that is imaginable which makes it that although one has for Him some intellectual love, it does not seem that one would be able to have any sensitive love because it ought to pass by the imagination in order to come from the understanding to the senses. (AT IV, 607)

One may mistake one's passion for an idol for love of the true God, but, strictly speaking, this is not sensuous love of God (AT IV, 607). It is God's lack of embodiment that in part precludes us from having sensuous love for Him. Moreover, the attributes of God are so high above us that we cannot think of them as appropriate for ourselves, and so do not join ourselves to them (AT IV 607). With regard to the passion of love, what we cannot imagine as being part of ourselves, we cannot form a union with.

The extended conception of the self that the soul obtains through the passion of love, and which is one source of altruistic motivation, thus presupposes both our own embodiment and that of others. To be an object of love, one must be the kind of thing to which the senses have access, and of which the imagination can construct an image. Love also bears an internal relationship to esteem directed at the self and others. Descartes distinguishes three kinds of love according to differences in the esteem in which an object is held: simple affection, which we may have for a flower or horse, involves having less esteem for the object than for ourselves; friendship, which entails esteeming the other as equal to one-self; and devotion (principally for the Deity), in which the object is esteemed more highly than oneself (PS, art. 83; AT XI, 390). The esteem that the soul has for other persons cannot be based merely upon the natural movements that express passions, for these can be imitated by machines or animals, and so cannot be based on our perceptions of their physical appearance. It is others' use of language or speech, which, in the *Discourse on Method,* Descartes identifies as the only sure sign of ration-ality, that principally reveals to us what kind of person another is, feeds into our image of the other and structures our esteem accordingly (AT VI, 58–9).

These distinctions between different kinds of love based on esteem suggest that the process of esteeming oneself and one's own actions is intimately connected through imaginative comparisons with the process of esteeming others. In esteeming our own actions and our own selves we naturally compare ourselves to others, and thereby develop certain pas-sions towards them. When others arouse esteem and love in us, their reactions to us become important and contribute to our own self-esteem, which defines the boundaries of our selves. My shame at what I have done to another puts in sharp relief that it was both I who performed a certain action and my other self who has been harmed by it. Without both lines of identification, I would not be ashamed. Out of these interconnected processes of self and other-esteem, each person forms a variety of unions which are as much a part of the Cartesian 'self' from the soul's point of view as the 'I' of the *Second Meditation,* the mind aware only of itself and its thinking.

CONCLUSION

Love makes us feel a close connection with others and drives us to act for their sake, even at some cost to ourselves, but because the senses are more susceptible to beautiful things than good things, and because we are prone to confuse our attraction to beauty with love of something good, love is also highly fallible (PS, art. 85). Love is particularly bad when combined with other passions such as 'rash desires and badly founded hopes' (AT IV, 614). Nor will love motivate us to act for others we do not 'in volition' join ourselves to. For all these reasons, love cannot be relied upon to lead one to virtue as other more rationally influenced methods can. But we have begun to see a pattern in Descartes' thinking about the place of the passions in the good life. Our knowledge and mastery of ourselves as embodied beings depends crucially on the functions of the imagination and those species of wonder connected with our assessments of ourselves and other persons. This is not the thinking of a hyper-rationalist but of someone sensitive to the fact that our embodiment is important to our identities as individual and socially related persons. Any successful programme for mastering the self must recognise these facts and enlist the sensitive faculties to bring the passions and intellectual faculties into alignment. In the next chapter, we shall see how this programme of self-mastery begins by restraining that most ornery of passions, desire.

CHAPTER 7

Several strange passages on desire and fortune

'Now I know,' she said, 'that other, more serious cause of your sickness: you have forgotten what you are. So I really understand why you are ill and how to cure you. For because you are wandering, forgetful of your real self, you grieve that you are an exile and stripped of your goods; since indeed you do not know the goal and end of all things, you think that evil and wicked men are fortunate and powerful; since indeed you have forgotten what sort of governance the world is guided by, you think these fluctuations of fortune uncontrolled. All these are quite enough to cause not merely sickness but even death. But I thank the author of all health that you have not yet wholly lost your true nature. The best kindler of your health we have is your true opinion of the governance of the world, that you believe it to be subject not to the randomness of chance events but to divine reason: do not be afraid, then, for presently out of this tiny spark your vital warmth will glow again.

(Boethius, *Consolatio*, I. Prose 6)

Recent debates about the nature of rational action have tended to take for their starting point a certain model, referred to as the belief-desire model. On Donald Davidson's account, rational action is behaviour that has conjointly a desire or 'pro-attitude' towards a certain end and a belief about the means to obtaining the end as its significant cause (Davidson, 1963). The model is one self-avowedly indebted to Aristotle's account of the practical syllogism, at least to the extent that it shares the idea that once one has the right conception of the end as good and deliberation about how to obtain the end, nothing more is required for action. The model is fitting for Aristotelians who traditionally struggled to reconcile two intuitions: (1) that human beings belong in the class of self-movers, beings moved by a special kind of internal principle of motion, and (2) that no action is possible in the absence of a previously given external stimulus to motion. The second intuition reflects a constraint on Aristotle's theory of motion, as developed in *Physics* VIII, that everything that is

moved is moved by something else. Since movement is just the actualisation of a potentiality to move, what is moved must be moved by something already in motion, from which it seems to follow that nothing
moves itself. Together these intuitions generate a dilemma for the account
of self-motion, for if every action is dependent upon a stimulus in the
sense of following automatically upon it, nothing can properly be
described as a self-mover, but if action is independent of an external
stimulus, the stimulus cannot be said to be a necessary condition for
action. According to some interpreters of Aristotle, this dilemma is
resolved through the concept of desire, which is the concept of a natural
impulse harnessed by a self-mover in pursuit of its ends (Furley, 1980;
Nussbaum, 1978). The object of desire is the unmoved mover, and what
makes desire a reason for acting (as opposed to a mere stimulus) is that it
is a stimulus towards an object conceived under the aspect of good.
Desire transforms the natural into the normative, and makes it a reason
for acting.[1]

It is not too much of a stretch to suppose that the concept of desire
plays a similar role in modern belief–desire models of action. Desire (or
some pro-attitude) is the impulse that moves the agent to undertake the
means to obtaining some end. But the rationality of a given desire is not
itself usually in question, even when whether one should act upon it or
not is, and for good reason. If desire is part of the explanation of rational
action, it cannot itself be the product of rational action, on pain of regress,
and so in some sense must be given to the agent. But the very passivity of
desire generates a paradox for the view in which desire has the role of
explaining what makes someone a self-mover, and accounting thereby for
the difference between mere behaviour and action. Being determined to
act by something belonging to one's self is not the same as being self-
determining, although exactly what the difference amounts to is obscure.

Descartes' own account of desire belongs within this nexus of concerns
about self-determination. Desire is a morally significant passion because it
is the passion that terminates in action. To be a rationally self-determining
being requires, therefore, the rational control of desire. Desires 'for things

---

[1] Aristotle attempts to explain self-motion by distinguishing within an animal moving and moved
parts. The motion-causing part, the soul, is moving, for there is a straightforward sense in which it
moves as part of the whole which it moves; *Physics* VIII.5, 257b12–22; *De anima*.I.3, 406a30–b8. But it
is better to think of this as necessarily involving an environmental stimulus also, which sets in
motion the intellect or appetite; *Physics* VIII.2. 253a15–18. For a critique of the 'intentionality escape'
from this dilemma, see Freeland, 1994. Freeland prefers a broader teleological approach. On her
reading, animals are self-movers insofar as their motions have final causes.

which do not depend upon us' are, however, natural impulses, and the principal effect of such desires (and other passions) is 'to move and dispose the soul to want the things for which they prepare the body' (PS, art. 40). The will can initiate action but it does so by virtue of the fact that 'each volition is naturally joined to some movement of the (pineal) gland', and so produces its effects through harnessing motions of the animal spirits already in place (PS, art. 44). Moreover, the pleasures common to the soul and the body 'depend entirely upon the passions' (PS, art. 212), suggesting that whatever actions the soul initiates through the body as good for it and the body as a whole, must ultimately be connected with what it perceives as good for this union, and so, with what it desires. In this respect, desires for things that do not depend on us are necessary motivators of action in our embodied state, and in themselves are neither rational nor irrational. It is what one does with such desires, or how they factor into one's rational decision-making, that can be rational or irrational.

The control of desires for things that do not depend upon us is 'the principal utility of morality' (PS, art. 144). But since such desires arise through sense, imagination, the temperament of the body and 'the multitude of accidents', which Princess Elisabeth complains carry a person, however virtuous, to perform actions of which they later repent, such control by the will is inevitably limited and indirect (PS, arts. 45–7). Elisabeth herself is characteristically pessimistic about the control of desire. The very contingency of the future, and our inability to know all the goods about which we are constrained to make choices in this life, in the absence of an 'infinite science', convince Elisabeth of the inevitability of discontent (AT IV, 289). Not surprisingly then, the *Passions* takes seriously the problem of desire. At article 145, Descartes informs us that there are two general remedies for 'vain' desires, desires for outcomes beyond our control that may not, therefore, come to be. The first is generosity, a topic he postpones until the third part, and the second is frequent reflection on divine providence. So that we do not 'desire with passion' things that do not depend upon us, he writes:

[W]e ought often to reflect upon divine providence and consider [*répresenter*] that it is impossible that any thing happens in any fashion other than that which has been determined from all eternity by this providence; so that it is like a fate or an immutable necessity that it is necessary to oppose to fortune to destroy it as a chimera which comes only from an error of our understanding. For we can only desire that which we think in some way possible, and we think possible only the things which do not depend on us inasmuch as we think that they depend upon fortune, that is to say, we judge that they can happen and that similar things have happened in the past. This opinion is founded only on the fact that we do not know all the causes which contribute to each effect; because when a thing we have thought depends upon fortune does not occur, this testifies that some one of the causes which was necessary to produce the thing was absent, and consequently, the thing was absolutely impossible, and no similar thing ever happens, that is to say, for the production of which such a cause was also missing; so that if we had not ignored this previously, we would never have thought the thing possible, nor, consequently, have desired it. (AT XI, 438)

Appealing to providence in a therapeutic mode had a long history prior to Descartes. Reflection on providence was generally thought to have the power of restoring the tranquillity of the soul in the face of its thwarted desires, and indeed, on Stoic accounts, to have the power of freeing us from those very desires themselves. Since, on Descartes' view, to desire some outcome, x, presupposes that x is metaphysically possible, knowing that x is metaphysically impossible because God has not willed it should be enough to kill the passion. Desires are, however, oriented towards the future, a future that is in large measure unpredictable. We typically do not know, therefore, whether a desired outcome is metaphysically possible or not, and thus the most we can say is that a precondition for desiring some outcome, x, is that x is epistemically possible – that is, for all we know, x may come to be if we strive to bring x about. Nor is it the case, given the essential role desire plays in preserving the union, that we can avoid having such desires. Insofar as he recommends against desiring things that do not depend upon us 'with passion', Descartes seems sensitive to these problems while at the same time remaining optimistic of reducing the disturbing effects of vain desires on the soul. But how exactly is embracing the Providential order supposed to enable us to avoid 'desiring with passion' things that do not depend on us? And what would it be to desire such things without passion?

Descartes' answer to these questions is even more puzzling:

But because the greatest part of our desires extend to things which do not depend wholly on us nor wholly on others, we ought precisely to distinguish those of them which depend only on us, so as to extend our desire only to those alone. As for the remainder, we ought yet to estimate the success of them entirely fated and immutable, and so that our desire does not occupy itself with them at all, we ought not to fail to consider the reasons that make them to be hoped for more or less so that these serve to rule our actions. For example, if we have business in some place where we are able to go by two different roads, the one of which is accustomed to be much safer than the other, although the decree of providence could be such that if we go by the road that we think the safer, we shall not avoid being mugged, and, on the contrary, we can pass by the other without any danger, we ought not for that [reason] to be indifferent to choose the one or the other nor to rest on the immutable fatedness of that decree. Reason wishes that we would choose the road which is accustomed to be the safer, and our desire ought to be accomplished concerning that even if, when we have followed it, some evil has occurred to us, because this evil having been from our perspective inevitable, we do not have any ground for expecting to be exempt from it, but only to do the best that our understanding had been able to know how, as I suppose we have done. And it is certain that when one exercises oneself to distinguish fate from fortune, one accustoms oneself easily to rule these desires in such a way that to the extent that their fulfilment depends only on us, they are always able to give us complete satisfaction. (AT XI, 440)

The consolation that this passage offers in the face of thwarted desires is the satisfaction of having acted in accordance with reason. It is the kind of self-satisfaction that comes from exercising our noblest faculties. The acceptance of providence does not, for Descartes, mean abandoning oneself to fate in the sense of not deliberating or making rational choices, for that, the passage implies, is not likely to yield satisfaction. 'Complete satisfaction' depends on ruling desires so that 'their fulfilment depends only on us'. But what could this mean? If all my desires could be restricted to the choice of the best strategy for deciding how to act, which in the above case consists in calculating the probabilities of encountering trouble along the various routes available to me and choosing the one with the lowest probability, then, if I am maximally rational, all my desires would be satisfied. But this is reasoning about means not ends, and it is difficult to see how my desire to be rational could prevent me from also rationally desiring the end (e.g. that I arrive home safely), or prevent me from being disappointed when I instead meet the muggers. Indeed, the desire for the means not only fails to supplant the desire for the end but presupposes it. I will, for example, only have the desire to follow the path reason decrees safest because I desire to get home safely and believe that my best (long-term) strategy is to use my wits to determine the safest route. My desire for this outcome requires for its satisfaction the co-operation of the world and is thus not something that depends just upon my wits.

We cannot do without desires for outcomes that do not depend upon us, not merely for practical reasons but also, therefore, for conceptual reasons. Our desires for certain outcomes are presupposed by our desires for and exercise of our rational decision-making faculties, even if it is only the exercise of these faculties that is the ultimate source of self-satisfaction in the practical sphere. Nor is it possible for us to be indifferent to the outcomes that do not depend upon us, for it is not obvious that one could choose rationally or desire to be rational unless one cared about the outcome. What would be the point, after all, of rationally preferring one strategy over another if not that the one chosen increases the probability of bringing about a certain outcome? All this suggests that it is impossible in this life to avoid desiring outcomes that do not depend on us and the inevitability that some of our desires will end up being in vain. Without the 'infinite science' of which Elisabeth speaks or knowledge of God's ends (AT VII, 55), it is hard to see how complete satisfaction of all our desires is possible.

Embracing providence is a matter of accepting whatever happens as being for the best, but that is distinct from claiming that complete satisfaction of all our desires is possible.[2] I may have a general desire that things turn out for the best, believe that whatever happens is the best insofar as it is willed by God, and still have quite specific desires, like the desire to get home safely, which remain unsatisfied because the outcome was not willed by God. It is also one thing to claim that we shouldn't get so upset about the fact that things don't turn out as we had hoped, because what we had hoped for was, as it turns out, neither possible nor for the best, and another to claim that things always turn out as we hope because God is at the helm. The latter stretches credulity in a way the former doesn't.

I shall argue for a more plausible reading of these passages regarding desire, one in which the 'complete satisfaction' of which Descartes speaks and which he thinks is tied to abandoning certain metaphysical presuppositions about the contingency of the future, has less to do directly with the satisfaction of all our desires than with the control of the various species of sadness (regret, repentance and remorse) that are consequent upon our disappointed desires. The discussion of providence and its connection with desire from articles 144–6 is complicated, and to understand it more fully, we need to know what, for Descartes, God's governance of the world entails. We also need to know how embracing providence is supposed to affect us psychologically for the better. These are not easy questions to answer on Descartes' behalf, perhaps even

---

[2] What helps us control our desires is not merely the belief in providence but also the natural tendency towards community with and love of God.

One is naturally led to have this [thought] when one knows and loves God as is necessary: for then abandoning oneself wholly to His will, one strips oneself of one's own interests, and has no other passion than to do what one believes to be agreeable to [God]. (To Elizabeth, 15 September 1645, AT IV, 294; see also AT VII, 432 and AT XI, 477.)

impossible questions to answer, and I am likely here only to make a start. But the exercise is worth undertaking for the discussion of desire brings us to the heart of what it is, on Descartes' understanding, to be a self-determining embodied being, and what human happiness consists in. The place to begin this examination is thus with the traditional notion of providence and Descartes' place in that tradition.

FATE AND FORTUNE IN THE TRADITION

> Fame, honor, beauty, state, train, blood and birth,
> Are but the fading blossomes of the earth.
> (*Farewel, ye gilded follies.* Attributed to John Donne; Grierson, 1933/77: 396)

Fortuna, the ghostly Lady Philosophy advises Boethius, is nothing but a 'fleeting goddess' and a sure sign of misery to come (*Consolatio*, II. Prose I). The rejection of fortune or luck as a necessary condition for virtue and the good life had a long history prior to Descartes and represented something of a trend against the powerful figure of Aristotle. Those who rejected the existence of fortune could not wholly embrace Aristotle's eudaemonistic ethics, in which happiness, the exercise of virtue in a complete life, depended upon some degree of good fortune. During the Renaissance, the debate over the connection between virtue and fortune resurfaced, principally through the work of Roman historians, Tacitus and Livy, who granted fortune a role in the good life and fed some of these ideas into Renaissance intellectual life. A more sinister champion of fortune during the Renaissance was Machiavelli, whose conception of *virtù* was premised upon the inescapability of fortune, and whom Descartes regarded as having derived bad laws from hard cases.[3] By contrast, Christian philosophers tended, albeit controversially, to reinforce the Platonic view that goodness does not depend upon external circumstances. The controversial aspect of this stance stemmed from the fact that the ultimate good for Christians – union with God – was something that depended upon grace, which is a free gift and not something we can guarantee for ourselves. One way around this difficulty was to distinguish between the 'good for us' and the 'good for us in this life,' and to claim that the attainment of the latter depends only upon us. Showing that fortune is nothing but a 'chimaera'

---

[3] See Descartes' letter to Elizabeth, September 1646 (AT IV, 486–93) and her reply of 10 October 1646 (AT IV, 519–24). This topic is more fully discussed in the next chapter.

was one strategy for securing a rational foundation for the good in this life and the strategy chosen by Descartes and many of his predecessors.

There were essentially two strands of thought leading to the rejection of fortune, those involving arguments from fate and those relying on arguments from providence. Susanne Bobzien argues that from the second century AD onwards, these two originally independent lines of thought tended to converge (Bobzien, 1998: 5). For Chrysippus, the Stoic, fate – 'the Reason in accordance with which past events have happened, present events happen, and future events will happen' – and the notion of universal determinism were co-ordinate notions.[4] The antecedent causes of an action necessitate one and only one subsequent outcome for the world at any point in time. The notion of providence, meanwhile, subsumes two ideas: the idea that everything that happens does so of necessity, and the idea that everything happens for the best because it is part of a divine plan. The conflation of fate and providence enjoyed a natural fit in Stoic theories, which often identified fate with Zeus, and in Christian thought, where fate was simply one side of the equation according to which the natural world is necessarily structured according to God's will, the other side being that whatever God wills is good. Calcidius notes, however, in his commentary on Plato's *Timaeus*, that the conflation of fate and providence was not universally agreed upon: 'others, like Cleanthes, while holding the dictates of providence to come about also by fate, allow things which come about by fate not to be the product of providence' (quoted in Bobzien, 1998: 46).

Calcidius also notes that some, like Plato, retain a sphere of activity not governed by fate or providence in which we can speak of events as occurring by chance or fortune: 'things belonging to our own free choice [*liberum arbitrium*] and [under] our authority [*ius*] happen at our initiative [*sponte nostra*]; things outside our influence happening without a purpose [*sine ratione*] and unexpectedly [*inopinate*] are said to happen fortuitously when they began in our arrangement of matters and by chance when without our arranging' (Calcidius, 1963: 204–5). The distinction between chance and fortuitous events is the distinction between the confluence of events that occur as the result of events not involving deliberation and the confluence of events involving deliberation. 'Fortuitous,' as Suárez observes, 'is said especially in human affairs' or with respect to actions done from reason and intention.[5] Whereas it seems

---

[4] Bobzien, 1998: 57; see also pp. 31ff.
[5] Suárez, 1965: XIX. section XII.2. 744b.

appropriate to say that it was purely a matter of chance that lightning struck when the clock chimed, it seems more appropriate to say that two acquaintances encountering one another at the market was fortuitous rather than a matter of chance, since each had a reason for being where they were at the time in question. For Calcidius (or Calcidius' Plato), some realm of activity that is exempt from determination by efficient causes was also thought necessary in order to account for the actions of free agents.[6]

In line with this movement rejecting the existence of fortune, Boethius notes that there is an ambiguity in the notion of necessity – necessity relative to one's knowledge and necessity relative to the natures of things. Although it follows neither from the nature of human beings nor from our knowledge of human affairs that two individuals should meet in a certain place at a certain time, from God's point of view, their meeting is as necessary as if it had been a consequence of their nature (*Consolatio*, v. Prose 6, 27–33). In the classical example, the master knows that the two servants will meet, but what makes their meeting fated is neither this knowledge nor their natures, but the master's willing it. Although the event is contingent upon the master's act of will, his willing it makes it as unavoidable as if it were of natural necessity. On this picture, chance or accidental events are nothing but the way things appear to us because we do not know all the causes God has put in place.

The notions of fate and providence posed obvious obstacles to preserving a realm for human freedom, and the most common response among philosophers opposed to Fortune was compatibilism, according to which free acts are events with special kinds of efficient causes within the soul, *voluntates,* or a process of deliberation and choice. The concept of 'that which depends on us', which looms large in Descartes' account of desire, can be traced back to debates among the Stoics concerning the extent to which determinism is compatible with voluntary action and moral appraisal. Bobzien notes that some Stoics (e.g. Chrysippus) did not treat actions that depend on us as relying on a principle of alternative possibilities – that we could have chosen or acted otherwise – but simply as events which have among their causes an act of assent, which depends upon us not in

---

[6] Sorabji (1980: ch.1, especially, p. 18) notes that while Aristotle (e.g. *Metaphysics*, vi 3: 1027a29–1027b14) recognises the need for a category of chance or coincidental events, events which are not strictly speaking caused, he is not concerned in these discussions with preserving freedom of action and moral responsibility.

the sense of being undetermined, but in the sense of being caused by the rational soul (Bobzien, 1998: 281–3). (As in Diogenes' report of the view, the dog can be pulled along by the chariot or run ahead, but either way it's going to go.) According to Calvin Normore, a free act for Boethius is one that results from a process of deliberation about means, which is an internal causal process and unless interfered with (typically by a passion) concludes in an action. The more an action issues from a process of rational deliberation, the more free it is (*Consolatio*, v. Prose 2, 390; Normore, 2002: 32). But the fact that a free act is the outcome of an internal causal process (deliberation) or known in advance by God, does not make it necessitated in the sense of necessity according to our nature.[7]

A common form of compatibilism in the debates about free will and fate in the Stoic and medieval periods was thus to argue that a free action is one which has a certain kind of cause, a *voluntas* or judgement or process of deliberation, and whether this involved being able to do or choose otherwise or amounted to nothing more than freedom from external constraints or interference were separate and open questions. Whether freedom is restricted to deliberation and choice among means to one's happiness or extends to ends was also a matter of some debate. Whereas Aquinas argues that the will is not free to not will the good, happiness, but can only choose among means (just or unjust) to obtaining the good, Scotus, in line with what Normore refers to as the 'two wills' tradition originating in Anselm of Canterbury, argues that the will must also choose among the potentially incommensurate ends of justice and happiness.[8] Others argue that what is definitive of the will is its power to choose in the absence of a 'sufficient reason'. Al-Ghazali, for example, held that the will has the power to simply pick, and it is precisely in willing one thing over an equally compelling alternative that the will demonstrates its absolute freedom (Normore, 1998).

Descartes' own position with regard to determinism and free will is nothing short of obscure. On the one hand, human beings enjoy a liberty of indifference (albeit 'the lowest degree of freedom'), through which the will may always withhold assent, even in the perverse case in which it withholds assent to a clear and distinct idea (though probably only by

---

[7] Boethius, *Consolatio.* v. Prose 6. With respect to God's foreknowledge, we may thus say that from God's knowing that x will occur, it is necessary that x will occur, but not that x is necessary. Compare: from seeing that Tom is walking, it follows necessarily that Tom is walking, but Tom's walking is not necessary.

[8] Aquinas, 1968: I-II. x. 2; Scotus, *Ordinatio* III. For discussion, see Normore 2002; Boler, 2002; Kent, 1995 and Alanen, 2002.

distracting the soul before it assents) (AT IV, 173–4). On the other hand, Descartes seems, in the following passage, to subscribe to the necessitation of everything, including thoughts, by God's will. When Elisabeth suggests that the evil caused by the free will of others is beyond the reach of providence, Descartes responds:

All the reasons which prove the existence of God, and that he is the first and immutable cause of all the effects which do not depend upon the free will of human beings, likewise prove in the same manner that he is also the cause of all those that depend upon it. For we can demonstrate that he exists only by considering him as a sovereignly perfect being; and he would not be sovereignly perfect if something could occur in the world that did not come entirely from him. It is true that it is only faith which teaches us about the grace by which God elevates us to a supernatural blessedness; but Philosophy alone suffices for the knowledge that the least thought cannot enter the mind of man if God has not wished and willed from all eternity that it enter therein. (AT IV, 314)[9]

Reconciling the absolute freedom of the human will with the determination by the divine will is no small matter. One possible interpretation of Descartes' reply to Elisabeth is that he is not accepting God's antecedent willing of all human actions and choices, but only His consequent willing – that is, God's concurrence in what we (antecedently) will. It is undeniable, however, that the last line of the above passage suggests a stronger reading: that whatever happens (including all our volitions and all other thoughts) is determined 'from all eternity' by God. Yet, the very existence of the category of things that depend on us alone, which comes up in the discussion of desire, suggests a realm of human freedom free from external determination. A more likely possibility is that Descartes is toying with a Stoic position: although he does not endorse the principle of alternative possibilities for either actions or volitions, what makes an act free is that it is caused by an act of assent, which, by the very fact that it originates in the soul, depends at least that much upon it. Since God's causal role extends to acts of assent as well, this is not a very satisfactory solution, but it has the comfort of familiarity. The important distinction

---

[9] Here Descartes is responding to Elisabeth's letter of 30 September 1645, in which she objects to his advice that the 'first and principal' truth to bear in mind in order to judge well is the existence of God. She argues that while she is consoled by the knowledge of God in regard to 'evils that come to us in the ordinary course of nature and from the order which is established', she is not so easily consoled in regard to 'those imposed on us by human beings, whose wills appear to us entirely free, for it is only faith that can persuade us that God takes care to regulate wills, and that he has determined the fortune of each person before the creation of the world' (AT IV, 302). Descartes rejects the libertarian streak in Elisabeth's objection.

for Descartes' account of human happiness is the distinction between those acts that depend on the soul in the sense of originating within the soul and those acts or behaviours produced by a stimulus originating outside the soul. We shall have to see whether this distinction is adequate to the task he assigns the idea of providence in preventing us from desiring things in vain, and securing the kind of self-satisfaction he deems central not only to human contentment but to virtue itself.

WHEREIN PASSIONS ARE DEFECTIVE

In the second part of the *Passions,* from article 137 to article 148, Descartes gives an overview of the uses of the passions insofar as they pertain to the body and to the soul and to the union. Their natural use in the union is to incite the soul to consent and contribute to actions that preserve and perfect the body (PS, art. 137). Sadness and joy are the first two passions because the soul is first informed of things useful to the body through pleasure, and of things harming it through pain. At article 138, the defects of the passions with respect to the body are connected with misleading effects of associated pains and pleasures: some things are harmful to the body but cause no sadness, and some things are useful which distress it. The discussion from 137 to 148, which relates principally to the passion of desire, constitutes the first of Descartes' reason-dominant remedies for controlling the passions.

Until article 143, Descartes is working with two standards of correctness for the passions: utility and truth. Questions concerning the utility of the passions are divided according to whether a passion is useful for the soul or useful for the body. The truth or falsity of a passion is connected with what it signifies. Because the passions 'almost always make as much the goods as the evils they represent seem much greater and more important than they are' it is necessary 'to use experience and reason in order to distinguish good from evil and know their true value' (PS, art. 138; AT XI, 431). The two criteria generally produce divergent results: a false passion may, in some circumstances, be more useful than a true passion. Because we cannot avoid the risk of being mistaken, inclining towards passions that have good as their object (e.g. love and joy) even when false is better for the soul than inclining towards those which have evil as their object (hatred and sadness). Hatred separates the soul from the good in each thing as much as from its evil (PS, arts. 140; 142). With respect to the body, love and joy are more conducive to health but sadness and hatred more conducive to survival. Unless accompanied by sadness or strong desire, joy and love promote circulation of the blood and digestion, whereas hatred and sadness constrict the flow of alimentary juices, which affects the digestive organs and diminishes the fuel needed to maintain the heat of the heart (PS, arts. 97, 98, 102, 103, 108). In terms of the preservation of the body, however, hatred and sadness are more important because it is better to avoid harmful things than to obtain goods one can live without (PS, art. 137).

At article 143 Descartes applies these considerations to the passion of desire and it is here where the two standards of correctness, truth and utility, converge. All 'false' passions that terminate in desire are harmful.

And it is necessary precisely to note that what I say now about these four passions [joy, sadness, love and hate] holds only when they are considered precisely in themselves and do not carry us to any action. For in as much as they excite desire in us by the intermediary of which they rule our mores, it is certain that all those of which the cause is false can harm and that, on the contrary, all those of which the cause is appropriate (*juste*) can help, and even that apart from being equally badly founded, joy is ordinarily more harmful that sadness because by producing restraint and fear, [sadness] disposes us in a certain way to prudence in the same measure as the other [joy] renders those who abandon themselves to it rash and temerarious. (PS, art. 143; AT XI, 435–6)

Desire is singled out for special treatment partly because of its volatility (PS, art. 101), especially when arising from attraction (*agréement*) or repulsion (*horreur*) (PS, art. 90), and partly because desire acts directly upon the will to act (PS, arts. 47; 143). Desire is 'an agitation of the soul caused by the spirits, which disposes the soul to want for the future the things it represents to itself as agreeable' (PS, art. 86; AT XI, 392). Although all desires are future-oriented, some are directed towards the preservation of goods already possessed or the absence of present evils (PS, art. 86). Descartes rejects the traditional idea that the opposite of desire is aversion, on the grounds that the pursuit of good and avoidance of evil are two aspects of every action. Pursuing wealth is tantamount to avoiding poverty, and can be explained through one and the same desire (PS, arts. 87; 89). This is important to the role he assigns regret and repentance in decision-making, for the desire for happiness is one and the same thing as the desire to avoid that which principally militates against happiness, regret and repentance. The utility of desire consists in its making the body more mobile and agile, preparing it to perform the action required to obtain some good or avoid some evil, keeping the sense organs attentive to the task, and bolstering the will (PS, arts. 106; 111). But because desires are so often false and then always harmful, control of desire is paramount to rational self-mastery.

Controlling our desires is part of seeking virtue, because without knowledge of the goodness of what depends on us, our virtuous desires cannot exist, and without the latter, we cannot be virtuous. The first task of moral philosophy is thus to 'free the spirit' from vain desires, a sentiment which echoes the third maxim of the *morale par provision* of the *Discourse*. I must aim to 'conquer myself rather than fortune, and to change my desires rather than the order of the world' (AT VI, 25).

DESIRE, REGRET AND PROVIDENCE

What makes us think that our desires for things that do not depend on us are legitimate is the false metaphysical presupposition that the desired outcomes are always at least possible, even if they fail to come to be. But is the relevant sense of possibility required for desire metaphysical, as Descartes believes, or merely epistemic? If, for all we know, a certain outcome is possible, and if the outcome would be good for the union, doesn't it makes sense to strive to bring it about? True, what we desire may not come about, but so what? It seems just plain silly to think that we can or should eradicate all desires for outcomes that do not depend entirely on us.

The principal obstacle to happiness on Descartes' view is not the existence of vain desires per se, however, but the regret, repentance or remorse that so often accompanies their being thwarted. 'For it is nothing but desire, and regret or repentance, that is able to prevent us from being content' (letter to Elisabeth, 4 August 1645; AT IV, 266; see also 284; 288). This is a theme not only of the *Passions* but also of the *Discourse on Method*, where the point of following merely probable opinions is proposed as the only way to free oneself 'from all the regrets and remorse that customarily agitate consciences' (AT VI, 25). In contrast with desire, regret and its ilk are mediated more directly by intellectual thoughts, particularly thoughts about what would have happened had one acted or chosen otherwise, and thus are more directly targets for moral therapy utilising the idea of providence.

On the reading advanced here, reflection on providence is a remedy for vain desires not because it enables us to extirpate such desires, but because it undermines the conceptual foundations for regret, repentance and remorse – passions that are direct responses to unfulfilled desires and the source of our greatest discontent. Regret is for goods lost (PS art. 209), repentance is for one's own mistaken past actions (PS art. 191) and remorse is for past actions performed while irresolute about the goodness of one's actions (PS arts. 60; 177). These are passions opposed to the kind of self-satisfaction Descartes regards as crucial to our happiness. The satisfaction we receive when we are robbed despite having chosen our routes carefully is not the satisfaction of all our desires principally but the satisfaction of having nothing to regret because we have acted from reason and a firm disposition of the will. If we regret our actions and choices or the goods we have lost, we presuppose that we could have acted or chosen otherwise to produce a better outcome, whereas, metaphysically speaking, neither an alternative action nor a better outcome was possible (this is the best of all possible worlds). Morally speaking, one has nothing to regret, for if one has applied one's rational faculties in the best way possible and acted resolutely, there is nothing more or else one could or ought to have done. Not getting exactly what you want is compatible with not wanting that things had turned out as you had wanted, and is compatible, therefore, with having no occasion for regret.

As Descartes writes to Elisabeth, 'there is no person who does not desire to become happy; but many do not know the means' (to Elisabeth, 1 September 1645; AT IV, 282). The end, happiness, is a given for human beings and the question then is: what can we do to maximise our happiness in the face of uncertainty about the future? To maximise our happiness requires choosing actions that hold the greatest promise not of maximising our good fortune (for that we cannot control), but rather of minimising regret, repentance and remorse. In this regard, Descartes shares with modern decision theorists who advocate principles for reducing or avoiding regret, the intuition that regret is a serious opportunity cost, and one that can be diminished by the knowledge that even though one did not obtain exactly what one wanted, a worse outcome (one in which one's regrets are higher) is imaginable (Savage, 1954; Loomes and Sugden, 1982; Acker, 1997). This may be as far as the similarities go – the cases Descartes considers are often too simple or under-described to yield interesting differences between regret rules and classical decision rules – but it is interesting, nonetheless, that he should target the minimisation of regret as a central goal of rational decision-making. (A comparison of these decision-making strategies and analysis of one of Descartes' cases as an application of a regret strategy is provided in the postscript to this chapter, which can be safely ignored if not of interest.)

There are two kinds of decision-making situations implicit in Descartes' examples, ones where the agent has information about the objective probabilities of various outcomes, and ones where the agent is in total ignorance of the probabilities. Of the first kind of situation, our inability to know God's ends does not rule out the possibility of making predictions about the likelihood of certain outcomes and letting such predictions influence our decisions. Because there is a rational plan to the universe, it is possible to exploit the immutable necessity of events to estimate the probability of future outcomes. This is evident in the passage at AT XI, 440 where we are advised to choose the route that reason decrees to be usually the safest, and in Descartes' remark to Elizabeth (of May 1646) that one should 'trust to divine providence *and allow oneself to be driven by it*' (AT IV, 415; my emphasis).[10] Abandoning oneself to God's plan is not abandoning oneself to fate by choosing randomly or not choosing at all, but involves using all one's faculties to try to determine from past patterns of events what the chances of various outcomes are. When, despite our best efforts, we get it wrong, we have the consolation of having reasoned well. A worse outcome is one in which things go badly and we haven't reasoned well, for in such a situation there is nothing from which to derive any self-satisfaction.

When we desire what God decrees in this fashion we find the highest form of satisfaction. But given our limited knowledge and the inevitability of error, this strategy is not guaranteed to ensure that we won't end up vainly desiring things that have not been willed by God. In cases where we are deciding under conditions of total ignorance, Descartes advises that acting resolutely is required to avoid regret, repentance and remorse. Irresolution is a vice (PS, arts. 170; 177). Acting resolutely is itself a source of self-satisfaction even in situations where we are unlikely to obtain what we desire.

The importance of resolution is demonstrated in the notorious example of the Prince, who has to choose between persevering with a course of action that could cause great harm, and not persevering and thereby risking the evil of being perceived as irresolute (AT IV, 490). Irresolution is, Descartes suggests, a greater cause for concern, 'for such harms (caused by persevering) can hardly be as great as the reputation of being irresolute and inconstant' (AT IV, 490). Descartes is not arguing that it would never make sense to change one's mind in light of new information, but in the absence of adequate information that would alter one's decision, the best

[10] More formalised methods for utilising probabilities in decision-making would not emerge until shortly after Descartes' death in the correspondence between Pascal and Fermat in 1654, and in the infamous 'wager' (Pascal, 1958).

course of action having made a decision is to stick with it. The explanation depends on certain empirical assumptions that Descartes' readers then might have been more inclined to share than they would now, for example, that stability of office depends on being resolute (rather than merely appearing so) and that it is more important to preserve stability than avoid the harms caused by irresolution.[11] Only by making firm decisions and acting resolutely, Descartes writes, may we avoid the regrets and remorse of 'those weak and faltering spirits who allow themselves to go about inconstantly engaging in things they judge afterwards to be bad' (AT VI, 25).

Whether Descartes is right about the connection between irresolution and regret or remorse is, however, beside the point. It is interesting that he was looking for some form of compensation – a measure of self-satisfaction and a way of reducing regret – for when things go badly. This reading has the advantage that we do not need to attribute to Descartes the implausible idea that reflection on providence enables us to derive complete satisfaction from all our desires or to render them all as desires that depend solely upon us. The only idea we need attribute to him is the idea that it is possible to derive complete satisfaction from all our actions, provided we reason as best we can and act resolutely, for then we have no reason for regret, repentance or remorse. Because we always have available a form of compensation in the satisfaction we derive from our practical reasoning, mastering desire turns out to be a matter of mastering those passions that obstruct our happiness when our desires are thwarted. But now it looks as if we have another problem. Can one fully embrace providence and take seriously this prescription to use reason well and act resolutely? If it is never the case that I could have chosen or acted otherwise, is there ever a situation in which regret, repentance and remorse are appropriate?[12]

---

[11] On the moral and political disorder of the late sixteenth and early seventeenth century which made stability at the cost of justice appealing to some authors, see Copenhaver and Schmitt, 1992: ch.4. The issue was, however, controversial. Erasmus argued strongly against forgoing justice, even when this requires changing one's position in such a way that might lead to the loss of power or the collapse of one's realm (Copenhaver and Schmitt, 1992: 272–3). Whether one would regret one's irresolution if one got away with it, so to speak, is not obvious and suggests that it is not irresolution per se that is the cause of regret. More often than not, political leaders demonstrate more attachment to the appearance of resolution than to the substance of it, and too few regrets about mistaken decisions and actions.

[12] Whether one thinks of them as rational or not, regret, repentance and remorse have a useful educative function. Spinoza treats repentance as a vice for 'he who repents of an action is twice as unhappy or as weak as before', but this is compatible with their having instrumental value in one's moral development (1982: IV. Prop.56.).

In the *Discourse,* Descartes makes the enigmatic remark that to render one's desires for things which depend upon oneself in this fashion is to make 'a virtue of necessity' (AT VI, 26). What room is there for virtue, we might ask, when everything, right down to our acts of assent, is governed by an immutable necessity? Is the self-satisfaction which comes from having nothing to regret, the key to my preserving my happiness in the face of my thwarted desires, based only on an illusion that I am in control of what I assent to, how I reason and whether I act resolutely or not? Without a clear solution to the problem of how to reconcile human freedom with Descartes' strong conception of providence, there is no obvious way to answer these questions. What is clear, however, is that were this problem to somehow go away, what would be left would be an interesting analysis of how human satisfaction and self-determination is possible, despite the fact that we are, in this embodied state, compelled to desire things that it is beyond our control always to bring about.

POSTSCRIPT: A RUDIMENTARY DECISION THEORY

Contemporary decision theories seek to define principles by which agents may rationally choose from a range of 'live options' an action that is optimal. To represent different theories theorists usually begin with a payoff matrix. A payoff matrix is a way of representing the utility of each action under consideration across a range of different possible states of the world. Once a matrix has been constructed, which action is optimal depends on the specific decision rule being applied. When the chances of particular outcomes cannot be estimated, the two most studied classical rules are 'maximax' and 'maximin'. 'Maximax', a rule which advocates maximising one's gains or the gambler's strategy, instructs the agent to choose the action from the matrix that promises the highest payoff (a_1 in fig. 7.1). Maximin instructs the agent to choose the action with the highest minimum payoff (a_3 in fig. 7.1). Regret principles differ from rules such as Maximax and Maximin in ways which can perhaps best be seen by considering not a standard payoff matrix but a regret matrix that measures the regret associated with each action in each state (fig.7.2). The regret associated with an action x in state S is calculated as the difference between the highest payoff of any other action represented in a given S column in the standard payoff matrix and the payoff for x in S (Acker, 1997: 208). So if x has the highest payoff, for example, 20 utiles in a state, S, the amount of regret

	S_1	S_2	S_3
a_1	20	0	4
a_2	4	15	1
a_3	2	14	12

Figure 7.1. A payoff matrix (Acker 1997, 209)

	S_1	S_2	S_3
a_1	0	15	8
a_2	16	0	11
a_3	18	1	0

Figure 7.2. A regret matrix

for x in S is zero, whereas if x has a payoff of 3 in S, and some other action, y, has a payoff of 20, the regret associated with x in S is 17.

A range of regret principles mirroring non-regret-based decision rules may then be formulated. L. J. Savage's original regret principle was a kind of *maximin regret* rule, which instructs the agent to choose the action with the lowest maximum regret (a_1 in fig. 7.2.) But other principles, which are variations on the regret principle, would recommend different choices. For example, a lowest average regret rule instructs an agent to choose the action with the least amount of associated regret on average (a_3). Such a rule may help deflect one serious objection to the maximin regret rule, namely that it considers only the outcomes and only the extremal values of the outcomes (Cohen and Jaffray, 1980; Acker, 1997: 210). Choosing the action that promises the lowest maximum regret is not optimal if it also promises a greater amount of regret on average than some other action.

There are also different ways of constructing the regret matrix that may avoid the problem of considering only the extremal values of the outcomes. Mary Acker has argued for a 'tempered regret' rule that considers the fact that some actions can be the cause for both regret and relief, and may therefore have the edge over those that promise the lowest maximum regret or lowest average regret. Under this proposal, an individual compares each outcome to both extremes 'and considers the sum of the gains and losses under all possible states of the world' (Acker, 1997: 210). The tempered regret (*Tr*) associated with each action is the difference between the best conditional outcome (Xmax) in a given state minus the payoff (X) of an action, and the payoff (X) minus the worst conditional outcome (Xmin) or:

$$Tr = (Xmax - X) - (X - Xmin)$$

The amount of tempered regret associated with an action represents a difference between differences and thus reflects the intuition that one's regret can be minimised by reflection on the fact that although one didn't achieve the best outcome, one didn't achieve the worst either. Applying the tempered regret rule is then simply a matter of choosing the action with the lowest maximum tempered regret. On this matrix (fig. 7.3), the tempered regret rule recommends the agent choose action a_2, which no other rule under consideration recommends (Acker 1997, 210).[13]

It is not easy to map Descartes' cases into this contemporary discussion about regrets. The belief that non-actual outcomes are not metaphysically possible (even if they are epistemically possible) is not a feature of modern decision theories, and it is difficult to imagine that one's reasoning wouldn't be affected by such a belief. But that aside, if Descartes' reasoning is based on the intuition that regret is a significant cost, there should be cases where applying a regret rule recommends different actions from applying a classical rule.

---

[13] Scepticism about the role regret plays in decision-making is a feature of a debate spanning both philosophy and the social sciences. For recent philosophical criticism and discussion of the rationality of regret see Bittner, 1992 and Hurka, 1996. The idea that negative emotions like regret and repentance only make a bad situation worse is reflected in the criticism that in being attached to past actions regret and its ilk are sunk costs, whereas only incremental costs and benefits should affect decisions. Foes often cite, for example, irrational decisions made on the basis of anticipated regret such as consumer preferences for more expensive brand names over less expensive, generic brands (Landman, 1993; Arkes and Blumer, 1985; Simonson, 1992). Allies, more often found in the social sciences than in philosophy, respond with the argument that from an empirical point of view, the influence of anticipated regret on individual decisions, particularly in the economic sphere, does not produce irrational decisions on the whole. Some psychologists and economists argue, for example, that it can be both rational and functional to factor past and anticipated regrets into one's choices, particularly where doing so affords learning from past mistakes – e.g. making investment decisions which are neither too risky nor too conservative, and engaging in various kinds of self-protective behaviours (Zeelenberg, 1999; Zeelenberg *et al.*, 1998; Richard, *et al.* 1996).

	S_1	S_2	S_3
a_1	−18	15	5
a_2	14	−15	11
a_3	18	−13	−11

Figure 7.3. A tempered regret matrix (Acker 1997, 211)

Consider the following (modified) case from part three of the *Discourse*, where Descartes argues for the virtue of acting resolutely despite having only doubtful opinions, and uses the analogy of the *voyageurs* lost in the forest (AT VI, 24–5).

My second maxim is to be as firm and as resolute in my actions as I am able, and to not hold any less constantly the most doubtful opinions, when I am once fixed on them, than if they had been the most certain. Imitating in this the *voyageurs* who, in finding themselves lost in some forest, ought not to wander around and around as much this way or that, nor yet even less to stay in one place, but rather to walk always as straight as they are able in the same direction, and not to alter course for weak reasons even though it has perhaps been only chance which has determined their choice at the beginning: for by this means, if they do not go exactly where they desire, they will arrive at least somewhere at the end where probably they would likely be better off than in the middle of the forest . . . And this would be capable of delivering me from all the repentances and remorse which customarily agitate the consciences of those weak and faltering spirits who allow themselves to go inconstantly to carry out as good the things that they judge afterwards to be bad. (AT VI, 24–5)

Let us suppose that we have to choose between the following three courses of action: (a₁) staying put, (a₂) picking a direction and walking resolutely in a straight line and (a₃) walking off but reconsidering one's direction every few hundred yards or so. The last of these three is intended to reflect the option of 'wandering this way or that', the irresolute action. Suppose also that you know that the forest is long in one direction, (not an unreasonable assumption generally), but not which direction that is. Descartes prescribes action, (a₂), but that action carries the risk that if you happen to choose the direction in which the forest extends the most, you could end up lost for a long period of time. Suppose that having picked a₂ you are still lost at the end of the day. Descartes seems to suggest that even

	S_1	S_2	S_3
a_1	20	1	0
a_2	16	12	4
a_3	8	8	5

Figure 7.4. A payoff matrix for the lost *voyageur*

this is better than having stayed put in the middle of the forest. In what way, exactly, would you be better off?

Acting resolutely seems to have for Descartes both a practical value (one is more likely to achieve one's goals this way) and a personal payoff (even if one doesn't achieve one's goals, one still has the satisfaction of having acted resolutely.) Let us build these assumptions into our analysis of the case of the lost *voyageurs*. Suppose that walking in a straight line is difficult – it requires hacking through thick undergrowth – and the third option, letting fortune guide your steps without making firm decisions about which direction to take, amounts to following the easiest route, but is more taxing than staying put. Suppose that you have no information about whether a rescue party will be looking for you but believe it is possible. You might then start by considering the two options that either the rescuers know your location or they don't. And then there is the third option that there are no rescuers.

Consider now the following outcomes: S_1, a rescue party goes to your starting point, A; S_2, a rescue party looks somewhere other than in the vicinity of A; and S_3, there is no rescue party looking for you. In S_3, the only chance of getting out of the forest is by walking out. A payoff matrix for such a case may look like the one above (fig. 7.4).

In S_1, a_1 has the highest utility, because no work is done and one gets rescued. a_1 has a minimal payoff in S_2, let us suppose, because you might reason that the rescuers could eventually find you, and no payoff in S_3, because in this scenario only leaving A offers any hope of getting out of the forest. a_2 has a fairly high payoff in S_1, because even though the rescuers go to A, and you have to do the hard work, you have the chance of intersecting the rescuers, and if that fails, you can always leave signs, carved arrows or marks in the dirt indicating the direction you are travelling. a_2 has not as high a payoff in S_2, because there is a much reduced chance that the rescuers will be in any place that you have been, but you can still leave signs, your direction is clear and there is always the possibility that you make it out on your own. a_2 has a minimal payoff in S_3, where nothing you do enhances the possibility of rescue and where you have to work hard, but you still might get out on your own and you have the satisfaction of acting resolutely. The payoff is tempered by the fact that if you choose the direction in which the forest is longest, you will be worse off perhaps than if you had changed your direction along the way. a_3 has a payoff of 8 utiles in S_1, let us suppose, because even though you leave A, you might intersect the rescuers and perhaps you increase your chances of intersecting the rescuers by meandering about in several directions, but there is no point in leaving signs marking your direction since it constantly changes. a_3 has the same payoff in S_2, for similar reasons. You might encounter the rescuers, and in both S_1 and S_2, you might stumble out on your own. a_3 has a slightly reduced payoff in S_3, where the only hope is that you get out on your own, where you do not have to work too hard and where, by changing your direction every so often you do not lock yourself into a direction that may prove to be the longest part of the forest, but where doing so may also lead to a lot of unnecessary meandering.

When we do the calculations from this matrix, we get the following results. Maximax instructs the agent to choose a_1, the action with the highest payoff overall, and maximin, a_3, because it has the highest minimum payoff. Savage's original regret strategy and Acker's tempered regret strategy instruct the agent to choose a_2, Descartes' preferred option. Intuitively, regret strategies give us the action Descartes wants us to choose because they build into the decision-making process the recognition that even if one doesn't get exactly what one wants, the occasion can still be one for a fair amount of self-satisfaction, provided one is able to compare the outcome with others in which one is worse off or unable to draw as much self-satisfaction from one's action. In the event that the *voyageur* is neither rescued nor finds his own way out, he will have fewer regrets if he has chosen the straight route and acted resolutely, than if he chooses an option where this form of compensation is unavailable.

CHAPTER 8

Generosity breeds content: self-mastery through self-esteem

Have we, in this, lost more than a mere word? Is there also some quality so far faded from our world and our literature that we find it hard to recognize in the writings of men long dead, so that when they would speak to us over the abysm of time we cannot clearly hear what they are saying?

(Margaret Greaves on the passing of 'magnanimity'
(Greaves, 1964: 14)

Managing our desires and regrets through reflection on providence and the illusory *fortuna* takes us only so far towards the rational self-mastery Descartes deems necessary for attaining the good in this life. It assists us in maintaining our equilibrium when things don't turn out as we had hoped, but it cannot prevent our being affected by things that induce in us the wrong kinds of desires or other kinds of unruly passions. Nor do we through this process move beyond the realm of self-regarding desires to become definitively moral beings. A stronger medicine is required to overcome these defects – *générosité* – which is first a passion of the soul and then, through habituation, a virtue as well. Since *générosité* is both the key to all the other virtues and a general remedy for all defects of the passions, it is an essential component of emotional health and moral development (PS, art. 161). It is the final fruit to be picked from the Cartesian tree of knowledge, an ethical notion combining the supreme power of the will with a passionate disposition to use it well.

The discussion of *générosité* signals a retreat from earlier ideals and promises made, when it seemed as if the new science really would yield the kind of technological control sufficient for mastery of our bodies and nature.[1] The *généreux* are not masters of nature, nor do they have the

---

[1] In the *Discourse on Method*, the principles of mechanistic physics are presented as laying the foundation for a practical knowledge of the world, one which would render us 'maîtres et possesseurs de la nature' (AT VI, 61–2). As Cottingham (1998, 72) notes, the idea of mastering the machine of nature through knowledge of mechanics represents a new form of alienation from

degree of self-control envisaged by the Stoics. They guide themselves in the full recognition of their practical limitations and the uncertainty of the world which impacts upon them. What remains immune to external forces are only the values of the *généreux*, in particular, the value of the free will, and their innate mental faculties. The restricted 'moral certainty' of the sage presages an emerging cult of the will, with surprising and puzzling consequences.

MAGNANIMITY AND GENEROSITY

The moral tone of the *Passions* until Part Three is one relatively congruent with Aristotelian virtue ethics, with the qualification that virtue is, as it was for the Stoics, independent of fortune. *Magnanimitas* is introduced at article 54 as a species of esteem. The notion of *magnanimitas* in the Latin tradition or *megalopsychia* in the Greek was long connected with the concept of legitimate self-esteem to the extent that the terminology has often appeared in modern English editions of Greek texts translated as 'pride'.[2] Aristotle defines the virtues or moral excellences as habits of acting in accordance with right reason, and it is only for such habits that one can justly esteem oneself.[3] The great-souled person esteems her own greatness, which consists of a unity of virtues (the four cardinal virtues: prudence, temperance, justice and fortitude), and the rightness of them according to the mean – neither too much (for this is stupid and ignorant vanity) nor too little (unjustified humility).[4] Being for the most part self-sufficient, the *megalopsyche* is not excessively self-interested but rather assists others and never displays her superiority over those less fortunate.[5] Because of this virtue, the *megalopsyche* warrants the greatest of desserts among external goods – honour – and for this reason Aristotle refers to *megalopsychia* as the 'crown' of the virtues. *Megalopsychia* makes one's virtues greater and cannot exist without them.[6]

---

nature. The *Passions* stands as our reconciliation with nature, and respect for its complexity and power. Submission to providence and self-mastery alone can make us content. Little wonder then that Descartes should write to Chanut in 1646 that it is more certain and easier to learn how not to fear death than to seek to preserve life (AT IV, 442).

[2] The conflation of magnanimity and pride would not have impressed Descartes, for whom pride is a vice (PS, art. 157; cf. Aristotle, 1984: 1773).

[3] Aristotle, 1980: II. 1. 1103a14–25.

[4] *Ibid.*, II. 7. 1107b23; IV.3. 1123b1–25.

[5] *Ibid.*, IV.3. 1124b7–20.   [6] *Ibid.*, IV.3. 1124a1–3.

By introducing magnanimity as a species of self-esteem, Descartes prepares the reader to expect an endorsement of the ancient notion of virtue (*arete*) and its connection with self-esteem. But at article 153 there is a sudden terminological shift, and it is the notion of *générosité* that is suddenly equated with virtue. The true generosity (as opposed to pride) of a person consists:

partly in that he knows there is nothing that truly appertains to him other than this free disposition of his volitions, nor ought he to be praised or blamed for anything except that he uses it well or badly, and partly in that he senses in himself a firm and constant resolution to use it well, that is to say, to never fail to use the will to undertake and execute all the things he judges to be the best. And this is to follow virtue perfectly. (AT XI, 446)

Generosity has a cognitive component, the knowledge of the freedom and value of the will, and a conative element, the feeling within oneself of the firm and constant resolution to use the will well. Prima facie, there is little in this definition of *générosité* to justify the terminological shift. The idea that only actions that are in some sense voluntary are the subject of moral approbation and disapprobation and thus the only legitimate cause of self-esteem, was subsumed under the traditional concept of *magnanimitas*. The rise to prominence of the notion of the will in the medieval period, particularly among followers of Augustine, seems only to have reinforced the conception of magnanimity as connected with one's free acts.[7] In the following passage from Augustine's *De libero arbitrio voluntatis*, I. 95, we can see themes very similar to those Descartes uses in connection with *générosité*.

We agree that the happy man is the lover of his own good will, a man who spurns, by comparison, every other good, which can still be lost even when the will to keep it remains . . . to love one's good will and to esteem it as highly as we have said – is this not the good will itself? . . . What, therefore, is the cause of our doubting (even if we have never been wise before) that it is by will that we deserve and live a praiseworthy and happy life, and by will that we deserve and live a disgraceful and unhappy life. (St. Augustine, 1964: 27)

Augustine defines the good will in terms of the esteem and love we have for the will, the happiness it produces and its independence from fortune. Similarly, Descartes explains the link between virtue and happiness as arising from the composition of passions that make up generosity: love

---

[7] Levi has traced the Augustinian influences on Descartes to the neo-Stoic French moralists of the period, particularly du Vair, Charron and Justus Lipsius (Levi, 1964: chs. 11 and 12).

(self-love), wonder (self-esteem) and joy (PS, art. 160). But if these were common themes associated with the traditional use of magnanimity, why then does Descartes feel the need to abandon the traditional notion in favour of a local term, *générosité*, and what work is the latter supposed to do that magnanimity cannot?

THE FOX AND THE LION

Descartes' explanation for the shift in terminology is as curious as the shift itself. As Lisa Shapiro has argued, the term *générosité* in seventeenth-century French literary culture carried connotations of noble birth but also of self-mastery and good will towards others (Shapiro, 1999a: 250–1). Descartes accepts that good birth can contribute to one's esteeming one's true worth and that God does not create all souls equally noble and strong, and for this reason, he tells us, he has chosen to follow the vernacular instead of 'magnanimity', which is used in the Schools 'where it is not well understood' (PS, art. 161). Like Aristotle, Descartes believes in the power of 'a good upbringing' to correct defects of birth, and despite the elitist terminology, therefore, the account of virtue is intended to have an equalising effect. The passion of generosity becomes a virtue through a habitual resolve to use the will well. Since virtue does not depend upon fortune but upon the free will that each of us possess, virtue is something everyone can strive to attain.[8] The break between virtue and fortune is one significant departure from Aristotle's account of virtue, but since this is not offered as a reason, it does little to explain the shift in terminology.[9] Against the background of what seems to be an overwhelming isomorphism between the notion of *générosité* and the traditional conception of magnanimity, the explanation offered at article 161 is unsatisfactory.

One possibility is that the term *générosité* signals not a radical departure from the traditional conception of magnanimity, but a shift in emphasis within the traditional conception of virtue. In particular, the notion of prudence or practical wisdom (*phronesis*) moves into prominence in a way that differs from its place in the ancient conception of virtue. It is the second component of the definition of *générosité* – acting with a firm and constant resolution to use the will well – which represents a distinctively Renaissance theme in the history of *magnanimity*. Two aspects of the

---

[8] Cottingham argues that regardless of the state of their fortune, anyone can, on Descartes' ethics, attain a state of virtue (Cottingham, 1998: 99–100).
[9] See Rodis-Lewis, 1987.

intellectual climate of the seventeenth century are resonant with Descartes' conception of virtue. One is the increasing valorisation of heroic virtues, lauded by Roman historians and celebrated in romantic literature. The other is a growing suspicion among moralists of the period that the classical conception of virtue, with its reliance on a strict conception of right reason, is practically useless for us in this life.

Descartes' repeated insistence on the necessity to follow 'firm and decisive judgements', and on the viciousness of acting from fear or irresolution (which the tone suggests is morally worse than doing the wrong thing but doing it decisively (PS, arts. 48, 170)) is reminiscent more of the heroic virtues than the cardinal virtues of the Greeks and Scholastics (Greaves, 1964: 19–27). The heroic virtues include charisma, liberality, love, courage (including courageous sacrifice), generosity, noble ambition and forbearance. Margaret Greaves identifies the point at which *megalopsychia* enters the Latin tradition as *magnanimitas* as containing the seeds of its heroic connotations insofar as *animus* stands ambiguously for either 'soul' or 'courage'. This extension in the meaning of *megalopsychia* is, for example, explicit in Cicero, for whom great courage in the service of the common good is *virtus* (cf: Cicero, *De Officiis* I, 19; Greaves, 1964: 17). The heroic virtues are also important for Machiavelli, whose conception of *virtù* derives much of its content from his peculiar reading of Roman historians, especially Livy.[10]

Machiavelli makes necessity a virtue in quite a different manner from Descartes. Descartes argues that to conjecture about God's ends and the providential order is appropriate only in ethics, and then only barely so (AT VII, 375; AT VIIIA, 81). But whatever happens is, as we discovered in the last chapter, both necessitated by God and the best possible outcome, and so virtue consists in part in submitting oneself to this immutable fate. Machiavelli, by contrast, regards fortune as real and tameable. The future is open to manipulation by strong hands. Virtue and political necessity are indistinguishable. Machiavelli's heroes are successful tyrants – Agathocles the Sicilian (1950:8), Scipio [1996:I. 29), Hannibal (1950:17), Severus (1950:19), Caesar (1996:I. 29) and, in his own time, the brutal and conniving Cesare Borgia (1950:7) and Pope Julius II (1950:25). Pope Julius' impetuousness and boldness in battle demonstrated for Machiavelli one key component of *virtù*. The three main components of *virtù* are (1) the recognition of the inescapability of fortune, (2) the importance of boldness and decisiveness and (3) the

---

[10] See Machiavelli, 1950.

necessity of adapting one's behaviour to prevailing circumstances (1950:25). Boldness and adaptability are necessary because of the unpredictability and capriciousness of Fortuna. 'I certainly think that it is better to be impetuous than cautious, for fortune is a woman, and it is necessary, if you wish to master her, to conquer her by force; and it can be seen that she lets herself be overcome by the bold rather than by those who proceed coldly.'[11]

Machiavelli recognises as 'good qualities' other traits, such as liberality or generosity, mercy, humanity, chastity and piety, and advises princes not to depart from these goods where possible. When the state is corrupt, however, it is not virtuous for the Prince to possess such qualities. The crowning virtue for Machiavelli is prudence, which stands alone from other cardinal virtues, including justice. *Virtù* consists in choosing the best means, whatever they are, to preserving power. To think anything else is a virtue is to be deceived by appearances.

[As the above-named qualities] cannot all be possessed or observed, human conditions not permitting of it, it is necessary that he [the Prince] should be prudent enough to avoid the scandal of those vices which would lose him the state, and guard himself if possible against those which will not lose it him, but if not able to, he can indulge them with less scruple. And yet he must not mind incurring the scandal of those vices, without which it would be difficult to save the state, for if one considers well, it will be found that some things which seem virtues would, if followed, lead to one's ruin, and some others which appear vices result in one's greater security and wellbeing.[12]

The prudent ruler combines elements of both man and beast, the use of law and of force, and, on the beast side, must be both 'a fox and a lion' – 'a fox to recognise traps and a lion to frighten wolves' (1950:18). The beast side of the Prince knows how to use deception and, above all, to avoid detection.

This 'politicised virtue' of Machiavelli, as Harvey Mansfield has described it, is not one Descartes agrees with in principle.[13] He writes to Elisabeth that it should not be necessary for the Prince to ruin himself in order to maintain the health of the earthly state.[14] But in the same letter, Descartes shows his own willingness to condone joining the fox with the lion, using 'artifice as well as force', in certain political contexts (AT IV, 488). The Prince must exercise a firm will, regardless of the rightness or wrongness of a particular action.

[11] Machiavelli, 1950: 94.   [12] *Ibid.*, p. 57.   [13] Mansfield, 1996: 20.
[14] Letter to Elisabeth, September 1646.

Finally [the Prince] should remain immutable and inflexible, not to the first designs which he would have formed within himself, for since he is not able to have a view of anything, it is necessary that he ask counsel and understand the reasons of several others before resolving himself, but that he be inflexible concerning those things which he has announced to have resolved even though they cause problems for him, for could they be harming him so much as to be worth the reputation of being lightweight and fickle? (AT IV, 490)

Machiavelli and Descartes are examples of a general trend in moral thinking away from the unity of virtue and knowledge found in the Greeks and Stoics, and towards a notion of virtue in which resolution is central, a trend which comes dangerously close to granting prudence the status of an end in itself.[15] This slide from thinking of prudence as concerned only with means to thinking of it as an end in itself is quite explicit in Machiavelli – 'in actions . . . from which there is no appeal, the end justifies the means'(1950:18)[16] – as are the diabolic consequences of this way of thinking. The opposite is true for Aristotle, for whom prudence is concerned with means not ends, and is only a virtue, indeed only prudence, when guided by the right conception of the good. There is something that looks superficially like prudence when action is not guided by right reason, cleverness (*deinotes*), which is accidentally praiseworthy if the end happens to be right, and villainous if it is not. But cleverness is not prudence. On the Aristotelian picture, it is thus impossible to have practical wisdom without a true conception of the good. Machiavelli's departure from what he takes to be the ancient (Greek) conception of virtue consists, as Mansfield argues, in collapsing the Aristotelian distinction between prudence and clevernesss (Mansfield, 1996: 39). Well might we ask then whether Cartesian virtue is subject to the same pitfalls as Machiavellian *virtù*?

Descartes' own position on the place of prudence in the conception of virtue is not entirely clear. There are several texts that together produce a somewhat confused picture of the connection between virtue and knowledge. Anthony Levi has drawn our attention to the Preface of the French edition of the *Principia*, written concurrently with the first draft of the *Passions*, in which Descartes distinguishes *sagesse* from 'mere prudence' in practical matters (Levi, 1964: 261; AT IXB, 2). *Sagesse* presupposes an adequate knowledge of Cartesian metaphysics and physics. Wisdom and

---

[15] Levi identifies the virtue of resolution as definitive of moral treatises of the period influenced by the Neostoic debate, especially Montaigne, du Vair and Charron (Levi, 1964: 246).

[16] Machiavelli, 1950: 66.

virtue and the sovereign good are interdependent notions, and presuppose an understanding of first causes and principles. Other texts stress that the wise person is one who does all that true reason tells him (e.g. AT IV, 490), and there is, from Descartes' earliest writings, a commitment to right action depending on right reason. The fourth maxim of the moral code outlined in the *Discourse on Method, IV* , states that since the will tends to pursue or avoid what the intellect represents as good or evil, we need only judge well in order to act well, do our best and acquire all the virtues (AT VI, 28). Yet, in the same text there is the analogy of the lost *voyageur*, who does not know which is the right way to go, but who acts well if he acts with a firm and resolute will (AT VI, 24–5). By defining virtue as the good use of the will, Descartes too could be accused of elevating prudence above the intellectual virtues, whose job it is to produce the right conception of the end, and of being caught between conflicting intuitions: that a true conception of the good must bear some internal connection to the goodness of an action, and that it suffices for the goodness of an action that it be performed by a firm will.

Descartes' reasons for identifying virtue with the good use of the will are explicit in other texts. Insofar as circumstances rarely permit more than a probabilistic judgement about what is good, the moral worth of our actions cannot always depend on true moral judgements. As Descartes writes to Queen Christina, although the goods of the soul include both to know and to will, 'knowledge is often beyond our powers', and there remains 'only our will, which is absolutely within our disposal' (AT V, 83; see also PS, art. 170). And as he writes to Elisabeth, even if our reason errs, there is nothing for which we may be blamed provided we act in good conscience. Acting in good conscience consists in a resolute use of the will in following the direction of reason (AT IV, 266; 530).

All sorts of desires are not incompatible with beatitude, only those accompanied by impatience and sadness. It is not necessary also that our reason does not make any mistakes. It suffices that our conscience testifies to us that we have never lacked resolution and virtue to execute all the things that we have judged to be the best, and thus virtue alone is sufficient to render us content in this life.

(AT IV, 266)

But how, given these limitations of reason, can one engage in anything but prudential conduct? What more could there be to Cartesian virtue than willing resolutely the best means to whatever one takes to be the good end? And why is it sufficient for both virtue and happiness that one wills an end that appears good, regardless of whether it is in fact good?

HUMAN REASON AND MORAL CONDUCT

Like other moralists of the period, Descartes is caught in a trap of ancient construction. The problem is how to conceive of *sagesse* in the absence of omniscient knowledge. Faced with this difficulty, the Stoic sage withholds assent to all propositions that are not clear and distinct and minimises the chances of being presented with false goods by extirpating her passions.[17] Descartes dismisses the Stoic solution as neither realistic nor desirable. One has to act and it is only the 'cruel philosopher' who wants the sage to be insensible (AT IV, 201–2). In accepting the classical formulation of the problem, however, Descartes cannot easily maintain both the hegemony of reason in ethical matters and a more than prudential conception of virtue.

Levi argues that it is this 'dissociation' of reason from the will in early seventeenth-century ethical theories that constitutes a 'rationalist dilemma' for moralists of the period. But Levi sees no contradiction in subscribing to a formally valid principle of moral activity based on judgements of reason, while allowing it to be materially true that the content of the good cannot always be ascertained (Levi, 1964: 287–306). Levi is correct that there is no contradiction in holding a normative principle of acting in accordance with right reason together with the recognition that, in particular moral contexts, the right action may elude us, but reconciling these ideas is not the main problem. The problem is that there is no conception of the good beyond the good (i.e. resolute) use of the will. [18] The notion of goodness that attaches to how one wills the means to one's ends is independent from any conception one might have of the goodness of one's ends. Without an independent conception of the goodness of one's ends, Descartes' notion of the good is, as Calvin Normore has argued, circular.[19] To act well or perform the good action is to have used one's will well. But how are we to identify an act of the will as good or bad? Notice that we cannot answer this question by appealing to the independent goodness or badness of the action that is willed. We cannot say, for example, that we will well when the action we perform is good, and badly when the action is bad, where the goodness or badness of the action is independent of the fact that it was willed in a certain way. So

---

[17] Levi argues that the solution adopted by Lipsius is similar in that it requires the sage to suspend judgement in all practical matters that are not clear and distinct (Levi, 1964: 287).

[18] Descartes lists a range of goods for humans in this life, including virtue, health and knowledge, but virtue or the supreme good consists just in the good use of the will (AT v, 55–6).

[19] Calvin Normore, 'Generosity' (unpublished).

all we can say is that the will is good when it wills the good action, and the action is good when it is willed by the good will, which is no answer at all. Appealing to the idea of the good will as the resolute will does not help either, because saying that the will is good because it is resolute only raises the question what it is to will resolutely, and the answer to that can only be that it is to resolve to will well. But if willing well just is willing resolutely, we again fail to escape the circle.

There is, of course, an independent conception of the good in Descartes' system and that is the goodness of God. But since this is not a good we can will, it is unclear how this concept of goodness is going to connect with our actions.[20] There may be no way to resolve this problem of circularity in Descartes' account of virtue but we can, perhaps, save it from some of the excesses of Machiavellian *virtù*. Since the passions are the most likely source of error in practical reasoning, bringing them under rational control will significantly reduce the likelihood of cases that involve gross moral errors. Since Machiavelli places no constraints on the moral psychology of those exercising *virtù*, his notion is open to much greater abuses that Descartes'. But if mastery of the passions is crucial to any success Cartesian ethics may aspire to, how exactly is mastery over the passions to be achieved, and how, moreover, are we to recognise it?

THE WONDER CURE

Generosity is a species of esteem and love and joy directed at oneself. The components of love and joy follow upon the esteem that one bears for oneself. In contrast with pride, generosity is legitimate self-esteem. It consists in understanding that nothing belongs to oneself but the free

---

[20] Perhaps I am underestimating the fact that God is the measure of all goodness. In the *Fourth Meditation*, Descartes describes how we err by misusing the gifts that God gives us by extending our will to assent to those things that we do not clearly and distinctly perceive. Stephen Menn has argued that Descartes' treatment of error and sin follows closely the Augustinian line: error is a privation because it is a deviation from the standard to which God intends us to conform (Menn, 1998: 306). It is only against the background of an understanding of God as Nous, as an objective standard of truth and right action, that this explanation of error makes sense. But it is difficult to see how Descartes' concept of God is going to inform our ordinary moral judgements. God's ends are incomprehensible to us, the matter of particular moral judgements is inherently obscure and identifying errors is much more hit-and-miss than it is in the theoretical domain, even if one aims above all else to love God. Our moral deficiencies are forced on us partly because of the urgency to act, often without even a probable grasp on things (AT VII, 149), and partly because our ideas of morality, even if they come by revelation, do not have the mark of metaphysical certainty. The moral truths that come to us from religion, perhaps even directly from God Himself through divine illumination, are no less obscure for having the sanction of grace. See Menn's (1998: 322–36) excellent discussion of why the truths of faith do not belong in Cartesian science.

control over one's volitions and feeling within oneself a firm and constant resolution to use the will well (PS, art. 153). It is first a passion and then, through habit, a virtue. By defining generosity in this way, a question arises as to the sincerity of Descartes' claim that generosity is first a passion. For generosity to be a passion in the strict sense, it must be caused directly by motions of the animal spirits, whereas the definition suggests that it arises from a judgement about the freedom of the will, a source more appropriate for an internal emotion. Is embodiment a precondition for virtue?

Consider the meditator, who has progressed through the first five *Meditations* without supposing that she has a body, reflected on the divine nature of the will and who has developed a range of intellectual virtues. Are these not sufficient for virtue, and if not, why not? If an intellectual awareness of the power of the will and determination to use it well is the key to self-control and virtue, why is it necessary to think of virtue as depending on a passion at all? Why a passion, and why that passion?

The emotions and passions divide primarily according to their origins: passions, strictly speaking, have origins wholly external to the mind (they arise solely from movements of the spirits), internal emotions are wholly internal (they arise solely from the soul's acts), but some passions arise from both sources – i.e. from the body, and so are passions, but through the mediation of thought. In this third category we may include generosity. Thinking about things one takes to be good about oneself is something that originates within the soul, but such thoughts can affect the spirits in the body in such a way that they, in turn, produce species of (self-) esteem. The same movements of the spirits can produce either legitimate self-esteem (generosity) or illegitimate self-esteem (pride), which are distinct thoughts (PS, art. 160). The fact that generosity and pride are distinct suggests either that they contain the same passion but are distinct ideas because of their distinct thoughts, or that they are distinct passions, and the thoughts from which they originate are components of the passion. Descartes is inclined to the former interpretation, and thus to the idea that one and the same passion may be virtuous or vicious depending on its relationship to other thoughts (PS, art. 160). Similar considerations apply to the pair of passions, (virtuous) humility and (vicious) servility: both involve the same movement of the spirits but differ in the content and truth-value of the opinion upon which each is based (PS, art. 160). It might seem somewhat risky to make our moral development depend on a passion that we could thus so easily confuse with its unvirtuous counterpart. Hence the need to stress that generosity, as opposed to pride, is dependent upon the recognition of the free will and the resolve to use it well.

What this comparison between pride and generosity demonstrates is that the moral therapy of the passions does not require obliterating passions, but establishing the right connections between passions and other thoughts. If the proud could be trained to associate habitually this movement of the spirits that sustains their pride with the thought of their free will instead of their perceptions or thoughts of things they possess or which happen to them, they could, in effect, train themselves to become generous. Such realignment could have the consequence of reshaping their entire moral psychology. With the free will as the locus of self-esteem, other causes of esteem that produce unruly desires, hatred, servility, anger, jealousy, fear, etc. should seem less important, and with these readjustments would come greater control over action (PS, art. 156). But how are new associations to be forged, especially when passions are solely and proximally dependent upon movements in the brain over which one has no direct control?

Associations between passions and thoughts are governed by a principle of habituation. They are formed throughout a person's history and can, through various cognitive exercises, be undone at least to some degree. Just as, when we acquire a language, certain sounds become associated with certain meanings, so too the scenarios in which our passions are initially induced establish connections between movements of the spirits (and their immediate effects on the soul) and particular thoughts about objects and their relationship to the self (PS, 50). We can train ourselves to associate new thoughts with these feelings, much as we can learn to associate new meanings with particular sounds. The dependence of passions on individual histories and the temperament of the body explains why different individuals will have different reactions to the same events. Forming new associations depends on first understanding something about the causal genesis of a passion and second on techniques for reconditioning one's responses. As John Cottingham has argued, Descartes' account of what is involved in controlling the passions thus anticipates psychoanalysis, techniques for uncovering the history of a disposition to respond in a certain way, while providing the agent with enough distance from the response so that it may be modified (Cottingham, 1998: 91–3). By recalling his affection for a cross-eyed girl in his childhood, Descartes claimed, for example, to cure himself of his attraction to women with squints (AT v, 57). Someone will not seem worthy of love just because of a superficial similarity to a childhood friend. A new association between a movement of the spirits and the thought of a defect, one's own included, may be just enough to kill the passion, just as the taste of something foul while eating something one previously relished may be enough to turn one off a dish for a long time (PS, art. 50). Other passions demonstrate more inertia, but just as hunting dogs can be trained against their natural inclinations, so too we can train ourselves to respond differently to perceptions which produce certain passions in us (PS, art. 50). As Lilli Alanen argues, the fact that we can train ourselves to join more useful thoughts to the feelings produced by movements of the spirits is sufficient for bringing the passions under rational control (Alanen, 2003: 199).

But how exactly is the process of reconditioning ourselves to connect more useful thoughts to certain movements of the spirits possible, and what role does reflection on the free will play in this process? The process of rehabituating ourselves to make new associations between brain motions and thoughts requires a mechanism for separating out corporeal 'images' which result in passions of the soul from their usual cognitive and behavioural associations so that new connections may be formed. John Sutton has argued that wonder plays a crucial role in this process, and I think we may extend his insights on this matter to better understand the functions of generosity as a passion. On Sutton's reading, Cartesian memory works through the superposition of corporeal images (understood here as just arrangements of matter) that are similar to one another in the same region of the brain. The reception of similar images results in many overlapping memory traces without successive temporal ordering or the laying down of discrete representations in individual storage cells. This dynamic process by which memories are formed makes them highly susceptible to interference from adjacent folds of the brain, to confusion with superficially similar images and obscures their role in shaping our emotional dispositions (Sutton 1998a: 123–7). Because of the way they are embedded in the memory structures of the brain, these connections between images and passions and thoughts are lasting and difficult to undo. Wonder is unique among the passions for Descartes (and Malebranche), according to Sutton, because of its independence from these embedded memory structures. In being a representation of novelty, and thus free from interference from a past embodied as it is in these dynamic processes of memory, wonder isolates an image and renders it temporarily independent from other images (Sutton 1998a: 127).

The problem with this account is that modifying our emotional dispositions is hard precisely because the images that trigger emotional responses automatically tend not to be new. This is not to say that seeking out new wonders wouldn't help us weather emotional storms. Wonder at novelty may be useful in rehabituating our emotional dispositions – it may distract us from things long enough for us to pull ourselves together – but since we cannot control what will strike us as new, it is an unstable strategy to rely upon. As noted in chapter 6, however, there is another kind of wonder, or esteem for something valuable or extraordinary, which can perform the same functions of holding the sense organs and body in a state of attention while the soul considers some object. What the soul needs in order to get control over its passions is to attend to the freedom of its will, or to put it more concretely, to those things which depend on it alone, and to esteem them more highly than things which do not depend upon it. What needs to be 'separated out' are the impressions or experiences of doing things by our own volitions, in contrast to those things that happen to us. Thus Descartes writes that wonder for novelty will not do for moral progress, depending as it does on surprise, for then it is easily abused by those who wonder at themselves every time something new happens to them, as if it were their own doing, and thus vacillate between esteem or contempt for themselves depending on whether they view what happens as advantageous or not (AT XI, 452). It is perhaps for this reason that Descartes' wonder cure isn't available to the disembodied soul or the meditator of the first five *Meditations.* To free ourselves from those images that present themselves as good, we need to compare them with images caused by our acting through our bodies, where we feel the power and goodness of the will. Disembodied souls aren't subject to images of apparent goods, and so don't need the wonder cure, but the meditator will have to get in touch with her body again if she is going to master the sensations and passions that come to her against her will. To control the body, one needs an agent in the body, and this is what wonder, or more precisely, generosity, is supposed to be.

In light of this argument about the function of wonder in rehabituating our emotional responses, let us reconsider the case of Descartes' attraction to women with squints. When he begins to wonder about this attraction of his, his ability to uncover its source does not depend on any new figure being traced on the brain. It is when his attention is turned rather to himself, to his role in the affective process, when he looks for a reason for his attraction and finds nothing in the story that depends on his will, but only things which have happened to him, that he is in a position to recover past influences and the old associations begin to come unstuck (AT V, 57). The image of cross-eyed women is not isolated because it is new but because it is seen in a new light, connected with new thoughts, which can have the same effect as if it were new. The isolating function of wonder in this case depends on the fact that we are the kind of being who is able to act for reasons, the observation of which causes esteem and the absence of which can reduce our esteem for ourselves and an object. But there is no difference for Descartes between that kind of wonder and generosity.

To master the passions, therefore, we must master esteem and we master esteem by mastering our self-esteem. The first step towards virtue is to apply the 'rule of reason': to measure each pleasure according to the quantity of perfection that produces it (letter to Elisabeth, 1 September 1645, AT IV, 283–4). This involves considering not just the pleasure but also its source and, hence, the importance of examining the causes of the passions. The pleasures of the body are fleeting, most often dependent upon the acquisition of things outside us, whereas the pleasures of the mind – goods whose acquisition depends just on us – are immortal (AT IV, 286). If reason can master esteem, it can control indirectly desire and all the other passions that proceed from esteem.

It is important to see that in developing a calculus of esteem, Descartes directs moral development from within the sensuous realm from which Elisabeth complains she cannot extract herself (22 June 1645, AT IV, 233–4). Recall her question of how it is possible to know the true worth of goods and evils that customarily arouse us without possessing an infinite science (13 September 1645, AT IV, 288–9). As we can now see, Descartes' response concedes that complete knowledge of the value of all things is not possible, but we can identify a locus of esteem around the free will that should enable us to measure the value of a thing according to the extent to which it depends on us or not. This is the kind of self-esteem that is practically advantageous because it enables one to change and direct one's bodily dispositions. Hence, the need for the sage to enlist the aid of the senses, in particular, imagination, 'to have imagined in general things more vexing than those which have happened and be prepared to suffer them' (AT IV, 411). Descartes' point here is not that the function of the imagination is to facilitate worst-case scenario reasoning, but to prepare the very folds of the brain, so that when things happen one hasn't experienced before, one isn't unduly surprised, and, if subsequently harmed or benefited by the thing, 'disposed to think those goods and evils greater than they are'. We may not be able to affect whether or not things over which we have no control happen to us, but we can minimise the extent to which they influence our actions by limiting the effects of wonder.

It is because virtue is a notion tied to right action and right action depends on mastering the processes of the body that affect one's reason and capacity to will well, that it is crucial that generosity be a passion. In its role as master passion, generosity is not to be confused with the traditional idea of using one passion to counteract another, an idea Descartes denounces at article 48. When counteracting passions pull the will in opposite directions, the soul is left in a hopelessly deplorable state (Alanen, 2003: 213). The 'proper weapons' of the soul are its ' firm and determinate judgements' about good and evil, but imagination is also required to buffer us against the shocks of unpredictable events (AT XI, 367). To use the imagination in the right way requires experience and engagement with the world. The imagination cannot represent to the soul scenarios *ex nihilo,* but must draw upon memory and past experience to construct ideas of situations worse than those it has encountered. Although the meditator can recognise that the will is the most divine part of the soul, the resolve to use it well requires conditioning the whole person, body and soul, to prefer and remain focused on those things that depend upon us.

The general prognosis that generosity works to control other passions precisely because it is dependent upon certain motions in the body, fits with the account offered in article 156 of the ways in which generosity serves as the remedy against all disorders of the passions. By mastering esteem, we master all the other passions that depend upon esteem or its opposite, contempt. Through generosity, we master jealousy, envy, fear and anger – all those passions which involve valuing things which do not depend upon oneself – hatred because one never scorns others and desire because without great esteem for things which do not depend upon oneself, one never desires these things with passion.

Not only does generosity as a passion serve as a remedy for all disorders of the passions that are based on false esteem but it also takes us into a less egoistic realm of moral motivation. The good will is the same thing as good will towards others, but exactly why this should be so is puzzling. Why should my legitimate self-esteem be sufficient for my esteeming others and acting for their sakes, particularly when doing so incurs some cost to myself?

THE GOOD WILL AND GOOD WILL TOWARDS OTHERS

At article 154, Descartes observes that the *généreux* neither think themselves inferior nor superior to others because all such differences are 'much less considerable in comparison with the good will for which alone they esteem themselves, and which they suppose also to be, or at least to be able to be, in every other man' (AT XI, 447). The qualification that everyone is at least capable of a good will is surprising given the discussion of why the *généreux* never scorn anyone that precedes this explanation.

> Those who have this understanding and this feeling concerning themselves persuade themselves easily that each other man is also able to have it concerning himself because there is nothing in it that depends on another. This is why they never scorn anyone, and granted that they see often that others commit errors which show their weakness, they are always more inclined to excuse them than to blame them and to believe that it is more particularly through lack of knowledge than through lack of good will that they commit them. (AT XI, 446)

Every action, no matter how morally blameworthy, results not from a bad will but from ignorance of the good, and the *généreux*, who understand the nature and value of the will, are thus more inclined to excuse wickedness. Regarding the phenomenology of generosity, this seems correct. The generous are always inclined to give others the benefit of the doubt and it seems true that one's capacity for esteeming others is influenced by the esteem one has for oneself. 'J'ai mauvais caractère,' Eugene Ionesco once remarked, explaining why he hesitated meeting the sculptor, Brancusi, 'C'est, sans doute, la raison pour laquelle je déteste le mauvais caractère des autres.'[21] But although Descartes' Socratic response is unremarkable – it was common to think that since the will cannot will objects except under the aspect of good, *akratic* and immoral acts must be the result of ignorance about the true worth of the object rather than a bad will – the qualification that some are merely capable of a good will needs explaining. What, after all, could the difference be between being capable of a good will and having a good will, if all wills tend towards the good?

We might find some clues to these puzzles by turning to article 48, where the comparative strengths of wills are discussed. Descartes describes those who fail to act from firm and decisive judgements as allowing themselves to be carried away by present passions (AT XI, 367). His discussion there suggests that the person who is merely capable of a good will is not one who acts from a bad will, but one whose actions follow their passions. This does not mean that the will is not active when one is carried away by one's passions; in acting, one assents. If it were possible to act from passion without assenting, as if, without judging, one's desire could have its head, so to speak, one would be more culpable than someone who wills evil out of ignorance, simply because in such a case

---

[21] Ionesco, 1966: 348.

one would not have willed what one judges to be best. By following the Stoic idea that all action occurs in the context of assent, Descartes subscribes to the oddly more generous interpretation of moral weakness as consisting in moral ignorance. And a principal source of moral errors is the false or exaggerated appearance of good as presented through the passions.

Judging others' actions reasonable or unreasonable requires one to have, as Descartes puts it, 'good will' towards them, and good will is part of generosity (PS, art. 187). Having good will towards others involves seeing others as the kind of beings for whom being reasonable is an end. Hence, the kind of self-understanding possessed by the *généreux* is internally connected with their understanding of moral nature generally, and befits them to be generous in the sense more familiar to us today.

CONCLUSION: THE RATIONALITY OF CARTESIAN PASSIONS

It was argued in chapter 1 that the unifying theme of the *Passions* is the reconciliation of reason and passion in the union of mind and body. It is now time to ask how far Descartes has come towards the realisation of that project. The discussion of generosity brings together in a poignant fashion the disparate themes of the book – the necessity of examining the physiological bases of one's passions; the classification of passions according to their relations to external objects, the self and other thoughts and dispositions of the agent; and the importance of having due wonder for one's position in the providential order and the freedom of the will. Self-mastery begins with understanding the source of one's motivations and in making use of a natural tendency to wonder about the self and its agency. In the end, however, we remain constrained to employ the will in circumstances we do not adequately know and cannot control, and in negotiating our world, we must rely on the very passions that generosity allegedly helps us master. But how do we identify the passions that are morally or practically appropriate in any given set of circumstances?

The conception of a passion we are left with after the first two parts of the *Passions* is of a mode of the soul that the soul passively receives from motions in the nervous system, that tends to exaggerate or misrepresent the value of external things, but which can be useful in strengthening the will when the action is one that accords with right reason. The very passivity of these modes does not rule them out as reasons for action any more than the passivity of ideas generally would rule them out as reasons, but they need special intellectual scrutiny. Descartes tends to justify passions in terms of their utility to the union as a whole, or to its components, the soul and the body, and we have seen that one and the same passion (particularly, love or hate) may have different use-values depending on whether it is considered in relation to the mind or to the body. This makes the nature of the 'truth' of passions a complicated business. There is no telling whether a particular passion on its own is 'true' in a given set of circumstances. To begin to answer such questions we would need to take into consideration not just the external causes of a passion, but other modes and dispositions of the agent as well. As we saw in chapter 4, the passions do not track mind-independent, objective values, and yet Descartes often describes them in terms of their representational adequacy, the degree to which they represent the values of external objects as they are. But without objective values, the intrinsic malice of the bad guys, for example, by what measure can we ascertain when our passions correspond appropriately to the circumstances?

Throughout this study of the passions, we have seen the importance to the moral project of a systematic study of the self as a union of mind and body, and I want now to suggest that this self-understanding provides us with an objective standard for judging the appropriateness of our emotional responses. What it means to understand ourselves as embodied beings is to have a firm grip on the distinction between goods that depend on us and those that don't, and to value the former above the latter to such an extent that we have some control over the effects that the contingencies of this life can produce in us. When this kind of self-understanding and self-control is lacking, the moral danger the passions present to us is that we will be inclined to project value on to objects that are unworthy. As Ronald de Sousa has argued, there is an important distinction between projected and relative values, and only the former threatens the objectivity of an emotional response (de Sousa, 1987: 150–1). Is there evidence of such a distinction at work in Descartes' account of the passions?

We could say that an object comes to have projected value in Descartes' schema when a passion 'makes us believe certain things to be much better and more desirable than they are' (letter to Elisabeth, 1 September 1645). When the only grounds for thinking that an object has a certain value is that one is having a certain kind of emotional response, we may say that the value is projected. Sensuous love is false when it causes the soul to see another as desirable when 'she would see only faults on another occasion' (AT IV, 603). Grief based not upon the suffering of a loved one but upon one's own felt loss is supported by 'neither religion nor reason' (AT III, 279). Envy that derives solely from one's own desire for a thing is unjust, but envy concerning an undeserved good belonging to another can be just (AT XI, 467). The appropriateness or 'truth' of envy depends on its association with a correct judgement about just desserts. When we look for a reason independent of the passion for ascribing a certain value to an object and find none, we have strong evidence that the value ascribed to the object is merely projected.

Discovering the source of a passion through an understanding of the psychophysiology of the union and our own personal histories can do much to reveal to us when the things we judge to be valuable on account of a passion are indeed valuable or not.[22] But we must exercise our judgement, where feasible, to consider the merits and demerits of the object on its own terms, independently of our particular emotional reaction to it, and generosity serves as a standard of correctness for making such judgements. Like the Stoic sage, the generous person stands as an ideal measure of appropriate passions.[23] Since their passions are constrained by the importance attached to their wills, it is the passions of the *généreux* that are reasonable or 'true' in Descartes' sense. Descartes argues that the sage will often have greater passions than others precisely because of her good will and greater understanding. She will be disposed especially towards compassion, indignation, gratitude and love, as well as the passions that are essential for preserving the union (PS, arts. 187; 202–3). One might think, therefore, that the concept of *générosité* works in a fashion similar to that of the reasonable person standard in law. The law does not suppose that the reasonable person is either omniscient or unaffected by passions, but will take into consideration the fact that certain emotional reactions in certain situations are reasonable for anyone of moderate intelligence to have. Define the reasonable person – for Descartes, the person who understands the value of the will and is resolved to exercise it according to right reason – and just as the actions of such a person are reasonable, so too will be their passions.

[22] A first step in this process requires being able to distinguish one's passions from other similar thoughts. But Descartes does not directly address the question how we are able to distinguish phenomenologically or otherwise between passions and internal emotions. Typically, a passion of the soul will depend on some perception or imagination, and so the mind may be able through this association to distinguish its passions in the strict sense, but since some passions are mediated by judgements and the internal emotions may also coincide with other images and passions, this is not a reliable criterion. Taking into account these difficulties gives us further reason not to ascribe a transparency thesis to Descartes' account of the mind, as Alanen and Cottingham have both argued citing passages where Descartes denies that we are always directly aware of our mental acts. In the *Discourse*, for example, Descartes writes that many people do not know what they believe, because to believe and to know are distinct acts (AT VI, 23). See Cottingham, 1998: 92–3; Alanen, 2003: 206.

[23] See my 2002b: 259–78.

But how do we recognise the *généreux* among us? Although Descartes recommends taking those we find in our community who have proved themselves of good judgement as role models, our ability to recognise appropriate passions should not depend on that alone.[24] We need not go outside ourselves to find a standard of correctness for judging our passions, even if we have not yet joined the ranks of the *généreux*. The *Passions* is intended for an audience of aspiring sages, those who are seeking the kind of self-mastery Descartes recommends but who are far from having achieved it. The strategies it offers and which have been emphasised here – strategies for controlling attention, reflecting on one's place in nature and discriminating between what depends on the will and what is the result of external forces – are means of internalising the standard of generosity whether one recognises it as such or not. To embrace Descartes' conception of the will is to esteem it above all else, an esteem that cannot but serve as a measure of the worth of all one's other passions.

We are a long way now from those bogeymen of analytic philosophy of mind and critical theory, the 'Cartesian mind' and the 'Cartesian self'. Far from our embodiment being an impediment to the mind, were it not for the fact that we are bodies as well as minds, we would be deprived not only of the capacity for rational action, but also of the capacity to do science, to understand causality (both our own and God's) and to derive all the benefits we derive from social relations. If the mind of the *Meditations* is alienated from its body, nature and others, the mind of the *Passions* is one thoroughly embedded and better off because of it. But while the richness of Descartes' conception of the 'whole self' may be more palatable to us than the fragmented conception he is generally accused of having invented, there is still much work to be done to fit this picture with other tenets of the Cartesian system.[25] It is sobering that one of his most astute critics, Elisabeth, never quite bought the story about the passions. In shock still from Descartes' radical dualism and corpuscularian dissection of the natural world, Elisabeth never ceased to express reservations about his prospects for reuniting the human being. Did Descartes in

---

[24] Queen Christina serves as such an ideal – a model of merit and virtue, generosity and majesty, sweetness and goodness, as one who, through strength of mind, lacks jealousy and values honesty (9 October 1649, AT v, 429). Amelie Rorty argues that bodily health is an important indicator of a balance among the passions. See Rorty, 1986a.

[25] See Cottingham's interesting discussion of the way in which the combination of Descartes' dualism and the mechanistic science produced various new kinds of alienation from nature and within the self (Cottingham, 1998: 67–74).

his later years succeed in illuminating a truly integrated self or simply replace it with some monstrous concoction of divine will, fallible reason and machine body, acting out its inadequately informed plans in a way oblivious to the capricious bad fortune Elisabeth insists robs her of her very ability to reason? It is a sign of her integrity that Elisabeth would not settle for anything less than an account of human nature and flourishing completely compatible with Descartes' metaphysics and natural philosophy.[26] But it is disappointing that she could not see the adjustments being made to so much of his thought through her influence as progress rather than compromise. I would like to think that there is cause for optimism – that we might start with Descartes' conception of the whole human and work back to the concept of mind we find in the early *Meditations*. This we can do even if we think the roots and trunk of his system are a bit too spindly to sustain all that's hanging from the branches. After all, a tree planted in shaly soil may yield some surprisingly sweet fruit.

---

[26] John Cottingham has referred to ethical systems of the period in which Descartes was writing as 'synoptic', insofar as they integrate a conception of human flourishing into a unified metaphysical and physical account of nature (Cottingham, 1998: 12–13).

Bibliography

Acker, Mary H. (1997) 'Tempered Regrets Under Total Ignorance', *Theory and Decision* 42. 3: 207–13.

Adam, Charles. *La Vie de Descartes* in AT XII.

Alanen, Lilli. (1994) 'Sensory Ideas, Objective Reality, and Material Falsity', in John Cottingham, ed., *Reason, Will and Sensation*. Oxford: Clarendon Press: 229–49.

   (1996) 'Reconsidering Descartes's Notion of the Mind–Body Union', *Synthese* 106: 3–20.

   (2002) 'Descartes on the Will and the Power to Do Otherwise', in Lagerlund and Yrjonsuuri 2002: 279–98.

   (2003) *Descartes's Concept of Mind*. Cambridge, MA: Harvard University Press.

   (2004) 'Descartes and Elisabeth: A Philosophical Dialogue?' in Lilli Alanen and Charlotte Witt, eds., *Feminist Reflections on the History of Philosophy*. Dordrecht: Kluwer.

Al-Ghazali. (1997) *The Incoherence of the Philosophers*. Trans. and ed. Michael Marmura. Provo, UT: Brigham Young University Press.

Almog, Joseph. (2002) *What Am I?* Oxford: Oxford University Press.

Aquila, R. (1995) 'The Content of Cartesian Sensation and the Intermingling of Mind and Body', *History of Philosophy Quarterly* 12: 209–26.

Aquinas, St Thomas. (1938) *Summa Contra Gentiles*. Trans. English Dominican Fathers. London: Burns, Oates & Washbourne Ltd.

   (1964) *Treatise on Happiness*. Trans. John A. Oesterle. Notre Dame, IN: University of Notre Dame Press.

   (1966) *Treatise on the Virtues*. Trans. John A. Oesterle. Notre Dame, IN: University of Notre Dame Press.

   (1968) *Summa Theologiae*. Vol. XII. London: Blackfriars and Eyre and Spottiswood.

   (1975) *Questiones disputatae de veritate* in *Opera Omnia* XXXII, I. Rome: Leonine Commission.

Aristotle. (1961) *De Anima*. Trans. David Ross. Oxford: Clarendon, 1961.

   (1980) *Nichomachean Ethics*. Trans. David Ross. Oxford: Oxford University Press.

(1984) *The Complete Works of Aristotle*. Ed. Jonathan Barnes. Princeton, NJ: Princeton University Press.

Arkes, H. R. and Blumer, C. (1985) 'The psychology of sunk cost', *Organizational Behavior and Human Decision Processes* 35: 124–40.

Armstrong, David. (1980) *The Nature of Mind and Other Essays*. Ithaca, NY: Cornell University Press.

Arnauld, Antoine. (1990) *On True and False Ideas*. Trans. with an introduction by Stephen Gaukroger. Manchester: Manchester University Press.

Augustine, St. (1957–72) *The City of God Against the Pagans*. 7 vols. Cambridge, MA: Harvard University Press.

  (1964) *On the Free Choice of the Will*. Trans. A. S. Benjamin and L. H. Hackstaff. Indianapolis, IN: Bobbs-Merrill.

  (1996–7) *Confessions*. Trans. William Watts. Cambridge, MA: Harvard University Press.

Avicenna. (1608) *Canon medicinae*. Venice: Industria ac sumptibus Juntarum.

  (1968) *Liber de anima, seu sextus de naturalibus*. Vol. II. Ed. S. van Riet. Louvain: Peeters; Leiden: Brill.

  (1564) *De viribus cordis* reprinted in *Avicennae libri in re medica omnes*, II, pp. 324–42. Trans. Arnaldus de Villa Nova (d.1311). Venice: V. Valgrisium.

  (1952) *Avicenna's Psychology: An English Translation of Kital al-najat, Book II, Chapter VI with Historico-philosophical Notes and Textual Improvements on the Cairo Edition*. Trans F. Rahman. London: Oxford University Press.

Averroes. (1969) *Tahafut al-Tahafut*. Trans. and ed. Simon van den Bergh. Unesco Collection of Great Works Arabic Series. London: Luzac & Co. Ltd.

Ayers, Michael. (1998) 'Ideas and Objective Being', in Daniel Garber and Michael Ayers, eds., *The Cambridge History of Seventeenth-Century Philosophy*, 2 vols. Cambridge: Cambridge University Press. Vol. II: 1063–71.

Ayloffe, W. (1700) *The Government of the Passions, According to the Rules of Reason and Religion*. London: Printed for J. Knapton, at the Crown in St Paul's Church-Yard.

Baker, Gordon and Morris, Katherine, J. (1996) *Descartes' Dualism*. London: Routledge.

Beavers, Anthony. (1989) 'Desire and Love in Descartes's Late Philosophy', *History of Philosophy Quarterly* 6: 279–94.

Berkeley, George. (1709) *Essay Towards a New Theory of Vision*. Dublin: Jeremy Pepat.

Beyssade, J. M. (1983) 'La classification cartésienne des passions', *Revue Internationale de Philosophie* 136: 278–87.

  (1992) 'Descartes on Material Falsity', in P. Cummins and G. Zoeller, eds., *Minds, Ideas and Objects: Essays on the Theory of Representation in Modern Philosophy*. Atascadero, CA: Ridgeview Publishing.

Bittner, Rüdiger. (1992) 'Is It Reasonable to Regret Things One Did?' *The Journal of Philosophy* 89.5: 262–73.

Black, Deborah. (1993) 'Estimation *(Wahm)* in Avicenna: The Logical and Psychological Dimensions', *Dialogue* 32: 219–58.

Block, Ned. (1997) 'On a Confusion About a Function of Consciousness', in Ned Block, Owen Flanagan and Güven Güzeldere, eds., *The Nature of Consciousness*. Cambridge, MA.: MIT Press: 375–415.

Blom, John J. (1978) *Descartes: His Moral Philosophy and Psychology*. New York: New York University Press.

Bobzien, Susanne. (1998) *Determinism and Freedom in Stoic Philosophy*. Oxford: Clarendon Press.

Boethius. (1973) *Tractates, De Consolatione Philosophiae*. Trans. H. F. Stewart, E. K. Rand and S. J. Tester. Cambridge, MA: Harvard University Press.

Boler, John. (2002) 'Reflections on John Duns Scotus On The Will', in Lagerlund and Yrjonsuuri, 2002: 129–54.

Bolton, Martha. (1986) 'Confused and Obscure Ideas of Sense', in Rorty, 1986b: 389–404.

Brandom, Robert. (1994) *Making It Explicit*. Cambridge, MA: Harvard University Press.

Brentano, Franz. (1966) 'On the Concept of Truth', in Oscar Kraus, ed., *The True and the Evident*. Trans. Roderick M. Chisholm. New York: Routledge & Kegan Paul: 3–25.

　(1973) *Psychology From an Empirical Standpoint*. Ed. Oscar Kraus, trans. A. C. Rancurello, D. B. Terrell and L. L. McAlister. London: Routledge.

Bright, Timothy. (1969) *A Treatise of Melancholie, Containing the Cause Thereof.* Reprinted in *The English Experience* series, no. 212. Amsterdam and New York: De Capo Press.

Broughton, Janet. (2002) *Descartes's Method of Doubt*. Princeton, N.J.: Princeton University Press.

Broughton, Janet and Mattern, R. (1978) 'Reintrepreting Descartes on the Notion of the Union of Mind and Body', *Journal of the History of Philosophy* 16: 23–32.

Brown, Deborah. (1999) 'What Was New in The Passions of 1649?' in Mikko Yrjonsuuri and Tuomo Aho, eds., *Norms and Modes of Thinking in Descartes. Acta Philosophica Fennica* 64: 211–31.

　(2000) 'Immanence and Individuation: Brentano and the Scholastics on Knowledge of Singulars', *The Monist* 83.1: 22–46.

　(2001) 'Aquinas and the Flying Man Argument', *Sophia* 40.1: 17–31.

　(2002a) 'Thomas Aquinas: Saint and Private Investigator', *Dialogue* 41.3: 461–80.

　(2002b) 'The Rationality of Cartesian Passions', in Lagerlund and Yrjonsuuri, 2002: 259–78.

　(2006) 'Is Descartes' Body a Mode of Mind?' in Lagerlund and Yrjonsuuri, 2006.

Brown, Deborah and de Sousa, Ronald. (2003) 'Descartes on the Unity of Self and the Passions', in Williston and Gombay, 2003: 153–174.

Brown, Deborah and Normore, Calvin. (2003) 'Traces of the Body: Descartes on the Passions of the Soul', in Williston and Gombay, 2003: 83–106.

Burge, Tyler. (1979) 'Individualism and the Mental', in Peter A. French, Theodore E. Uehling and Howard Wettstein, eds., *Midwest Studies in Philosophy*, Vol. IV. Minneapolis: University of Minnesota Press: 73–121.

(1982) 'Other Bodies', in A. Woodfield, ed. *Thought and Object*. Oxford: Oxford University Press: 97–120.

(1986a) 'Cartesian Error and the Objectivity of Perception', in P. Pettit and J. McDowell, eds., *Subject, Thought and Context*. Oxford: Oxford University Press: 117–36.

(1986b) 'Individualism and Psychology', *Philosophical Review* 95.1: 3–45.

(1988) 'Individualism and Self-Knowledge', *Journal of Philosophy* 85.11: 649–63.

Burnyeat, M. F. (1982) 'Idealism and Greek Philosophy: What Descartes Saw and Berkeley Missed', *Philosophical Review* 91: 3–40.

(1983) 'Can the Sceptic Live His Scepticism?' in M. F. Burnyeat, ed., *The Sceptical Tradition*. Berkeley: University of California Press: 117–48.

Burton, Robert. (1949) *The Anatomy of Melancholy*. Vols. I-III. Eds. Floyd Dell and Paul Jordan-Smith. New York: Tudor Publications Co.

Calcidius. (1963) *Platonis Timaeus interprete Chalcidio cum eiusdem commentario*. Ed. Ioh Wrobel. Frankfurt: Minerva.

Carriero, John. (1990) *Descartes and the Autonomy of the Human Understanding*. New York: Garland.

Casini, Lorenzo. (2002) 'Emotions in Renaissance Humanism: Juan Luis Vives *De anima et vita*', in Lagerlund and Yrjonsuuri, 2002: 205–28.

Charleton, Walter. (1674) *Natural History of the Passions*. London: printed by T. N. for James Magnes.

Chomsky, Noam. (1966) *Cartesian Linguistics*. New York: Harper & Row.

(1967) *Aspects of the Theory of Syntax*. Cambridge, MA: MIT Press.

(1972) *Language and Mind*. New York: Harcourt Brace & Jovanovich.

Churchland, Paul. (1984) *Matter and Consciousness*. Cambridge, MA: MIT Press.

Cicero, Marcus Tullius. (1961) *De Officiis*. Cambridge, MA: Harvard University Press.

(1989) *Tusculan Disputations*. Vol. IV. Trans. J. E. King Loeb Classical Library. Cambridge, MA: Harvard University Press.

Clarke, Desmond. (1999) 'Causal Powers from Descartes to Malebranche', in Gaukroger, S. Sutton, J. and Schuster, J., eds., *Descartes' Natural Philosophy*. Cambridge: Cambridge University Press: 131–48.

Clatterbaugh, K. (1980) 'Descartes' Causal Likeness Principle', *Philosophical Review* 89: 379–402.

Coeffeteau, Nicholas. (1620) *Tableau des passions humaines, de leurs causes et de leurs effets*. Paris: Chez S. Cramoisy.

Cohen, M. and Jaffray, J-Y. (1980) 'Rational Behaviour Under Complete Uncertainty', *Econometrica* 21: 1281–99.

Cook, Monte. (1987) 'Descartes' Alleged Representationalism', *History of Philosophy Quarterly* 4: 179–93.

Copenhaver, Brian P. and Schmitt, Charles B. (1992) *Renaissance Philosophy* Oxford: Oxford University Press.

Cottingham, John. (1985) 'Cartesian Trialism', *Mind* 94: 218–30. Reprinted in *René Descartes, Critical Assessments*, ed. G. Moyal. London: Routledge, 1991. Vol. III, pp. 236ff.

  (1986) *Descartes*. Oxford: Basil Blackwell.

  (1998) *Philosophy and the Good Life*. Cambridge: Cambridge University Press.

Cottingham, John, ed. (1992) *The Cambridge Companion to Descartes*. Cambridge: Cambridge University Press.

  (1994) *Reason, Will and Sensation: Studies in Descartes's Metaphysics*. Oxford: Clarendon Press.

Cumming, Robert. (1955) 'Descartes's Provisional Morality', *Review of Metaphysics* 9: 207–35.

Curcellæi, Stephani. (1702) *Synopsis ethices*. Edition 3a, Cambridge.

Damasio, Antonio. (1994) *Descartes' Error: Emotion, Reason and the Human Brain*. New York: Grossett/Putnam.

Daston, Lorraine and Park, Katherine. (1998) *Wonders and the Order of Nature: 1150–1750*. New York: Zone Books.

Davan, Kingsmill. (1799) *An essay on the passions: Being an attempt to trace them from their source, describe their general influence, and explain the peculiar effects of each upon the mind*. London: Vernor and Hood.

Davidson, Donald. (1963) 'Actions, Reasons and Causes', *Journal of Philosophy* 60: 685–700.

  (1987) 'Knowing One's Own Mind', *The Proceedings and Addresses of the American Philosophical Association* 60: 441–58.

de la Chambre, Marin Cureau. (1658–63) *Les charactères des passions*. Amsterdam: chez Antoine Michel [i.e. L. & D. Elzevier].

de la Forge, Louis. (1664) *Traité de l'esprit de l'homme, de ses facultez et fonctions, et de son vnion auec le corps, suiuant les principes de René Descartes*. Amsterdam: Abraham Wolfgang.

de la Primaudaye, Pierre. (1972) *The French Academie*. Trans. Thomas Bowes. New York: Georg Olms Verlag Hildesheim.

Dennett, Daniel. (1987) 'Cognitive Wheels: The Frame Problem in A. I', in Zenon Pylyshyn, ed., *The Robot's Dilemma: The Frame Problem and Other Problems of Holism in Artificial Intelligence*. Norwood, NJ: Ablex Publishing: 41–64.

  (1991) *Consciousness Explained*. New York: Penguin.

Dennett, D. and Kinsbourne, M. (1972) 'Time and the Observer'. *Behavioral and Brain Sciences* 15: 183–247.

Descartes, René. (1897–1913) *Oeuvres de Descartes*. Vols. I–XII. Eds. Charles Adam and Paul Tannery. Paris: Leopold Cerf.

  (1984–91) *The Philosophical Writings of Descartes*. Vols. I–II Trans. and ed. John Cottingham, Robert Stoothoff and Dugald Murdoch. Cambridge:

Cambridge University Press, 1985. Vol. III. Trans. and ed. John Cottingham, Robert Stoothoff, Dugald Murdoch and Anthony Kenny. Cambridge: Cambridge University Press, 1991.

(1989) *Correspondance avec Elisabeth et autres lettres.* Introduction, bibliography and chronology by Jean-Marie Beyssade and Michelle Beyssade. Paris: Flammarion.

(1989) *The Passions of the Soul.* Trans. Stephen Voss. Indianapolis, IN: Hackett.

des Chene, Dennis. (1996) *Physiologia: Natural Philosophy in Late Aristotelian and Cartesian Thought.* Ithaca, NY: Cornell University Press.

de Sousa, Ronald. (1987) *The Rationality of Emotion.* Cambridge, MA: MIT Press.

Duns Scotus, John. (1639) *Ordinatio in Opera Omnia.* Ed. L. Wadding. Lyous: Durand.

Field, R. (1993) 'Descartes on the Material Falsity of Ideas', *The Philosophical Review* 102: 309–33.

Fine, Gail. (2000) 'Descartes and Ancient Scepticism: Reheated Cabbage?' *The Philosophical Review,* 109.2: 195–234.

Finset, A. (1988) 'Depressed Mood and Reduced Emotionality after Right-hemispheric brain damage', in M. Kinsbourne, ed., *Cerebral Hemisphere Function in Depression.* Washington: American Psychiatric Press: 51–64.

Flanagan, Owen. (1991) *The Science of the Mind.* Cambridge, MA: MIT Press.

Fodor, Jerry A. (1987) *Psychosemantics.* Cambridge, MA: MIT Press.

(1990) *A Theory of Content.* Cambridge, MA: MIT Press.

Freeland, Cynthia A. (1994) 'Aristotle on Perception, Appetition, and Self-Motion', in Gill and Lennox, 1994: 35–63.

Frierson, Patrick R. (2002) 'Learning to Love: From Egoism to Generosity in Descartes', *Journal of the History of Philosophy* 40.3: 313–38.

Furley, David. (1980) 'Self-movers', in Rorty, 1980: 55–68.

Gainotti, G. (1989) 'The Meaning of Emotional Disturbances Resulting from Unilateral Brain Injury', in Guido Gainotti and Carlo Caltagirone, eds., *Emotions and the Dual Brain.* Berlin: Springer-Verlag: 147–67.

Galen, Claudius. (1821–33) *Opera Omnia.* Ed. C. G. Kühn. Lipsiae: C. Cnobloch.

(1928) *On the Natural Faculties.* Trans Arthur John Brock. London: William Heinemann.

(1963) *On the Passions and Errors of the Soul.* Trans. Paul W. Harkins, introd. Walther Riese. Columbus, OH: Ohio State University Press.

Garber, Daniel. (1987) 'How God Causes Motion: Descartes, Divine Sustenance, and Occasionalism', *Journal of Philosophy* 84: 567–80.

(1992) *Descartes' Metaphysical Physics.* Chicago: University of Chicago Press.

(1993) 'Descartes and Occasionalism', in S. Nadler, ed., *Causation in Early Modern Philosophy: Cartesianism, Occasionalism and Preestablished Harmony.* University Park: Pennsylvania State University Press: 9–26.

(2001) *Descartes Embodied.* Cambridge: Cambridge University Press.

Gaukroger, Stephen. (1995) *Descartes: An Intellectual Biography.* Oxford: Clarendon Press.

(2002) *Descartes' System of Natural Philosophy*. Cambridge: Cambridge University Press.

Gaukroger, Stephen, ed. (1998) *The Soft Underbelly of Reason*. Indianapolis, IN: Hackett.

Gibson, A. Boyce. (1932) *The Philosophy of Descartes*. London: Methuen.

Gill, Mary Louise and Lennox, James G., eds. (1994) *Self-Motion From Aristotle to Newton*. Princeton, NJ: Princeton University Press.

Gombay, André. (1988) 'L'Amour et jugement chez Descartes', *Revue Philosophique de la France et de l'Étranger* 178: 447–55.

Greaves, Margaret. (1964) *The Blazon of Honour: A Study in Renaissance Magnaminity*. London: Methuen & Co.

Greenspan, P. (1988) *Emotions and Reasons*. London: Routledge.

Grene, Marjorie. (1985) *Descartes*. Indianapolis, IN: Hackett.

Grierson, Sir H. J. C., ed. (1933) *The Poems of John Donne*. London: Oxford University Press.

Griffiths, Paul. (1989) 'The Degeneration of the Cognitive Theory of Emotion', *Philosophical Psychology* 2.3: 297–313.

(1997) *What Emotions Really Are: The Problem of Psychological Categories*. Chicago: University of Chicago Press.

Groarke, L. (1984) 'Descartes' First Meditation: Something Old, Something New, Something Borrowed', *Journal of the History of Philosophy* 22: 281–301.

Gueroult, Martial. (1968) *Descartes selon l'ordre des Raisons*. Vol. II. Paris: Aubier-Montaigne. Trans. Roger Ariew, *Descartes' Philosophy Interpreted According to the Order of Reasons, vol. II: The Soul and the Body*. Minneapolis: University of Minnesota Press, 1985.

Harman, Gilbert. (1977) *The Nature of Morality*. Oxford: Oxford University Press.

(1997) 'The Intrinsic Quality of Experience', in Ned Block, Owen Flanagan and Güven Güzeldere, eds., *The Nature of Consciousness*. Cambridge, MA: MIT Press: 663–75.

Harvey, Ruth. (1975) *The Inward Wits: Psychological Theory in the Middle Ages and the Renaissance*. London: Warburg Institute Surveys no.6.

Hatfield, Gary. (2003) *Descartes and the Meditations*. London: Routledge.

Haugeland, John. (1985) *Artificial Intelligence: The Very Idea*. Cambridge, MA: MIT Press.

Hoffman, Paul. (1986) 'The Unity of Descartes's Man', *The Philosophical Review* 95: 339–70.

(1990) 'Cartesian Passions and Cartesian Dualism', *Pacific Philosophical Quarterly* 71: 310–33.

(1991) 'Three Dualist Theories of the Passions', *Philosophical Topics* 19: 153–200.

(1996) 'Descartes on Misrepresentation', *Journal of the History of Philosophy* 357–81.

(1999) 'Cartesian Composites', *Journal of the History of Philosophy* 37.2: 251–70.

(2002a) 'Descartes's Theory of Distinction', *Philosophy and Phenomenological Research* 64.1: 57–78.

(2002b) 'Direct Realism, Intentionality, and the Objective Being of Ideas', *Pacific Philosophical Quarterly* 83: 163–79.

Hurka, Thomas. (1996) 'Monism, Pluralism and Rational Regret', *Ethics* 106: 555–75.

Inwood, B. (1985) *Ethics and Human Action in Early Stoicism*. Oxford: Clarendon Press.

Ionesco, Eugène. (1966) *Notes et contre-notes*. Paris: Gallimard.

Irigaray, Luce. (1993) *An Ethics of Sexual Difference*. Trans. Carolyn Burke and Gillian C. Gill. Ithaca, NY: Cornell University Press.

James, Susan. (1994) 'Internal and External in the Work of Descartes', in James Tully, ed. *Philosophy in an Age of Pluralism: The Philosophy of Charles Taylor in Question*. Cambridge: Cambridge University Press: 7–19.

(1997) *Passion and Action: The Emotions in Seventeenth-Century Philosophy*. Oxford: Clarendon Press.

Jeannerod, M. (1994) 'The Representing Brain: Neural Correlates of Motor Intention and Imagery', *Behavioral and Brain Sciences* 17.2 187–202.

Kambouchner, Denis. (1995) *L'homme des passions: Commentaires sur Descartes*. Vols. I–II. Paris: Albin Michel.

Kaufman, Dan. (2000) 'Descartes on the Objective Reality of Materially False Ideas', *Philosophical Quarterly* 81: 385–408.

Keating, Laura. (1999) 'Mechanism and the Representational Nature of Sensation in Descartes', *Canadian Journal of Philosophy* 29: 411–30.

Kennedy, L. A. (1977) 'The Soul's Knowledge of Itself: An Unpublished Work Attributed to St. Thomas Aquinas', *Vivarium* 15: 31–45.

Kenny, Anthony. (1962) *The Anatomy of the Soul*. Oxford: Blackwell.

(1963) *Action, Emotion and Will*. London: Routledge & Kegan Paul.

(1968) *Descartes*. New York: Random House.

Kent, Bonnie. (1995) *Virtues of the Will: The Transformation of Ethics in the Late Thirteenth Century*. Washington, DC: Catholic University of America Press.

Kerr, N. H. (1983) 'The Role of Vision in "Visual Imagery" Experiments. Evidence From the Congenitally Blind', *Journal of Experimental Psychology* 112: 265–77.

King, Peter. (1994) 'Scholasticism and The Philosophy of Mind: The Failure of Aristotelian Psychology', in Tamara Horowitz and Allen I. Janis, eds., *Scientific Failure*. Oxford: Rowman & Littlefield: 109–38.

(2002) 'Late Scholastic Theories of the Passions: Controversies in the Thomist Tradition', in Lagerlund and Yrjonsuuri, 2002: 229–58.

Kinsbourne, Marcel. (1989) 'A Model of Adaptive Behavior Related to Cerebral Participation in Emotional Control', in Guido Gainotti and Carlo Caltagirone, eds., *Emotions and the Dual Brain*. Berlin: Springer-Verlag: 248–59.

Knuuttila, Simo. 'Passions from Avicenna to Aquinas' (unpublished).

(2002) 'Medieval Theories of the Passions of the Soul', in Lagerlund and Yrjonsuuri, 2002.

(2004) *Emotions in Ancient and Medieval Philosophy*. Oxford: Clarendon Press.

Kohly, Radha P. and Ono, Hiroshi. (2002) 'Fixating the Wallpaper Illusion: A Commentary on "The Role of Vergence in the Perception of Distance: A Fair Test of Bishop Berkeley's Claim" by Logvinenko, *et al.* (2001)', *Spatial Vision* 15.3: 377–86.

Kolb, B. and Milner, B. (1981) 'Performance of Complex Arm and Facial Movements after Focal Brain Lesions', *Neuropsychologia* 19: 491–503.

Kripke, Saul. (1972) *Naming and Necessity*. Cambridge, MA: Harvard University Press.

Lagerlund, Henrik and Yrjonsuuri Mikko eds. (2002) *Emotions and Choice from Boethius to Descartes*. Dordrecht: Kluwer.

(2006) *Forming the Mind*. Dordrecht: Kluwer.

Landman, J. (1993) *Regret: The Persistence of the Possible*. Oxford: Oxford University Press.

LeDoux, Joseph. (1996) *The Emotional Brain*. New York: Simon and Schuster.

Lennon, Thomas. (1974) 'The Inherence Pattern and Descartes' Ideas', *Journal of the History of Philosophy* 12: 43–52.

Levi, Anthony. (1964) *French Moralists: The Theory of the Passions 1585–1649*. Oxford: Clarendon Press.

Lewis, David. (1973) 'Causation', *Journal of Philosophy* 70.17: 556–67.

(1983) 'Attitudes *De Dicto* and *De Se*', in David Lewis, ed., *Philosophical Papers*. Oxford: Oxford University Press: 513–43.

Loeb, Louis. E. (1974) 'Causal Theories and Causal Overdetermination', *Journal of Philosophy* 71.15: 525–44.

Logvinenko, Alexander D., Epelboim, Julie and Steinman, Robert M. (2001) 'The Role of Vergence in the Perception of Distance: A Fair Test of Bishop Berkeley's Claim', *Spatial Vision* 15.1: 77–97.

Logvinenko, Alexander D. and Steinman, Robert M. (2002) 'Fixation on Fixation Impedes Cognition: Reply to Kohly and Ono', *Spatial Vision* 15.3: 387–91.

Long, A. A. (1974) *Hellenistic Philosophy*. Bristol: Duckworth.

Loomes, G. and Sugden, R. (1982) 'Regret Theory: An Alternative Theory of Rational Choice Under Uncertainty', *The Economic Journal* 92: 805–24.

Lyons, W. (1977) 'Emotions and Feelings', *Ratio* 19: 1–12.

Machiavelli, Niccolò. (1950) *The Prince and The Discourses*. Trans. Luigi Ricci, revised by E. R. P. Vincent. New York: Random House.

(1996) *The Discourses on Livy*. Trans. Harvey C. Mansfield and Nathan Tarcov. Chicago: University of Chicago Press.

MacKenzie, Ann Wilbur. (1990) 'Descartes on Sensory Representation', *Canadian Journal of Philosophy*, supplementary vol. 19: 109–47.

(1994) 'The Reconfiguration of Sensory Experience', in Cottingham, 1994: 251–72.

Malebranche, Nicholas. (1992) *Philosophical Selections*. Ed. Steven Nadler. Indianapolis, IN: Hackett.

(1997) *The Search After Truth*. Trans. Thomas M. Lennon and Paul J. Olscamp. Cambridge: Cambridge University Press.

Mansfield, Harvey C. (1996) *Machiavelli's Virtue*. Chicago: University of Chicago Press.

Marks, J. (1982) 'A Theory of Emotion', *Philosophical Studies* 42: 227–42.

Marion, J. L. (1993) 'Generosity and Phenomenology', in Stephen Voss, ed., *Essays on the Philosophy and Science of René Descartes*. Oxford: Oxford University Press:

Marshall, John. (1998) *Descartes's Moral Theory*. Ithaca, NY: Cornell University Press.

Matheron, Alexandre. (1988) 'Amour, digestion, et puissance selon Descartes', *Revue philosophique de la France et de l'eEtranger* 178: 433–45.

McDowell, John. (1994) *Mind and World*. Cambridge, MA: Harvard University Press.

Menn, Stephen. (1995) 'The Greatest Stumbling Block: Descartes' Denial of Real Qualities', in Roger Ariew and Marjorie Grene, eds., *Descartes and His Contemporaries: Meditations, Objections and Replies*. Cambridge: University of Chicago Press: 182–207.

(1998) *Descartes and Augustine*. Cambridge: Cambridge University Press.

Merleau-Ponty, Maurice. (1962) *Phenomenology of Perception*. Trans. Colin Smith. London: Routledge & Kegan Paul.

Mesnard, Pierre. (1936) 'Essai sur la Moral de Descartes', *Ancienne Librarie Furne*. Paris: Boivin.

Monnoyer, Jean-Maurice. (1988) *Les Passions de l' âme précédé de la pathétique cartésienne*. Paris: Editions Gallimard.

Morgan, Vance. (1994) *Foundations of Cartesian Ethics*. Atlantic Highlands, NJ: Humanities Press International.

Nadler, Steven. (1995) 'Occasionalism and the Question of Arnauld's Cartesianism', in Roger Ariew and Marjorie Grene, eds., *Descartes and His Contemporaries*. Chicago: Chicago University Press: 129–44.

Nagel, Thomas. (1974) 'What is It Like to Be a Bat?' *The Philosophical Review* 83: 435–50.

(1986) *The View from Nowhere*. Oxford: Oxford University Press.

Navarro, Juan de Huarte. (1594) *Examen de Ingenios, The Examination of Mens Wits*. Trans. Richard Carew. Reprinted in The English Experience series, no. 126. Amsterdam and New York: De Capo Press, 1969.

Nelson, Alan. (1996) 'The Falsity of Sensory Ideas: Descartes and Arnauld', in E. Kremer, ed., *Interpreting Arnauld*. Toronto: University of Toronto Press: 13–32.

Neuburger, M. (1910). *History of Medicine*. Trans. Ernest Playfair London: Henry Frowde, Hodder and Stoughton for Oxford University Press.

Normore, Calvin, (1986) 'Meaning and Objective Being: Descartes and His Sources', in Rorty, 1986b: 223–41.

(1998) 'Picking and Choosing: Anselm and Ockham on Choice', *Vivarium* 36: 23–39.

(2002) 'Goodness and Rational Choice In the Early Middle Ages', in Lagerlund and Yrjonsuuri, 2002: 29–48.

(2003) 'Duns Scotus's Modal Theory', in Thomas Williams, ed., *The Cambridge Companion to Duns Scotus*. Cambridge: Cambridge University Press, 2003: 129–60.

Nussbaum, Martha C. (1978) *Aristotle's De motu animalium*. Princeton, NJ: Princeton University Press.

(1994) *The Therapy of Desire*. Princeton, NJ: Princeton University Press.

Oesterle, Jean, ed. and trans. (1962) *Aristotle: On Interpretation. Commentary by St Thomas and Cajetan*. Milwaukee, WI: Marquette University Press.

O'Neil, B. E. (1974) *Epistemological Direct Realism in Descartes's Philosophy*. Albuquerque: University of New Mexico Press.

O'Neill, E. (1987) 'Mind–body Interaction and Metaphysical Consistency: A Defense of Descartes', *Journal of the History of Philosophy* 25: 227–45.

O'Toole, F. (1993) 'Descartes' Problematic Causal Principle of Ideas', *Journal of Philosophical Research* 18: 167–91.

Pascal, Blaise. (1958) *Pensées*. Trans. W. F. Trotter. New York: Dutton.

Papin, Nicolas. (1653) *Considerations sur le traité de Mr. Des-Cartes, des passions de l'âme*. Paris: Chez Simeon Piget.

Perry, John. (1979) 'The Problem of the Essential Indexical', *Nous* 13: 3–21.

Plato. (1961) *Republic*. Trans. Paul Shorey, in Edith Hamilton and Huntington Cairus, eds., *The Collected Dialogues of Plato*. Princeton, NJ: Princeton University Press.

Pylyshyn, Zenon. (1984) *Computation and Cognition*. Cambridge, MA: MIT Press.

Putnam, Hilary. (1975) 'The Meaning of "Meaning"', in K. Gunderson, ed., *Language, Mind and Knowledge, Minnesota Studies in the Philosophy of Science*, VII. Minneapolis: University of Minnesota Press. Reprinted in *Philosophical Papers: Mind, Language, and Reality*. Cambridge: Cambridge University Press. Vol. II: 215–71.

Radner, Daisy. (1971) 'Descartes' Notion of the Union of Mind and Body', *Journal of the History of Philosophy* 9: 159–70.

Rahman, F. (1952) *Avicenna's Psychology*, see Avicenna.

Ramachandran, V. S. and Blakeslee, Sandra. (1998) *Phantoms in the Brain: Probing the Mysteries of the Human Mind*. New York: William Morrow.

Ramachandran, V. S., Rogers-Ramachandran, D., and Cobb, S. (1995) 'Touching the Phantom Limb', *Nature* 377–489.

Reid, Thomas. (1896) *The Philosophical Works of Thomas Reid*. Ed. W. Hamilton. Edinburgh: James Thin.

Reynolds, Edward. (1971) *A Treatise of the Passions and Faculties of the Soul of Man*. Gainesville, FL: Scholars Facsimilies & Reprints.

Richard, R., van der Pligt, J. and de Vries, N. K. (1996) 'Anticipated Regret and Time Perspective: Changing Sexual Risk-taking Behavior', *Journal of Behavioral Decision Making* 9: 185–99.

Robinson, Victor. (1943) *The Story of Medicine*. New York: The New Home Library.

Rodis-Lewis, Genevieve. (1957a) *La Morale de Descartes*. Paris: Presses Universitaires de France.

(1957b) 'Maîtrise des passions et sagesse chez Descartes', in *Descartes: Cahiers de Royaumont*. Paris, Edition de Minuit: 208–27.

(1987) 'Le dernier fruit de la métaphysique cartésienne: la generosité', in *Le Sens actuel de la métaphysique de Descartes*, n° spécial, *Les Etudes Philosophiques*: 43–54.

(1995) *Descartes Biographie*. Paris: Calmann-Lévy.

(1998) *Descartes: His Life and Thought*. Trans. Jane Marie Todd. Ithaca, NY: Cornell University Press.

Rorty, Amelie Oksenberg. (1986a) 'Cartesian Passions and the Union of Mind and Body', in Rorty, 1986b: 513–34.

(1992) 'Descartes on Thinking With the Body', in John Cottingham, ed., *The Cambridge Companian to Descartes*. Cambridge: Cambridge University Press: 371–92.

Rorty, Amelie Oksenberg., ed. (1980) *Essays on Aristotle's Ethics*. Berkeley: University of California Press.

(1986b) *Essays on Descartes' Meditations*. Berkeley: University of California, Berkeley Press.

Rorty, Richard. (1979) *Philosophy and the Mirror of Nature*. Princeton, NJ: Princeton University Press.

Ryle, Gilbert. (1949) *The Concept of Mind*. Chicago: Chicago University Press.

Savage, L. J. (1954) *The Foundations of Statistics*. New York: John Wiley.

Senault, Jean-François. (1649) *De l'usage des passions*. Suivant la copie imprimee a Paris. Written in French by J. F. Senault. Translated into English by Henry Earl of Monmouth as *The use of passions*. London: printed for J. L. and Humphrey Moseley.

Sextus Empiricus. (1990) *Outlines of Pyrrhonism*. Trans. R. G. Bury. Buffalo, NY: Prometheus Books.

Shapiro, Lisa. (1999a) 'Cartesian Generosity', in Tuomo Aho and Mikko Yrjonsuuri, eds. *Norms and Modes of Thinking in Descartes*. Acta Philosophica Fennica 64: 249–75.

(1999b) 'Princess Elisabeth and Descartes: The Union of Soul and Body and the Practice of Philosophy', *British Journal for the History of Philosophy* 7.3: 503–20.

(2003) 'The Structure of The Passions of the Soul and the Soul–body Union', in Williston and Gombay, 2003: 31–79.

Simmons, Alison. (1999) 'Are Cartesian Sensations Representational?' *Nous* 33.3: 347–69.

(2001) 'Sensible Ends: Latent Teleology in Descartes' Account of Sensation', *Journal of the History of Philosophy* 39.1: 49–75.

Simonson, I. (1992) 'The Influence of Anticipating Regret and Responsibility on Purchase Decisions', *Journal of Consumer Research* 19: 105–18.

Sirven, J. (1987) *Les annees d'apprentissage de Descartes.* Albi: Imprimerie coop-érative du sud-ovest, 1928; reprinted New York: Garland.

Solomon, R. (1988) 'On Emotions as Judgements', *American Philosophical Quarterly* 25: 183–91.

Sorabji, Richard. (1980) *Necessity, Cause and Blame: Perspectives on Aristotle's Theory.* Ithaca, NY: Cornell University Press.

Spinoza, Baruch. (1982) *Ethics.* Trans. and ed. Samuel Shirley with an introduction by Seymour Feldman. Indianapolis, IN: Hackett.

Strawson, Peter F. (1959) *Individuals: An Essay in Descriptive Metaphysics.* London: Methuen.

Stoutland, Frederick. (1999) 'The Real Reasons', in J. Bransen and S. Cuypers, eds. *Human Action, Deliberation and Causation.* Dordrecht: Kluwer Academic Publishers.

(2002) 'The Belief–Desire Model of Reasons for Action'. *Uppsala Prints and Reprints in Philosophy* 4: 1–100.

Suárez, Franisco. *Tractatus de anima* in *Opera Omnia* (1856–78), v. iv–vi. Ed. D. M. André. Paris: D. M. André.

(1965) *Disputationes Metaphysicae, Opera Omnia,* xxv. Hildesheim: Georg Olms Verlagsbuchhandlung.

Sutton, John. (1998a) 'Controlling the Passions: Passion, Memory, and the Moral Physiology of the Self in Seventeenth-century Neurophysiology', in Gaukroger, 1998: 115–46.

(1998b) *Philosophy and Memory Traces.* Cambridge: Cambridge University Press.

Tachau, Katherine H. (1988) *Vision and Certitude in the Age of Ockham.* Leiden: E. J. Brill.

Temkin, Owsei. (1973) *Galenism: Rise and Decline of a Medical Philosophy.* Ithaca, NY: Cornell University Press.

Titchener, E. B. (1914) *A Primer of Psychology.* New York: Macmillan.

Tucker, D. M. and Newman, J. P. (1981) 'Verbal Versus Imaginal Cognitive Strategies in the Inhibition of Emotional Arousal', *Cognitive Theoretical Research* 5: 197–202.

Van-den-Bos, Esther and Jeannerod, Marc. (2002) 'Sense of Body and Sense of Action Both Contribute to Self-recognition', *Cognition* 85.2: 177–87.

Vinci, Tom. (1998) *Cartesian Truth.* New York: Oxford University Press.

Voss, Stephen. H. (1989) *René Descartes: The Passions of the Soul.* Indianapolis, IN: Hackett, 1989.

Wee, Cecilia. (2002) 'Self, Other and Community in Cartesian Ethics', *History of Philosophy Quarterly* 19.3: 255–73.

Wells, Norman J. (1984) 'Material Falsity in Descartes, Arnauld and Suarez', *Journal of the History of Philosophy* 22: 25–50.

Williams, Bernard (1978) *Descartes: The Project of Pure Inquiry.* Atlantic Highlands, NJ: Humanities Press.

Williston, Byron and Gombay, André, eds. (2003) *Passion and Virtue in Descartes.* Atlantic Highlands, NJ: Humanities Press International.

Wilson, Margaret Dauler. (1978a) *Descartes.* New York: Routledge.

(1978b) 'Cartesian Dualism', in M. Hooker, ed. *Descartes: Critical and Interpretative Essays.* Baltimore: Johns Hopkins University Press: 197–211.

(1990) 'Descartes on the Representationality of Sensation', in J. A. Cover and Mark Kulstad, eds., *Central Themes in Early Modern Philosophy.* Indianapolis, IN: Hackett: 293–323. Reprinted in *Ideas and Mechanism.*

(1991) 'Descartes on the Origin of Sensation', *Philosophical Topics* 19: 293–323. Reprinted in *Ideas and Mechanism.*

(1999) *Ideas and Mechanism: Essays on Early Modern Philosophy.* Princeton, NJ: Princeton University Press.

Wolf-Devine, Celia. (1993) *Descartes on Seeing.* Carbondale: Southern Illinois University Press.

Wolter, A. (1996) *John Duns Scotus: De primo principio.* Chicago: Franciscan Herald Press.

Wright, Thomas. (1986) *The Passions of the Mind in General.* Ed. William Webster Newbold. London: Garland.

Wundt, W. (1961) *Bietrage zur Theorie der Sinneswahrnehmung.* Leipzig: Wintersche, trans. *Contributions to the Theory of Sensory Perception,* in T. Shipley, ed., *Classics in Psychology.* NY: Philosophical Press: 51–78.

Yolton, John W. (1974) 'Ideas and Knowledge in Seventeenth-Century Philosophy', *Journal of the History of Philosophy* 13: 145–66.

(1984) *Perceptual Acquaintance from Descartes to Reid.* Minneapolis: University of Minnesota Press.

(1996) *Perception and Reality: A History from Descartes to Kant.* Ithaca, NY: Cornell University Press.

Yrjonsuuri, Mikko (2002) 'Free Will and Self-Control in Peter Olivi', in Lagerlund and Yrjonsuuri, 2002: 99–128.

Zeelenberg, Marcel. (1999a) 'The Use of Crying Over Spilled Milk: A Note on Rationality and the Functionality of Regret', *Philosophical Psychology* 12.3: 325–40.

(1999b) 'Anticipated Regret, Expected Feedback and Behavioral Decision-making', *Journal of Behavioral Decision Making* 72: 93–106.

Zeelenberg, M., van Dijk, W. W., van der Pligt, J., Manstead, A. S. R., van Empelen, P. and Reinderman, D. (1998). 'Emotional Reactions to the Outcomes of Decisions: The Role of Counterfactual Thought in the Experience of Regret and Disappointment', *Organizational Behavior and Human Decision Processes* 75: 117–41.

Index

224

Lightning Source UK Ltd.
Milton Keynes UK
UKOW052013190412

191114UK00001B/7/P